POETIC INQUIRY
UNEARTHING THE RHIZOMATIC ARRAY BETWEEN ART AND RESEARCH

Adam Vincent
University of British Columbia; University of the Fraser Valley

Series in Education
VERNON PRESS

Copyright © 2023 Vernon Press, an imprint of Vernon Art and Science Inc, on behalf of the author.

All rights reserved. No part of this publication may be reproduced, stored in a retrieval system, or transmitted in any form or by any means, electronic, mechanical, photocopying, recording, or otherwise, without the prior permission of Vernon Art and Science Inc.
www.vernonpress.com

In the Americas:
Vernon Press
1000 N West Street, Suite 1200,
Wilmington, Delaware 19801
United States

In the rest of the world:
Vernon Press
C/Sancti Espiritu 17,
Malaga, 29006
Spain

Series in Education

Library of Congress Control Number: 2022935728

ISBN: 978-1-64889-561-6

Also available: 978-1-64889-343-8 [Hardback]; 978-1-64889-509-8 [PDF, E-Book]

Product and company names mentioned in this work are the trademarks of their respective owners. While every care has been taken in preparing this work, neither the authors nor Vernon Art and Science Inc. may be held responsible for any loss or damage caused or alleged to be caused directly or indirectly by the information contained in it.

Every effort has been made to trace all copyright holders, but if any have been inadvertently overlooked the publisher will be pleased to include any necessary credits in any subsequent reprint or edition.

Cover design by Vernon Press.
Cover image created by denamorado / Freepik.

Written with an engaging, conversational tone, this book captures the best of both academic and creative expression. There is generative movement at the heart of practice that in this articulation of poetic inquiry has the ability to pause and listen deeply, and to attend to the self-in-relation with humility, awareness and sensitivity to practice.

In terms of contributing to the field of education, this book is both timely and definitive. Vincent identifies critical issues concerning poetic inquiry and arts research in general, and invites us to consider the integrity of poetic practice as an artist, researcher and teacher, resulting in a book with the needed coherence, rationality and style to facilitate opportunities to re-think and re-make innovative practices in schools, in university classrooms, and beyond.

The genealogy of thought documented in interviews with leading scholars offers an original contribution to historical understandings and recognises the vitality of learning and mentoring relationships that nurture such possible spaces as research. The analysis of specific works and identification of hallmark traits add new layers to the discourse of poetic inquiry and demonstrates further how this book makes an original contribution to knowledge. The concluding chapter is well-crafted, and serves as a guide to how poetic inquiry, as a rhizomatic array of diverse approaches, is contingent on the researcher's disposition to research questions.

This book offers a key contribution to the study of poetic inquiry, and in particular, it honours the legacies of those who have made poetic inquiry possible. Vincent's vision for the future is rooted in equitable, inclusive and diverse applications, and as a result, this book serves as an open invitation to students and scholars alike to take up these practices.

Vincent is indeed living poetically.

Dr. Anita Sinner
Program Coordinator, BFA Major
Art Education, Faculty of Fine Arts
Concordia University

Dr. Vincent takes a close look at four leading artist-scholars in the field of poetic inquiry with insight and grace in Poetic Inquiry: Unearthing the Rhizomatic Array Between Art and Research. *His analysis, coupled with his poetic response to their work, offers the reader a rich lens to better understand the complexity and possibilities of poetic inquiry as a research methodology. This book is invaluable for arts-based scholars, practitioners and educators who have a particular interest in poetic inquiry. Within the ten chapters, Vincent provides a detailed historical evolution of the field, a robust literature review, plenty of examples of engaging in poetic inquiry in diverse ways, and last but not least a convincing and compelling argument as to why this approach is much needed in scholarship and for community engagement.*

Dr. George Belliveau
Professor and Head
Faculty of Education, Department of Language and Literacy Education
The University of British Columbia

In this delightful book, Dr. Adam Vincent invites us to consider how poetic inquiry can form a methodology for educational audiences. Beneficial to educators, as well as scholars, readers and creators of poetry, and arts-based practitioners, this book will serve as a pioneering resource for years to come."

Dr. Derek Gladwin
University of British Columbia)
Author of 'Rewriting Our Stories: Education, Empowerment, and Well-being'

For JV,
for SV,
for BV,
and
for CV,
my muses,
my motivation,
my meaning,
my soul's poetic music.

Table of Contents

List of Figures and Tables	xi
Preface	xiii
Foreword:	
The Journey to Self-Discovery In/ Through Poetic Inquiry	xv
References	xx
Prologue	xxiii

Chapter 1
This book. The study. Why Poetic Inquiry? 1

Context and Purpose	2
My Research Questions	2
Significance of this Research	3
The Problem Addressed	4
Explicating Terms: What Is Poetic Inquiry? What Is Meant by Rhizome?	5
Outline of this Book: The Research and the Art	6
An Idiomatic Review	7

Chapter 2
Exploring the Literature: How Is Poetic Inquiry Being Used in Published Studies? 9

Introduction	9
The Proliferation of Poetic Inquiry	9
The Rhizomatic History of Poetic Inquiry	12
Poetic Inquiry in Fields of Practice	15
Synonymous Terms and Uses	21
Acknowledging Concerns With Poetic Inquiry	27
Poetic Inquiry Today	29
Concluding Thoughts on the Literature	32
Recognizing the Poetic Rhizomes	33

Chapter 3
Research Methodology: Theory, Design and Methods 35
Theoretical Stance: Where Am I Coming From? 36
Research Rationale 37
Selection and Description of Participants 38
Data Collection Methods 39
Interview Settings 41
Role of the Researcher 43
Data Analysis and Coding 44
Close Analysis of Poetic Inquiry Products 50
Trustworthiness? Something Else? 53
Application and Contribution 55
Summary of the Methodology 56
Musings on Method and Meetings 56
Preface to the Profiles: Crafting the Crafters 58

Chapter 4
Profile: Dr. Carl Leggo 61
What is this Work? Who Can Do It? 61
Reasons for Poetry in his Work 62
(No) Limits of Poetic Inquiry 63
Unique Features of his Work 63
Carl Leggo's Poetics: Love, Fun and the Process of Becoming 66
Common Themes and Purpose of Poetry in his Work 70
Carl Leggo's Teaching 71
Discussion 73

Chapter 5
Profile: Dr. Pauline Sameshima 75
What Is this Work? Who Can Use It? 75
Reasons for Poetry in her Work 76
(No) Limits of Poetic Inquiry 76
Unique Features of her Work 77
Pauline Sameshima Poetics: Ekphrasis, Responding and the Advocacy of Voices 77
Pauline Sameshima's Teaching 82
Discussion 83

Chapter 6
Profile: Dr. John Guiney Yallop   85

What Is this Work? Who Can Do It?   85
Reasons for Poetry in his Work   86
(No) Limits of Poetic Inquiry   87
Unique Features of his Work   88
John Guiney Yallop's Poetics: Stories, Identity and the
Act of Making Space for Others   90
John Guiney Yallop's Teaching   92
Discussion   93

Chapter 7
Profile: Dr. Monica Prendergast   95

What Is this Work? Who Can Do It?   95
Reasons for Poetry in her Work   96
(No) Limits of Poetic Inquiry   98
Unique Features of her Work   99
Monica Prendergast's Poetics: Vox, Performance and the
Propagation of Knowledge   99
Monica Prendergast's Teaching   103
Discussion   105
Where Does this Lead Us?   106
Profiling Prolific Poetic Practitioners   106

Chapter 8
Analyzing Poetics, Purposes and Teaching Praxis   109

Commonalities, Paradoxes and Differences in Views
(From the Interview Data)   110
Teaching Commonalities and Differences: Purpose and Praxis   117
Probing Poesis   119
Pondering the Poetic Analysis Process   127
Discussion of the Findings of this Process   128
Critical Cartography of Purposes and Poetics   130

Chapter 9
Implications, Applications and Conclusion   135
Implications   135
Poetry's Unparalleled Purposefulness   150
Application and Contribution   151
Limitations   154
Future Research   155
Concluding Thoughts on The Study   157
Study Postscript   160

Chapter 10
Epilogue, Post-Study Rumination on Theory and Findings   163
Does Poetic Inquiry Have a Theory?   163
Back to the Original Question: Does Poetic Inquiry Have a Theory?   164
Further Explorations and Applications in Poetic Inquiry and Across the Disciplines   165
Closing Thoughts   166
The Array of Rhythms   166

References   169

Appendix:
Interpretive Frameworks and Poetic Inquiry   181

Index   185

List of Figures and Tables

Figures

Figure 2.1: Öhlén's Poetic Method.   17
Figure 3.1: GTR Workbench Interface.   45
Figure 3.2: GTR Antonym Replace Function.   45
Figure 3.3: GTR List Example.   46
Figure 3.4: Poetic Play Example.   47
Figure 3.5: Data Table Example.   48
Figure 8.1: Commonality: Overarching View of Poetic Inquiry.   112
Figure 8.2: Difference: Limits of Poetic Inquiry.   114
Figure 8.3: Difference: Reasons for Poetry.   115
Figure 8.4: Commonality: Scholarship/Teaching.   117
Figure 8.5: Difference: Research Influences on Teaching.   118

Tables

Table 3.1: Interview Details.   41
Appendix Table 1: Poetic Inquiry and Philosophical/Interpretive Frameworks.   181
Appendix Table 2: Poetic Inquiry and Research Approaches.   183

Preface

This book is derived from the original intellectual and creative product of the author, Adam Vincent's, doctoral dissertation at the University of British Columbia. All participants have consented to the creation of this book and have provided full support in sharing the findings of the study.

The interviews and fieldwork that took place in the dissertation were covered by UBC Ethics Certificate (REB) Number H18-00402.

A version of the literature review appears in Art/Research International: A Transdisciplinary Journal:

Vincent, A. (2018). Is there a definition? Ruminating on poetic inquiry, strawberries and the continued growth of the field. *Art/Research International: A Transdisciplinary Journal*, 3(2), 48-76. doi:10.18432/ari29356

A version of the discussion around my poetic fieldnote practices appears in the following book chapter:

Vincent, A. (2020). The poetry of fieldnotes. In Burkholder, C., & Thompson, J. (Eds.). *Using fieldnotes in educational research: Approaches, practices, and ethical considerations* (138-150). Routledge. doi: 10.4324/9780429275821-12

Foreword:
The Journey to Self-Discovery In/ Through Poetic Inquiry

Kedrick James
University of British Columbia

"I thought I saw you before": In this book Adam Vincent takes the reader on his journey of discovery into the realms of poetic inquiry. As many great poets of antiquity had their guides or muses, Vincent presents four scholars whose work is germinal in the field of poetic inquiry, whose writing grows in the world of the academy. The academy is both germane to and distant from poetry, a genre that is "capacious", to quote one of those four key figures, the late Carl Leggo, in a way that academic writing is not. In this book, Vincent engineers a bridge between these two genres and the worlds they encompass by studying how they are situated both awkwardly and generatively, one within the other. It is possible to understand this relationship from a variety of angles and Vincent takes up more than one, much like seeking points where these opposite banks are closest, and testing the firmness of the ground on which to build the connecting points of that bridge. He not only writes about poetic inquiry, but he also utilizes poetic inquiry as both a reflective tool, as a way to summarize ethnographic interview notes, and as a relational tool, as a way to appreciate the person behind the poetry. He also employs some facets of literary criticism or close reading to fabricate a sense of the poetics that motivate these academic researchers to adopt poetry in order to conduct their inquiries into the human condition. But this is not typical literary critical writing, for it seeks to do something critics take for granted, that is, it seeks to know the utility of form and to understand poetry from an efferent stance (from the Latin "effer", *to take away*). What are the takeaways i.e. how does poetic inquiry contribute to banks of human knowledge and understanding?

Vincent borrows from a cornerstone of literary theory in education, Louise Rosenblatt (1978), in that his stance toward the poetry of academic inquirers leans toward the efferent as opposed to the aesthetic. He does not judge the poet and does not turn a critical eye upon the aesthetic value of their work as founders of a genre of academic poetry. In keeping with Rosenblatt's transactional approach, he "does not permit honorific use of the terms 'literary work of art' or 'literature'…. [so] we can thus leave open the evaluative question of whether the transaction has produced a poor or a good literary work of art" (p. 155). As such, he poses interesting questions that are timeless, partly because they are unanswerable and devious. For poetry to serve its aesthetic purpose, it must be free from the limiting interpretation of what is right or correct. Rather, it should create an ambience within which the reader, viewer, or listener pours their own experience and knowledge, making its linguistic space a habitus of their own imagining. But this is decidedly not the scientific, nor even the social scientific environment of discourse which relates repeatable findings that have specific kinds of applied meanings and uses. Indeed, the genre of academic discourse is notably verbose and largely of an impersonal tone, whereas much that is recognizable as poetry strives for the opposite – the compression of language into crystalline forms of meaning that resonate in a harmonic series of cognate associations, and whose fundamental tone is personal to the nth degree. Therefore, the challenge this book addresses from the outset is the central contradiction that confronts poetic inquiry when poetry is indentured to the service of so-called knowledge mobilization.

This dilemma, which Vincent introduces through his own youthful encounter with the relational power of poetry and his subsequent efforts to unshackle himself from the droll standard essay format, his cross-genre provocations as a student, but also as a university instructor boosting students' academic English or teaching Communications and Educational Studies courses, becomes apparent through his encounter with Carl Leggo and the subsequent masters and doctoral work under his tutelage until Leggo's death from cancer in 2018. It is indeed fortunate for Vincent and his readers that Vincent's research was already well underway before Leggo's tragic passing, and that this book contains the last sustained interview on the topic of poetic inquiry that Leggo gave. There can be no more central node in the distributed, rhizomatic network of poetic inquiry than Carl Leggo. As Vincent explains, Leggo, who always saw himself as a poet first and a scholar second, tirelessly advocated for the spirit of creative rebellion and resistance within the academy (e.g. he mocked notions of academic rigour, spoke of vigor as rigour, and would parenthetically add "mortis" when it was spoken of). In 2005-2007, Leggo supervised the postdoctoral appointment of Monica Prendergast, who is also one of Vincent's four "participants".

Prendergast's two-year postdoctoral work undertook two landmark projects: the first was an interdisciplinary survey of social science qualitative research publications for all instances where poetry was included, resulting in an annotated bibliography of over 1000 pages; the second, in collaboration with Leggo, Prendergast convened the first International Symposium on Poetic Inquiry (ISPI) held at the University of British Columbia in 2007. The event was modestly attended, with about 50 people who gathered at St. John's College atrium for three sunny days, but that special vigor that Leggo so admired was in great abundance. The event prepared the ground for the growth of a poetic inquiry network, like "a strawberry plant" (as Leggo describes it). To plant strawberry fields forever, one must begin with "starts", the nodes from which tendrils will branch out and start their own nodes in a strawberry patch. Among the "starts" who presented at the first ISPI were Vincent's two other interviewees, Pauline Sameshima and John J. Guiney Yallop, both education scholars nearing completion of their doctoral degrees and employing arts-based research methods in their dissertations. It should be noted that Leggo was also Sameshima's supervisor.

What captures Vincent's interest is not just the start of a particular network of arts-based scholars who explore the potential of poetry in research, but also their keen resistance to the whole notion that what they are doing as poetic inquirers can be easily assimilated or defined, either as research methodology or as practice of an artform. Each participant of Vincent's study is reluctant to speak when confronted with Vincent's quest for some consensus on what poetic inquiry actually is or does. And this might be one of the most revealing aspects of this book: poetic inquiry, at present, encodes an act of resistance to the norms that govern professional, disciplinary discourses. It demands room and cannot be boxed in to definitions or a specific repertoire of practices. It is as if each new inquirer to join the rhizomatic fold brings their own practices, needs, insights, origins, expectations, talents, and voices to this vigorous and fruitful field. In the case of the poet-academics Vincent focuses on, they come with varied disciplinary backgrounds: Guiney Yallop in sexuality and gender studies, Sameshima with visual arts and health studies, Prendergast with drama and theatre studies, and Leggo as a literacy scholar in the central role. What each has in common is their connection to education.

This book is therefore most specifically about the journey of educators and researchers who find their way to poetry and discover the po/e/tentials it holds for encoding more than just the facts; more, even, than the narrative of events and findings. What they discover is that poetry evokes otherness in the way we come to know and understand, and this otherness holds vital information which is not otherwise made accessible. Perhaps the biological corollary of poetry's role in academic writing is the strange phenomena of human heart cells: when a heart cell is put in a petri dish with another (different) heart cell, both cells begin to contract and expand in sync. Poetry is the medium which best allows two distant heart cells in different bodies to inhabit the same rhythm, to correspond as if one, to inhabit the same emotional and psychic space. Importantly, however, this is achieved precisely because it does not necessitate a limitation on the experience of that space. It does not tell the reader what to make of it. More than any other genre, poetry makes room for others to participate in the making of meaning; poetry celebrates what the New Criticism scholar, William Empson (1966), enumerated as the *Seven Types of*

Ambiguity, each of which is anathema to most mainstream academic discourses. Emerson states that "the machinations of ambiguity are among the very roots of poetry" (p. 3) and "so far as poetry can be regarded altogether dispassionately, so far as it is an external object for examination, it is dead poetry and not worth examining" (p. 248). This is very clearly not the goal or disposition of almost all other forms of knowledge production in the academy, which strive to do the exact opposite – to remove ambiguity and dispossess it of vigor in favor of rigorous object analysis.

*****

Much of what follows in this book is Vincent's doctoral dissertation, which incorporated portions of published articles on the topic of poetic inquiry that began to draw attention and was then quoted by the same people he saw advancing this interdisciplinary method, which ultimately helped Vincent find his own niche in the academy. Like Guiney Yallop and Leggo, Vincent has a Canadian maritimer heritage, and he had been publishing about his Acadian heritage through the lens of place and identity, and exploring the poetic use of field notes in addition to his literature reviews of poetic inquiry. For Vincent, there was a particular thrill to undertaking interviews with people whom he admired as leaders of the field, which he describes in illuminating detail, like the creaking of an office chair when interviewing Leggo or getting lost in the halls of the University of Victoria on his way to visit Prendergast. But once his ingénue anxiety subsided, he began to find his raison d'être. He structured this book on the combination of his poetic and academic sensibilities, as well as on the comparative analysis of his participants' uses of poetry and their poetics.

The last chapter (10) of this book undertakes a more reflective exposé based on his expanding network of affiliations who are also tackling the central issue of the book, which is to provide a working definition for this methodological field. Throughout the book, the question of poetics looms quite large but is obscured by purpose. One must regularly respond to the question of "why" in one's research in the academy. The purpose and potential outcomes are what get funding for research, get jobs, promotions and tenure, and awards and accolades. The same is not true of poetics. You do not get asked why you have a particular poetics or what its use-value is in the knowledge economy. "Poeisis", the art of making, is at its core integrated with praxis, the crafting of letters and words into a kind of *Tardis*, a time machine that is bigger on the inside than on the outside. Poetics comes as a jouissance, an excess produced by doing meaning-making in the embodied laboratory. Poetics describes what enables the poet not just to write a poem but to write many poems, to sustain a continuous mode of expression that can capture complexity and hold it long enough for someone else to crawl inside and witness it firsthand. And for the poetic inquirer, this requires (sometimes arduous) work. The jouissance of the academic poem is a struggle of the pleasure-pain principle where, Derrida (1987) writes,

> The imagination turns this violence against itself, it mutilates itself, ties itself, binds itself, sacrifices itself and conceals itself, gashes itself [s'entaille] and robs itself...But this mutilating and sacrificial violence organizes the expropriation within a calculation; and the exchange which ensues is precisely the law of the sublime as much as the sublimity of the law. The imagination gains by what it loses. It gains by losing. The imagination organizes the theft (Beraubung) of its own freedom, it lets itself be commanded by a law other than that of the empirical use which determines it with a view to an end. But by this violent renunciation, it gains in extension (Erweiterung) and in power (Macht). This potency is greater than what it sacrifices, and although the foundation remains hidden from it, the imagination has the feeling of sacrifice and theft at the same time as that of the cause (Ursache) to which it submits. (p. 131)

This sacrifice, combined with the promulgation of a cause, underlies the determination that poetic inquirers bring to the academy, by superimposing a poetics of expression on the work of scholarship, to the point where it is more than an idle fancy: it is a devotional practice which involves the whole of one's being.

Leggo's poetics were quite succinctly stated as "living poetically" (Leggo, 2005), a notion which he understood as the brave act of living with awareness, in synchrony with one's environment and all the beings in it. In particular, it was to dwell with language, not merely to use language to some other end, but to be and become with language as one's sustenance, a praxis he developed as a lived curriculum (Aoki, 1993), to invoke Leggo's mentor, Ted Aoki. Leggo's stance of living poetically within the academy is a lasting legacy that he passed on to all those who took guidance and inspiration from him, and that would include all the participants of the study this book articulates, its author, and indeed, myself. And this is a crux of the issue regarding poetic inquiry, one that Vincent provokes at various points in the following text. Many of the people who adopt the use of poetic inquiry at some stage in their research process come to poetry as academics, steeped in particular discourses and traditions from which they seek to liberate a sensuous, affective license to have an aesthetic experience in and through scholarship. But there are also those who come to the academy as poets, who adopt formal academic discourses as a way to dress up their feral language so as to disguise themselves. As teachers, instructors, and professors, we might recognize, from time to time, one of these language-obsessed creatures in our midst. To honour the work of Carl Leggo, as this book and its author do, is to recognize that Leggo was especially good at spotting and supporting those who brought to the academy the wild heart of poetry, and who try their best to keep it in a box, hidden in a desk, kept out of sight lest someone oust them as inherently unreliable, always destabilizing discourse, making it do something beyond its purpose and utility.

Perhaps then, poetic inquiry is a liminal zone where two kinds of wordsmiths meet, those for whom poetry is their ken, who move across the surface of disciplinary discourses like mimic octopi with intelligent legs camouflaged to blend in but capable of burrowing below, and those for whom the discourse of their field is a zone of comfort, who occupy it authentically but recognize the mystery that lurks beneath, and are drawn to it as sailors to sirens. Both navigate imposter syndrome for a period that is as long as it takes for a routine practice to develop, where doing and being something subconsciously blend. Whichever you, as a reader of this book, might align yourself with, you now have the opportunity to engage with poetic inquiry's special capacity as a form of aesthetic expression that escapes the tidy, expository, summarized spaces of discourse. When Vincent writes that poetic inquirers resist imposing "a singular view on what poetic inquiry should be" for fear that to do so causes poetry to lose "some of its power and some of its subjective e/affectiveness," he leaves room for both the academic poets and the poet academics to find a space of belonging. And in doing so, we expand the po/e/tential of the academy to be receptive to the mysteries of language (incorporating inspired, intuitive, emotive, reflective and deeply personal knowledge/wisdom), to pass on a space of belonging to the artists and to the scientists in which they might be appreciated equally as essential contributors. The use of language impacts more than just the human universe; it extends to the more-than-human life forms that comprise the world as we know it and as we have yet to comprehend it. To be exposed in all one's vulnerability, to have one's storied-self unsheltered to the scrutinous academy, to venture beyond certainty of a stable and predictable language in the realm of professional identity, is at the heart of Vincent's journey bound in these pages: "I now see for myself / the power of poetry / functioning as / method and methodology / research and poetry / art and epistemology / craft and tool. / I will use it more deftly. / I will show others. / I will tell others. / I will continue to look and hear."

Kedrick James, 2022

References

Aoki, T. T. (1993). Legitimating lived curriculum: Towards a curricular landscape of multiplicity. *Journal of Curriculum and Supervision, 8*(3), 255-268.

Derrida, J. (1987). *The truth in painting.* Translated by G. Bennington & I. McLeod. The University of Chicago Press.

Empson, W. (1966). *Seven types of ambiguity*. New Directions.

Leggo, C. (2005). Pedagogy of the heart: Ruminations on living poetically. *Journal of Educational Thought, 39*(2), 175-195.

Rosenblatt, L. M. (1978). *The reader, the text, the poem: The transactional theory of the literary text*. Southern Illinois University Press.

Prologue

Poetry. Yes, poetry. For some, the term brings to mind people wearing all black, snapping their fingers in a coffee shop (offbeat), with a beret wearing, patchouli-smelling bongo player. For others, it brings forth the fear of reading Shakespeare in grade nine English class, where you are trying to decipher iambic pentameter to better understand why in the world Romeo is so smitten by someone he just met. These are not my visions of poetry.

For me, poetry began in the seventh grade. The class was asked to write poetry by our teacher, Ms. Lumgair, "Just for fun." I began my foray into Shakespeare years earlier, inspired by the Saturday morning 90's TV show "Saved by the Bell." In the show, Zack Morris (who was the protagonist and the coolest kid in school) was Romeo in Bayside High's production of "Romeo and Juliet." I recalled Kelly Kapowski (who played Juliet and who was, for me, the prettiest girl at Bayside High) being smitten by Zack's words during the balcony scene. This was my first remembrance of language having power and impact. It sent me on a journey to find the play and learn the powerful poetic words. I thought if I were ever to find myself a Kelly that I would need some way to impress her; Shakespeare it was.

I went to the local library, figured out how to use the computer system, learned through trial and error how their collections were categorized and found a large Shakespeare anthology. I opened the book, careful to not further rip its already half-ripped dust jacket and flipped through until I found "Romeo and Juliet." I found a mention of a balcony. I read the scene over and over again and set a few key phrases to memory, "But soft, what light through yonder window breaks? It is the east and Juliet is the sun" (Shakespeare, 2.2, 2-3). That would do.

This now takes us to twelve-year-old Adam, scrawling parts of the balcony scene in lefty, chicken-scratch writing on lined paper, recalling how Juliet is the sun in an effort to impress Ms. Lumgair. With time left during the free-write, I took it upon myself to explore more of my poetic voice. Why not? Having recently felt the sting of unrequited love, which I did not realize then would be a recurring theme for years to come, I began writing and rhyming. What I scrawled on the page was something to the effect of, "Are these tears in my eyes?/Or the blackness of the black flies flying by?" I submitted my work and went home to write more. The next day, Ms. Lumgair spoke about the results of the previous day's free-write. As she did, she made direct eye contact with me and noted that there was "a poet in the class." She did not name me, but her eyes indicated that she was referring to me. Me, a poet?

I went through the rest of my high school education with few attempts at writing poetry in class. Instead, I wrote poems for myself at home. I sometimes created songs, usually about that familiar sting first recognized in the seventh grade. That sting of unrequited love had the most emotion behind it. I would also create poems by splicing together lyrics from songs (going from CDs to cassettes in my four CD changer) to say what I wanted to say, without ever having to say it myself. It was not until university, while in an Interdisciplinary Expressive Arts class, that I began to strengthen my voice as a poet. I began by weaving poetry or song lyrics (from popular songs) into personal narratives or formal essays to show different or deeper layers of meaning. The work was of my own creation. I had no idea that others were doing work of that nature as they were outside of my sphere. I joined creative writing groups, performed my poems in public spaces and sent pieces out for publication, yet I did not identify as a poet.

During my undergrad, with a focus on English and Creative Writing, I decided that I loved literature and wanted to become a high school English teacher. That dream lasted until I volunteered in a high school and swore to never return; it takes a certain person to work in that environment and I instead felt a calling towards adult education. I wanted to help others, like me, who had trouble finding their voice. I found work in my alma mater in the Admissions office and began an MA in interdisciplinary studies (focusing on the connections between academic and personal writing) taken at a Canadian university that was known for its online graduate programing, Athabasca University. I completed the majority of the program, making proposals for alternative assignments where I could; assignments that blended my academic voice with my poet's voice when I realized that something was missing. I no longer had my writing groups, no mentors in the flesh, no conference links, no opportunities to share my work with anyone except for occasionally with peers at work or the woman who would ultimately become my wife. I decided to look elsewhere.

After numerous searches for programs in Canada that would allow me to look more at what the practice of writing does for students, I found UBC's Language and Literacy Education program (LLED). At first, the program did not appear to be a home for me. I was not interested in EAL/ELL work specifically and did not yet see the ties between my work and literacy. I clicked through the LLED faculty page and stopped upon an image of man with long hair and a huge smile, facing into what appeared to be sunlight. Dr. Carl Leggo. I wondered what his story was. Why was he so happy? I clicked on his profile, saw his connection to poetry, read over a few of his published works and decided to email him to ask him if he thought I would fit in with the program. What did I have to lose?

I heard back a few days later from the man who I would come to know simply as "Carl." He requested samples of my writing to see if my work was in sync with his. I sent him some samples of my interdisciplinary work where I wove story and lyric with citations from the literature that linked to the theme of my writing. I also sent him work that used my own poems and stories, without academic links, and I sent him an academic essay. He quickly replied to ask if we could meet to discuss my application to the MA program. We decided to meet at a Starbucks midway between where I was working in the city of Richmond, BC, and his home in Steveston village, an area on the outskirts of the city. I did not know then, but this meeting over coffee would be instrumental in the trajectory of my future.

Tuesday, October 29, 2013, at 3pm I sat anxiously, printed copies of my writing samples in hand, waiting for Carl to arrive. Would I make a good impression? How should I speak to him? Should I try to sound more academic? Should I speak like a poet would? Would I recognize his face when he was not staring into the sunlight? Would he be as happy as he looked in his picture?

I watched each car that turned into the Starbucks parking lot, hoping to see what he drove. Somehow, what he drove would tell me something about him. Car after car drove in. No one had long hair. No one had a large grin. I looked down at my papers, trying to think through what I wrote and why I wanted to join an MA program at UBC after having already completed the bulk of an MA program online through Athabasca University. I heard another car, looked up, and saw Carl walking around the corner. He was in black pants, a blue shirt and a black vest, hair loosely floating in the breeze of the unusually bright October day. He was walking towards the light. He looked happy. I remember this moment vividly as it was the moment that I met the mentor who would support my growth as an artist, educator and researcher.

We spoke for thirty minutes about my career as staff in higher education, starting in the office of the registrar and ultimately supporting students in The Learning Centre at Kwantlen Polytechnic University (KPU) as a coordinator who worked with students and trained incoming tutors. We talked about my brief stint volunteering in a high school English class that sent me fleeing. He seemed pleased with my unique teaching experience and praised my writing samples, in particular those which braided story, poetry and citations from relevant literature. He said I was on the cutting edge of something and he gave me his full support for my MA application. We shook hands and parted ways. At the time, I was unsure of what it meant, but would later learn the significance of having this "full support."

I completed my MA in Literacy Education at UBC, with Carl as my supervisor. In my thesis, I explored ways in which poetry could be more a/effectively used in the teaching of literacy. I then moved into my PhD with a new set of advisors,

Dr. Anthony Paré and Dr. Kedrick James. I wanted to know more about a term that I stumbled upon, *poetic inquiry* (Prendergast, 2009). More than that, I wanted to know more about the people who used poetry in their academic work and what it did that other genre or approaches could not do. It was following my MA thesis that I finally described myself as a poet, embracing the title that others had called me along the way. I had also been conducting research, adopting the role of an academic researcher. Was I a Poetic Inquirer? Was that even a title? I had to know more about poetic inquiry. I believed that if I could glean exactly what poetic inquiry was, what it did, what the proponents of the work added to the academy, and where the work was going that I could offer insights into the work being done, and potentially unearth new understandings about teaching and learning. I could then share my findings with others, supporting their scholastic endeavours by giving them more information, and potentially find where I belonged.

Early in my PhD research, I identified that knowledge-creation approaches employed by poets, who are also academics, are unknown to many scholars or are omitted from significant discussions that have taken place in arts-based research (e.g., jagodzinski & Wallin, 2013). Despite this lack of overt visibility in the arts-based and qualitative research communities, the work being done through poetry appeared significant when I found it in the literature. I wondered: What capacities do poets bring to academia? What are academic poets doing that others are not? Why do they do it? How do they do it? How can what they are doing inform approaches to research and scholarship?

I began by exploring poetic inquiry, its definition and how it had been used. This was a start, but it did not answer all of my lingering questions. I needed to know more. I needed to complete this study, a multiple case study with critical analytical elements. This gave me an opportunity to speak with practitioners of poetic inquiry, analyze their poetics and delve more deeply into the diverse literature on poetic inquiry. Then, and only then, could I fully answer my questions and critically assess for myself (and others) the merits of poetic inquiry, informing what is known and potentially adding to its credence as an approach to research and scholarship.

Chapter 1

This book. The study. Why Poetic Inquiry?

Poetic inquiry is happening. Poets are using it. Researchers are using it. I know that it is being used in by practitioners of qualitative research under different labels and for diverse purposes (Prendergast, 2009; James, 2017; Vincent, 2018). Why then, I asked, is it not in my qualitative research textbook? Why am I reading about impactful studies that use poetry in their research processes in academic journals, but I cannot find a definitive definition or a canonical book that tells me how to use it (akin to books about case studies, narrative studies or phenomenology) or how it functions? Why is it overlooked in critiques of arts-based research when it is using art and research? I quickly came to realize that not enough is known about poetic inquiry and its place in qualitative research. It was undertheorized. Nowhere in the literature was there a starting point for those interested in using poetry in their research and scholarship. There were examples of how it was being used, there were products, but other than suggested ways to approach poetic inquiry (as in Faulkner, 2019 and Leavy, 2018), there lacked a critical consideration of what poetic inquiry does that other methods or methodologies could not do. There also lacked a procedure for extracting the depths of knowledge that exist in the poetry of academic-poetic studies that extends beyond conventional forms of literary analysis. These poetic products of poetic inquiry studies, poetry produced as part of the data gathering, analysis or dissemination processes, are not only meant to exclusively showcase findings in aesthetic and affective ways. They also contain complex findings of the inquiry that need further, and different, examination. Why is poetic inquiry seen almost exclusively as generative? What approaches do poet-researchers use in creating their poetry? What can be gleaned from their poetry as it relates to the crafting of research-powered poetry? What more can be learned by analyzing poetry as it relates to participants' experiences or diverse concepts highlighted in/through poetry? These questions need answering for they have glimpses of something more; they appear to hold insights into ways that research and scholarship could do more.

This book showcases my doctoral dissertation research and represents my scholarly effort to understand more about this undertheorized area of research and scholarship that is somewhat obscured in qualitative research, yet evidently impactful. The findings, implications and applications of the study are further explored in the epilogue, written six months after the formal completion of my doctoral program, which takes on the form of an explorative rumination on theory and practice.

Context and Purpose

The research discussed in this book is situated in discussions of qualitative research methods, with a focus on arts-based approaches and pedagogy. It describes the landscape of poetic inquiry by way of analyses of poetic inquiry as a method and methodology and identifies its unique attributes and impacts on qualitative research. At the same time, it focuses on ways that poetic inquiry is and could be adopted in curriculum development and how it influences teaching strategies. This study could be seen as a response to poetic inquiry's omission in research methods books (e.g., Creswell, 2013) and books that challenge the value of arts-based approaches to research (e.g., Slattery, 2003) or even be undertaken in response to strongly worded concerns that arts-based approaches are self-serving and lacking in academic merit (e.g., jagodzinski & Wallin, 2013). While the findings of this study may ultimately silence those claims, that is not its primary goal. This research moves away from refuting the claims of others and instead highlights ways that poetic inquiry scholars actively use poetry in their educational research and scholarship and to understand its unparalleled function(s) therein. Further, this study seeks to not only understand how and why they use poetry in their research and teaching, but also synthesize ways that their approaches can add greater substance to qualitative research and pedagogy. This study also seeks to support scholars, new or experienced, who wish to engage in their academic practices in different ways. It does this by providing various entry points into poetic inquiry and academic-poetic practices, including an example of a close reading (a form of hermeneutic analysis), of the poetry borne out of qualitative research, while also drawing attention to its versatility as a research methodology that is being used across disciplines to reveal new knowledge. While there is a primary focus on the Canadian context where this research occurred, there are greater implications on poetic inquiry's versatility for studies across the disciplines and for scholars across the globe. These notions are explored in even greater depth after the sharing of the study in the concluding chapter of this book.

My Research Questions

To strengthen what is known about poetic inquiry, to support the creation of an accessible definition, to provide entry points for others into poetic inquiry and to draw out understandings around how proponents create and share new knowledge, I had questions that needed answering:

- What is poetic inquiry?
- What do proponents believe poetic inquiry does that other approaches cannot do?
- How is poetic inquiry being used in research and scholarship today?
- What is the future of poetic inquiry in Canada? What does this imply for the future of poetic inquiry across the globe?
- In what ways do proponents' approaches to poetic inquiry impact their teaching approaches?

Significance of this Research

This study was initially undertaken in response to discrepancies between the work being done in poetic inquiry and its omission in qualitative research methods texts. It is evident that poetic inquiry is actively in use through publications in academic journals and books published by reputable international publishing houses and through its inclusion in special interest groups in professional organizations, such as the American Education Research Association (AERA) and the Canadian Society for the Study of Education (CSSE). Yet, it is obscured or overlooked in texts that discuss theoretical and practical applications of qualitative research methods. This study critically examined how poetic inquiry functions in research and scholarship, building on the research of Prendergast (2009a) and James (2017), with first-hand reports from four of Canada's well-known scholars in the area. This adds to what we know about poetic inquiry as an approach to research, as both a method and a methodology, further informing what is known about qualitative research methods and creates profiles of four notable and well-reputed poetic inquiry scholars that do not exist in the literature. It also provides an approach to delve more deeply the poetry of these academic-poetic studies, furthering what is known about these poems as research-informed products, while piloting a way of advancing what is known about the creation and implications of academic poetry. Further, through the critical analysis of these findings, this study not only advocates for a closer consideration of research findings but also provides a way of hermeneutically breaking down language and assessing meaning that may be of use in a variety of studies across the disciplines. Additionally, this study has significance for teaching through its initial findings around poetic inquiry's current and potential uses in curriculum development and delivery of content in the classroom. In providing discussions around poetry as a multimodal tool, one that supports students in their knowledge-creation processes by way of content delivery and by diversifying what is seen as an acceptable way to engage in course concepts, this study builds on what is known about arts-based approaches to pedagogy and student-focused teaching approaches which can be elaborated on in future research studies.

The Problem Addressed

Over twenty-five years ago, Barone (1995) cautioned that "the political realities remain such that, in many places, non-scientific inquiry projects are still not considered legitimate research endeavours" (p. 169). While political tensions have eased from external political resistance to qualitative research, there remains some skepticism of the value of this creative-academic work (as in jagodzinski & Wallin, 2013). Without criticality, research conducted through poetic inquiry is at risk of seeming invalid therefore putting valuable knowledge in jeopardy of being lost. These studies, and the approaches therein, have unearthed greater understandings of data that would otherwise be unattainable through any other approach. This data, often representing the complexity of lived experience, becomes more relatable and tangible by the choices made by the poet-researcher. This is because the poet-researchers who undertake these studies use language in both analytically and aesthetically evocative ways that strive to more authentically represent their interpretation of lived experience(s). They do this through the use of poetic devices such as metaphors and similes which hold multiple levels of meaning through fewer words, through choices of craft such as the use of line breaks, enjambment, spacing and appearance on the page to create or subvert meaning, and through using language in unique ways to explicitly illustrate or imply meaning.

The studies that risk being disregarded include those that use participant-written, participant-voiced or participant-inspired poetry that, when parried to inquiry, create impactful ways to understand lived experiences and find solutions to problems. These poetic inquiry studies use poetry to generate a visceral glimpse into the realities of domestic violence (Maarhuis & Sameshima, 2016), those that accentuate the experiences of health care workers as they strive to better understand their patient's mental health challenges (Furman & Cavers, 2005) and physical suffering (King, 1995; Öhlén, 2003), as well as those that highlight the experiences of incarcerated individuals (Hartnett, 2003; Fels et al., 2014). They also include studies that poetically share stories of those seeking to (re)define their identities (Orr, 2002; Wiebe & Guiney Yallop, 2010; Leggo, 2015). Poetic inquiry studies also provide ways for authentic voices to be shared and/or amplified, using poetry for autobiographical or autoethnographic reasons (see Smith, 2002), by those who have experienced marginalization throughout history. This includes poetry being used to magnify the voices and experiences of members of the 2SLGBTQ+ community (Teman, 2019), as well as to highlight issues facing members of the BIPOC community (De Vito & Johnson, 2017; Cutts, 2019). At the same time, should poetic inquiry be further overlooked or under-utilized, we may lose knowledge regarding how these unparalleled approaches to research can inform curriculum development and teaching approaches that could reach students for whom more traditional approaches have failed, or do not do enough to support their unique learning circumstances, styles or preferences. These include those by Leggo (1997; 2003), who uses his classroom teaching experiences and life as a poet to question how writing pedagogy can be adapted to better serve students, as well as the work being done by Morell and Duncan-Andrade (2002), who study ways that hip-hop music and popular culture can be integrated into English curriculum to support students' understanding of canonical poetry.

This study encompassed in this book seeks to identify and describe the unique attributes and functions that poetic inquiry approaches can bring to research and teaching. Based on the findings, this book posits ways to add further depth to qualitative studies and how poetic inquiry is used. Without a close examination of what poetic inquiry is and an exploration of how it is in use/how it functions for research and scholarship purposes, there remains a risk that current and future knowledge may be discounted or lost. That means that current and/or future scholars may also remain or become unnecessarily lost.

Explicating Terms: What Is Poetic Inquiry? What Is Meant by Rhizome?

In this book, I use the term "poetic inquiry" to describe the complex rhizomatic nature of this poetic-academic method, research approach, methodology and/or tool. Initially, in this study, poetic inquiry was used as a singular proper noun—Poetic Inquiry—to describe the perceived category or genre of poetic-academic research that uses poetry in the data gathering, data processing and data dissemination processes. What was discovered, as encompassed in this book, is that there is no singular or exclusive way to define poetic inquiry beyond demarcating its obvious elements of poetry and inquiry. This could potentially lead to all forms of poetry being defined as types of poetic inquiry. While there is little argument that all poetry reveals something and/or asks questions of the poet or reader, in the context of this study, poetic inquiry relates to poetry created purposefully by scholars as part of their research or knowledge creation process(es). This includes the use of poetic inquiry as a method, methodology, analytical tool or research product which both transpires and exists in the liminal spaces (Sinner et al., 2006) between disciplines or research traditions. As explored in Chapter Two, poetic inquiry is in use across and between the disciplines for a wide range of purposes and therefore requires a more open-ended definition, a common noun, that can represent its interminable nature—poetic inquiry. In this book, through highlighting examples of poetic inquiry in use in the literature and the ways that poetic inquiry is used by this study's participants, this somewhat paradoxical yet pragmatic definition of poetic inquiry will become more comprehensible.

In this book, I use the metaphor of the rhizome to explain this non-linear approach to research and scholarship. This term, explored in more depth in Chapter 2, often used in botany or in educational theory (see Deleuze & Guattari, 1988; Irwin et al., 2006) refers to nodes or underground stems from which further shoots, roots and/or new visible life grow (above ground), while continuing to simultaneously grow (often linearly) underground. These subterranean growths have no discernable center and cannot be traced back to a particular original plant. The notion of the rhizome, as explored in Chapter 2, may also be further explained using the metaphor of mushrooms growing in diverse places, yet being interrelated/connected. Mycelia (fungi) grow rhizomatically—centerless and vast.

The rhizome or rhizomatic array is how I have come to envision/understand poetic inquiry. An effort to trace it back to a founding theory, approach or individual scholar becomes an act of futility as poetry appears throughout qualitative research and across the disciplines. It is used in diverse ways and for a multitude of purposes, yet it produces or uses poetry in some capacity. Poetic products from studies appear across a vast array, yet they did not grow from one singular origin. This metaphor should become clearer as you engage in the following chapters.

Outline of this Book: The Research and the Art

This book is comprised of ten chapters, nine encompassing the study and one final chapter ruminating on the study, that seek to combine the tenor of the researcher with the craft of the poet. The first, the introduction, has sought to provide context for the book and the study that took place, including its purpose and where it is situated in ongoing discussions around arts-based research. Chapter 2 explores the complex definition of poetic inquiry, where it has appeared in the literature, how it has been used and how researchers have chosen to label their approaches. Chapter 3 centers on the research methodology undertaken for the study. This includes the theoretical framework, research rationale, information about my participant selection process, my data collection and data analysis processes, as well as discussions around my role as the researcher, which trouble the notion of a qualitative standard of trustworthiness of the study. Chapter 3 also includes an initial exploration of how this research, and the techniques applied herein, can be applied in other studies. Chapters 4-7 consist of participant profiles (or case profiles) based on the findings of the study. These profiles illustrate each scholar's views on poetic inquiry, what it does in their academic-poetic research and writing processes, how they do it and who they believe can/should do it. Each profile also includes descriptions of their poetic approaches and products and highlights their views on poetic inquiry's influences on their teaching praxis. Chapter 8 presents the findings of the cross-case analyses. It focuses on accentuating the participants' commonalities and differences in relation to their views on poetic inquiry and their approaches to teaching which are influenced by their writing as academic poets. Further, it highlights the poetic inquiry paradox, which sees poetic inquiry perceived as an inclusive yet exclusive approach to conducting research. This chapter also includes the trialing and exemplification of a close reading approach to poetic inquiry products, which is used in this study to analyze a sample of each participants' poetry. This previously unused approach to analyzing poetic inquiry products includes identifying the functions of word choice, poetic devices, line breaks and appearance on the page to not only create an aesthetic experience but accentuate the findings of the data therein. Chapter 9 includes a discussion of the findings of the study at the time of its completion, the diverse research processes employed in this study and its potential uses in future research and scholarship. This chapter also deals with the implications around the findings of the study and how they can potentially be immediately applied to research and teaching approaches. I end the chapter by discussing the limits of the study and making suggestions for future studies that can continue the trajectory of this study by bringing new insights about poetic inquiry and its functions in research and scholarship to light. Chapter 10 is an epilogue to the study which further explores the concept of the theory of poetic inquiry and offers further ruminations on poetic inquiry's place in research and scholarship across the disciplines.

In keeping with poetic inquiry, where it is integral that the researcher positions themselves in their practice as both a researcher, bound by rigour, and as a poet in the academy, bound by their poetic perspectives on the research and their sensibilities around creating meaning through language, each chapter ends with poetry. These poems act as a denouement, highlight findings or concepts from each chapter, while simultaneously exemplifying ways that poetry can enrich research and research can enrich poetry.

An Idiomatic Review
(Adam Vincent)

This thing
that plays with language,
that uses line breaks,
that uses metaphors to enliven lived experience,
breathing life into the lungs of deflated language,
formally drowning in third-person phrases
and

the other things that draw humanity
away from the surface
seems meaningful,
yet it can be hard to find.

That thing
called poetry
that usually only exists in literature class,
that you write about,
(not through)
(not in conjunction with)
has brought depth
that the other thing,
missed
(despite its best efforts)
but why can't I use it?
Why is it not an option?

The other thing
that it seems to do
is add criticality
that adds multiplicity
that adds polyphony
and adds that other thing
where the researcher,
the poet,
and
the researched
are symbiotically
enriching what is known.

This study examines
this
that
and the other thing
that makes poetic inquiry unique;
analyzing its existence,
considering its purpose
contemplating its function
and
bringing attention to some other things
that are going unseen
and
that it is doing.

Chapter 2
Exploring the Literature: How Is Poetic Inquiry Being Used in Published Studies?

Introduction

A review of the literature that uses poetry in research or reporting processes, comprised of academic journal articles, book chapters, anthologies, and poems published in peer-reviewed publications, reveals that poetic inquiry, at times capitalized other times not, does not have a fixed definition. This is because the work undertaken through the method/methodology is not limited solely to artistic, aesthetic, educational or traditional research-focused spaces. This widespread or transdisciplinary space has been referred to in the literature as a liminal space (Sinner et al., 2006; Neilsen, 2008; Leggo et al., 2011) that exists between multiple disciplines and disciplinary practices. With mentions in the literature of poetic inquiry going back nearly 70 years (Carruth, 1948; James, 2017), not including the spectrum of synonymous terms, it is first important to understand why the method arose in qualitative research. Its purpose needs to be established before there is an understanding of the basic tenets of poetic inquiry and its functions for research and scholarship as they exist today.

The Proliferation of Poetic Inquiry

Prendergast (2009a) found over 230 published, peer-reviewed journal articles or book chapters that identify poetry as a major element of the research processes or research presentation. She distilled the ways in which poetry was used, and what labels were given to the poetic research practices, into 40 key terms that encompassed poetic inquiry in the literature at that time. The number of published articles has increased significantly since she began the process in 2009. Prendergast has now compiled a bibliography and samples of "around 3000 pages of poems from social science peer-reviewed journals" (Prendergast, personal communication, January 27, 2017). As her compendium is not currently available for public consumption, her initial published findings continue to remain significant today.

In her article, published in 2009, Prendergast highlights that while a number of terms were used synonymously with poetic inquiry, most studies could be placed into three categories by using the concept of voice. These categories served as a way to better understand the landscape of the methodology and how poetry was being used in qualitative research. These initial categories were:

- Vox autobiographia/autoethnographia – researcher voiced poems (e.g., field notes)
- Vox participare – participant voiced poems (e.g., interview data)
- Vox theoria – literature voiced poems (e.g., written from or in response to the literature) (p. 545).

Prendergast (2015) has since adapted and expanded her original categorizations, from three to five, to include:

- Vox Theoria/Vox Poetica – Poems about self, writing and poetry as method
- Vox Justitia – Poems on equity, equality, social justice, class, freedom
- Vox Identitatis – Poetry exploring, self/participants' gender, race, sexuality
- Vox Custodia – Poetry of caring, nursing, caregivers'/patients' experience
- Vox Procreator – Poems of parenting, family and/ or religion. (p. 6)

These new categorizations better describe poetic inquiry's ever-expanding uses across multiple disciplines. Notably, vox theoria was changed from "literature voiced poems" (p. 545) to poems about self, writing and poetry as method. This change reflects that literature-voiced poems can, and do, exist in all categorizations. Prendergast's original categorizations are similar to those of Hanauer (2010) whose smaller-scale study found 66 sources that use poetry in their research. He suggested three categories that could aid in better understanding why and how poetry is/was used in qualitative research studies by looking at the focus of each study. He found that poetry was used: "1) to represent and reinterpret existing data; 2) to collect data; and 3) to collect field notes" (p. 75). Both researchers' categorizations reflect the multifaceted and dynamic nature of the methodology and provide ways to consider what sets poetic inquiry apart from other qualitative methods. This information aids in the exploration and discovery of more common characteristics of methodological approaches to poetic inquiry.

The increase in published research studies that use poetic inquiry, what Leavy (2015) calls a "turn towards scientific artistic expression" (p. 66), show that the methodology goes beyond a way of representing voices more vibrantly (which can also be demonstrated through well-written studies that use narrative inquiry or case study methodologies). Poetic inquiry, in literature, is selected as it promotes criticality, can make explicit the position or reflexivity of the researcher, and allows for different perspectives to be considered through the artistic medium of poetry. Prendergast (2009a) stressed the importance of a balance between both aspects of the methodology–aesthetically pleasing/evocative poetry and critical inquiry—writing, "My intention to articulate a methodology for poetic inquiry is to position it as an artistic practice carried out within a research framework that cannot and must not diminish the critical/aesthetic qualities of these kinds of poems as poetry" (p. 549). In her exploration of the dynamic ways that poetry is used in academic literature, she does not favour the aesthetically pleasing works over the critical works. She suggests that poetic inquiry is, "along with all arts-based inquiry approaches, deeply concerned with aesthetic issues around quality, qualifications, preparedness, elitism and expertise" (p. 563). poetic inquiry is not selected by researchers as a way to avoid the stringent nature of scientific studies or to diminish the need for thorough, well-supported studies. Instead, researchers choose poetic inquiry as a method to realize new or different ways of knowing with the potential for a variety of views/interpretation and voices to be represented at one time.

The mode of poetry, the act of writing poems or analyzing through poems, is represented in the literature as a way to expand perspectives on human experience. As a proponent of this idea, Brady (1991, 2004) stresses that the capaciousness of poetry is able to express and accounts for "life's exigencies" and that it "promotes robust discourse from ivy-covered halls to the hinterlands of humans *being*" (pp. xv-xvi) through its dynamic uses of language. Similarly, Leavy (2015) writes, "poetry is a form that itself brings attention to silence (or as a poet might say, to space) and also relies on emotional evocation as part of meaning making while simultaneously exposing the fluidity and multiplicity of meaning" (p. 66). Percer (2002) goes beyond appealing to the emotion brought forward through the use of poetry, arguing that the intersections of poetry and research extend beyond the usual range of educational scholarship by adding greater depth to the study. He, like Prendergast and others, maintains that poetry brings out new ways of understanding, but that it does not diminish the need for balance between the expressive and empirical elements that encompass the study. There need to be both elements for the study to be rigorous and purposeful. Informed by her own experiential and experimental practices, Cahnmann (2003) also suggests that the use of poetry can bring about new understandings, contending that "through poetic craft and practice, we can surprise both ourselves and our audiences with new possibilities" (p. 37). The practitioners of poetic inquiry, from various fields of practice, choose to use poetry in their studies for particular purposes and in particular ways, but the underlying reason is that they wish to interact through language (with themselves, the reader and the researched) in ways that are not commonly accepted in more traditional qualitative research methods. They seek different ways of knowing.

The Rhizomatic History of Poetic Inquiry

The literature indicates that poetic inquiry (at times capitalized as Poetic Inquiry) arose in response to what Denzin and Lincoln (2011) describe as a "crisis of representation" (p. 3). Prendergast and Galvin (2012) describe this crisis as a response to research that "appropriated, overpowered, fragmented, rendered-over summative or even silenced" participants' voices (p. 5). Through poetry, researchers have an alternative approach which seeks to add or amplify the voices of participants to the research and provide different ways to try to understand others' perspectives and experiences. This attempt to understand differently has yielded hundreds of published studies across the disciplines and a myriad of unpublished theses and dissertations that remain archived in universities around the world.

We now turn to address the question of how this method developed historically. The history of poetic inquiry is difficult to trace and organize thematically because it is not linear. Any attempt to convert the non-linear history of poetic inquiry into a linear history would diminish the richness and complexity of the methodology. As such, I posit that the history of poetic inquiry is *rhizomatic* (Deleuze & Guattari, 1988; Irwin et al., 2006) with various nodes that have no discernable center. This idea was echoed in correspondence with Dr. Carl Leggo who likened the rhizomatic nature of poetic inquiry to a strawberry plant (Leggo, personal correspondence, June 19, 2017), with fruit growing from its runners where you may not expect it. Dr. Kedrick James likened poetic inquiry to a mushroom, more specifically like a mycelium with no hierarchy (James, personal correspondence, June 19, 2017; June 29, 2017). The idea that strawberries grow in a variety of areas and mushrooms grow out of a variety of media also helps to further the understanding that the poetry created through poetic inquiry may be of the same textual genre, but the context – that is what feeds the poetry – differs and is as important as the products themselves.

Turning again to the literature, we would be remiss if we did not talk about sociologist Laurel Richardson, who is often cited as a major influence in the field of poetic inquiry (Pelias, 2004; Prendergast, 2009; Haunauer, 2010). In her article *Poetics, dramatics and transgressive validity: The case of the skipped line*, Richardson (1993a) explains how her creation of a five-page poem about Louisa May's lived experiences was written with the intent to explore how using a non-scientific form can "make visible the underlying labor of sociological production as well as its potential as a human endeavor" (p. 695). Inspired by DeShazer's (1986) feminist writing on language and power, Richardson explains that she felt inclined to explore her work through poetry as poetry can create checks and balances – that it has the ability to mitigate power struggles that occur in social science research. She wanted the freedom to explore her findings in ways that could bring the lived experiences of her participants to life. She writes:

> Poetics strips those methodological bogey-men of their power to control andconstrain. A poem as "findings" resituates ideas of validity and reliability from "knowing" to "telling." Everybody's writing is suspect – not just those who write poems.

In sociological research, the findings have been safely staged within the language of the fathers, the domain of science writing. [The poem] "Louisa May" challenges the language, tropes, emotional suppressions, and presumptive validity claims of masculinist social science. (1993a, p. 704)

Richardson sought to explore a way of better portraying her participant's story through poetic form, as she saw it as a way of giving voice and power to her participant by creating "a transcript masquerading as a poem/a poem masquerading as a transcript" (1994, p. 126). As in the expert of her poem, below (with original formatting to showcase her approach), Richardson (1993a) takes Louisa May's words, verbatim, and organizes them so that they display the core story and showcase Louisa's commentary (in parentheses and italics) on the original interview transcription.

> Well, one thing that happens
> growing up in the South
> is that you leave. I
> always knew I would
>   I would leave.
>   *(I don't know what to say ...*
>   *I don't know what's germane.)*
> My high school sweetheart and I married,
> and went north to college.
>   I got pregnant and miscarried,
> and I lost the child.
>   *(As I see it now it was a marriage*
>   *situation which got increasingly horrendous*
>   *where I was under the most stress and strain*
>   *without any sense of how to extricate myself.)* (p. 707)

While her play on form, showcasing Louisa May's words and reflections on their original interview, was seen as radical by some at the time, she contends that she was not seeking an elimination of social-scientific writing but was looking to expand her field and its "representational forms" (1997, p. 298). This led to her further conceptualization of forms of poetry used in research: narrative and lyric research poetry. Leavy (2015) interprets Richardson's identification and categorization of research poems in her discussion of poetic inquiry by explaining that for Richardson, narrative poetry is "closer to storytelling, where data gathered from interviews are transformed into a poem that tells the respondent's story, using his or her language" while "lyric poetry emphasizes moments of emotion and is less concerned with relaying a 'story' per se" (p. 66). This is an important distinction when trying to understand the purpose of using poetry in research, beyond experimental poetics, and the foundational texts that form approaches to poetic inquiry.

Despite her major contribution to the method, what Richardson's (1992) writing about *Louisa May* and subsequent publications about the poem, there lacked clear descriptions of her process(es) of writing research poetry. In response to this lack of method or guide, Glesne (1997), motivated by Richardson's transformation of interview transcripts into poetry (poetic transcription), developed a process that can be used to create poetry from transcript data. She calls this process "poetic rendering" (p. 206). Poetic rendering entails taking the participants' words, putting them into stanzas, and then deliberately removing words so that participants' intent and voice remain, but the text is more refined and evocative. Glesne, as an early adopter of poetic inquiry, was careful to discuss the hybridization of her texts by not defining them as poetry. She notes that her poem-like transcription texts "move in the direction of poetry but are not necessarily poetry" (p. 213) in order to have her work exist in the liminal space between art and research. Glesne and Richardson's ideas were later picked up by the likes of Walsh (2006). Walsh used her research transcripts to create found poems that "were both academic and artistic" in nature (p. 990) which highlights the need for balance between poetry and inquiry.

Other notable mentions in the literature that help to provide the context of poetic inquiry's functions in qualitative research are Poindexter (1998), who used poetry as a method of data analysis, and MacNeil (2000), who is cited as being one of the first researchers in the literature to use qualitative data analysis software to support the creation of poetic data transcription (p. 361). It should be noted that before the contributions and explorations of these researchers came the experimental work of Tedlock (1983) who experimented with the creation of "dramatic poetry" (p. 55) from transcription data. Gee (1989) also posited a process for breaking transcripts down into stanzas to generate understandings, while Eisner (1997) sought ways of integrating the creative and analytical. Eisner's argument that poetry could transcend language and possesses an "evocative presentation of data" (p. 5), one that is visceral and ephemeral for the reader, contributes to the conversations around the use of poetry in qualitative research studies across multiple fields.

These researchers work in different fields, yet, using the analogy put forth by Leggo (personal communication, June 9, 2017), they all grew "strawberries."

Each scholar seeks new ways of knowing and feels that poetry is the mode of writing that can help them learn more about their research processes and research participants. Acknowledging the simultaneous parallels that took, and take, place in various fields continues to develop our understanding of poetic inquiry and moves us closer to a working definition. Looking closer now at how poetic inquiry has developed and how it is used in the areas of health care, anthropology, sociology and education should assist in our conceptualizing of this ever-growing rhizomatic method.

Poetic Inquiry in Fields of Practice

Poetic inquiry is difficult to trace as it appears in some form or another across a multitude of fields. Appearing infrequently in the literature, though worth mentioning as researchers continue to explore ways in which poetry can be used to support their research, are the areas of advertising, organizational research, management and policy and music therapy (McCulliss, 2013). There are, however, four major areas, or fields, that appear recurrently in the literature: health care, anthropology, sociology, and education. Discussing poetic inquiry's use in the field of health care research requires mentioning the significant contributions of Rich Furman. Furman is frequently cited in the literature (Prendergast, 2009; Hanauer, 2010; McCulliss, 2013; Faulkner, 2016a) as a single author or as part of a small group of authors, who used poetry as a tool for healing for medical practitioners and their patients (Furman & Cavers, 2005).

Furman and Cavers (2005) share an example of a participant-generated poem, where the poet/participant (Cavers) describes some of his experiences with bipolar disorder. In the article, Furman describes how poetry can be a valuable tool where "[t]he author of a poem presents his or her truth; truth in terms of his or her day to day reality, wishes and fantasies, hopes and aspirations, and even emotional paradoxes that characterize the human psyche" (p. 317). Furman also highlights what he believes poetry does that other media cannot do, sharing that

> [t]hrough [Cavers'] poem, we enter into a world of conflict, of disappointment, of hope, and finally of the ultimate concerns of existence. Would we dare to reduce this rich data to a simple questionnaire response category such as "bipolar" or "mentally ill?" (p. 317)

Furman has also published studies that use poetry to explore loss in his personal life. He shares an evocative and visceral poem (with an excerpt shared here in its original single-spacing) relating to his powerlessness and apparent anger at his father's cancer diagnosis and perceived outcome,

> The shades are drawn by choice,
> snow-sealed by the madness of time,

of your death. Four days until they
slice your chest,

a cherry pie or deep ditch by lonely
road,
or thin slices of sandwich meat. They
will pick at you
    uncaring vultures;
devour the parts they save
    praising their success
whatever the outcome,
after they will drink dry Chardonnay.
Filtered cancer daydreams
    a ridiculous bar
high on coffee
    beer
and your end soon coming,
you perform now maybe your final
winks,
the last of your dreams.
There is all the beer I can drink,
but precious little time. (2004, p. 166-7)

Through his own lived experience, he demonstrates that the creation of poetry, which he considers a form of data, akin to that of this study, "helps various constituents consume research more effectively. [Where] [t]ogether, the use of qualitative and quantitative research can lead to the acquisition of a body of knowledge that has depth, breadth, reliability, and validity" (p. 196). This consideration of poetry as a form of data is not limited to this study but extends to other health-related studies that explore the uses of poetry as a form of research data (Furman, Lietz & Langer, 2006). The work that was done was both autoethnographic and ethnographic in nature (see Smith, 2002 for more on ethnopoetics), where poetry served as a major methodological process. These are but a sampling of studies that reflect the versatility of poetry as a tool in qualitative research.

   It should also be noted that the work being done through poetic inquiry echoes the work being done through writing therapy, which often explores identity and the concept of self (Anderson & MacCurdy, 2000; Furman, 2004; Lengelle, 2008; Orr, 2002; Zimmerman, 2002). Similarities lie in the reflective and reflexive nature of the writing, which is akin to autoethnographic and ethnopoetic ways of using poetry to explore self in societal or cultural contexts. Moreover, many of the theories, studies and explorations through poetry have parallels to the work done by arts-based researchers in education (Leggo et al.,

2011), as well as those exploring issues in the area of social work, where they strive to understand the lived experience of others (Black & Enos, 1981). Poetic inquiry has also been used in research relating to physiotherapy and the relationship between physiotherapist and client (Tasker, Loftus & Higgs, 2014) and to explore specific emotional facets of nursing such as empathy (e.g., King, 1995). These researchers seek to better understand human experience from a variety of viewpoints. For example, Öhlén (2003) took narratives of suffering and condensed them into poetic form in an attempt to better understand what suffering meant, thereby informing healthcare professionals approaches and practices when dealing with patients in mental and physical pain. He did this through a columnar approach where the verbatim transcript was represented on one side, with his poetic interpretation on the other (see Figure 2.1):

Figure 2.1: Öhlén's Poetic Method.

Verbatim Transcription in Dialogue Format	*Poetic Condensed Transcription*
Joakim: Would you like to tell me about how it was when you first got ill?	How it was when I got ill? Well, the thing is that I do not remember it That's what's so odd
Olga: Well, the thing is, that I do not remember it. That's what's so odd about it. I don't really know when it was. I do think (obvious consideration) that I must have become more tired little by little (raised her eyes like it was so definitely). I daresay I became more tired. Then I don't know, but it is possible, I usually go to him, the doctor in (the name of the place). He may have done a few tests, maybe that's the way it was. Then, then I don't know. You see, it was something.	I don't really know when it was I do think I must have become more tired little by little

I daresay I became more tired

Then I don't know but it is possible I usually go to him, the doctor He may have done a few tests maybe that's the way it was

Then then I don't know You see it was Something |

He argues that a hybridization of approaches – using narratives and poetry— can aid in understanding writing and that "scientific language needs to be enriched by everyday metaphoric and poetic expressions" (p. 565) if a complex phenomenon (e.g., a lived experience) is to be understood. Once again, there is an indicator of growth occurring without linear ties between fields of study.

Looking now to the field of anthropology, the initial use of poetic inquiry in research studies is often attributed (e.g., Prendergast, 2009; McCulliss, 2013) to Flores (1982) and her experimentation with "field poetry" (p. 22) and to Tedlock's (1983) and Rothenberg's (1994) creation of narrative poetry from transcript data. Flores (1982) writes that she used her field of poetry to highlight initially unseen issues with the Canguese people of northern Spain whom she was studying,

> one result of course, are poems which describe how a place looks, sounds and smells or how it feels physically to be in that place. Another, perhaps paradoxical result, is that sensually-apprehended details can give clues to more abstract problems. (p. 18)

While Flores remains cited in the literature, a deeper look at the field of anthropology also uncovers the work of biological anthropologist Loren Eiseley (1972) who is cited by poet and anthropologist Miles Richardson (1998) as a trailblazer in his field. According to Miles Richardson, Eiseley was not only able to use poetry as a way to portray significant discoveries in anthropology but also used it to explore and give dimension to everyday human behavior.

As mentioned previously, the poetic inquiry movement in sociology is attributed to Laurel Richardson and her experimental poetic renderings of her participants' stories. Richardson's work is often cited as a primary inspiration for poetic inquiry as we know it today (Butler-Kisber, 2002; Hanauer, 2010). Be it field note poetry, poetic transcription or poetic renderings, the uses of poetry in anthropology and sociology, as in health care, are further rhizomes that contribute to our understanding of poetic inquiry with each study growing and extending into other fields of practice and research.

Continuing the metaphor of the rhizomatic history of poetic inquiry, I now turn attention to the field of education. The academic-poetic works of Lynn Butler-Kisber, Carl Leggo, and Monica Prendergast are each significant in shaping and identifying the history of poetic inquiry in education. Butler-Kisber's notable work in poetic inquiry can be traced to the late 1990s where her experimentation with poetic transcription illuminated ways in which poetry and qualitative research could unite in education. Butler-Kisber (2002) cites Eisner (1991) and his discussions around the power of combining art and research as a major inspiration for her research. She writes that she feels as if Eisner's work gave her "permission" to explore her research through poetic representation (p. 231). Of her process, she writes:

> I began to experiment with poetic representation. I chose this route because what was emerging in my research demanded an evocative portrayal. I was familiar with the work of Richardson (1994) in which she used found poetry to represent sociological interviews. In this approach, the researcher uses only the words of the participant(s) to create a poetic rendition of a story or phenomenon. Because I was most comfortable working with words rather than other alternative forms, I decided found poetry might offer a viable way of portraying what I was finding. (2002, p. 232)

While her work in poetic transcription and poetic data analysis linked to the poetic exploration of Richardson (1993b; 1994), Tedlock (1983) and Glesne (1997), her work marks a pivotal shift in the acceptance of poetry within educational research that opened the doors for other artist-researchers.

Similarly, Leggo's work has contributed significantly to the literature around poetic inquiry and is cited in a variety of studies that employ poetry (Prendergast, 2009; Lahman et al., 2011). With obvious ties to autoethnography (Ellis, 1999), Leggo's research explores his positionality and reflexivity through poetry in a practice that he calls "living poetically" (2015, p. 145). His a/r/tographic work (as artist, researcher and teacher) in the literature also explores his development and growth as a person, educator (see Leggo, 1997, 2003, 2007) and poet (see Leggo, 2005, 2012a) while simultaneously exploring how education, writing and poetry enrich the lives of others. Leggo's concept of poetic rumination (1999) to process ideas through the creation of poetry and his discussions of the merits of writing poetry as a way of knowing (2008c), where the poet can "experiment with language, to create, to know, to engage creativity and imaginatively with experience" (p. 165), remain relevant in poetic inquiry. He was also instrumental in the propagation of the notion of "living poetically" (Leggo, 2005), a way of viewing the world through a poet's eyes that has helped to expand the definitions of academic writing and what it means to be a researcher. Further examples of Leggo's work and discussion of the influences of his approaches to poetry and inquiry appear in subsequent chapters of this book (Chapter Four and Chapter Eight).

Other notable pieces in the literature around the use of poetry in education and educational studies comes from Furman (2014) who describes how the use of poetry in his freshman course at the University of Washington Tacoma "allowed students to learn about the nonliterary uses of poetry using experiential, hands-on methods that help students develop new communication and analytical skills" (p. 206). Roberts, Brasel, and Crawford (2014) also discuss the benefits of using formula poems when working with in-service and pre-service teachers to help them reflect on their professional experiences as well as to identify struggles that students may have with test and assignment anxiety. Patrick's (2016) study also reveals a need for a space in qualitative educational research for poetry, as the findings indicate that found poetry written by teachers allowed them to refine information and seek greater scholarship around what can be done with poetic data. Her findings are: "[f]inding 1. The poetry experience supported the writing efforts of novice poets" (p. 391), [f]inding 2. The found poetry experience supported the transactional relationships between readers and texts" (p. 391) and "[f]inding 3. The found poetry experience supported prospective teachers of poetry"(p. 392). Through the writing of poetry, where inquiry happened in the writing process and the reflective/autoethnographic inquiry that followed, the participants were able to understand their perceived place in the teaching of poetry and their role as poets themselves. Similarly, Dobson (2012) argues for additional interactions through poetry in education suggesting that, "as an artefact, the poem offers valuable insights regarding the process of awakening in consciousness and of possibilities for the reinvigoration of education, from the Latin, *educo, educare*, to draw forth from within" (p. 132).

The uses of poetic inquiry in education is, however, not limited to research on practices, experiences or teaching methodologies. It also extends to exploring issues around curriculum development. Inspired by the presentations at the Provoking Curriculum Studies Conference in 2013, Ng-A-Fook et al. (2016) edited a collection of studies that consider the intersections between curriculum, the arts, and teaching strategies. Their exploration uses notions of "strong poetry" and "strong poets," building off Bloom (1973) and Rorty's (1989) discussions respectively, to frame their collection which emphasizes the work of those who "find themselves involuntarily straddling that which is realistic and that which is yet to come, which they help bring into being" (p. xvii). The collection presents the concept that scholars are poets and that using the poetic voice and poetic approaches in education could support curriculum development by complicating accepted practices and theories and by promoting change incited by meaningful and critical reflection.

Reviewing the history of poetic inquiry in education requires not only a consideration of published works, but also a look at the works that may not be published in international journals that still contribute to the rhizomes of poetic inquiry. Experimentation and exploration are actively occurring in universities around the world. Be it occurring through purely text-based explorations or through text and visual arts such as De La Lama's (2014) unpublished dissertation that took the form of a poetic graphic novel at the University of Florida. A cursory search for the specific term "poetic inquiry," in its proper or common noun form, limited to dissertations or theses, through the University of British Columbia's library online database generates 86 results between 1974 and 2018. An item of interest that stands out is that of the 86 dissertations that cite "poetic inquiry," 10 were authored in the latter two years. This gives a strong indication of the greater acceptance of such approaches in graduate studies and qualitative research. Taking a closer look at some of these 86 studies, I turn to the research of Sinner et al. (2006) who provides a glimpse into how Arts-Based Educational Research (ABER) has been used in graduate dissertations at one of Canada's top universities. The researchers explored over 30 arts-based dissertations in the Faculty of Education at The University of British Columbia (UBC) from 1994-2004 with the intent of identifying, describing and documenting the arts-based practices of graduate students. Among these dissertations were projects that used narrative inquiry and hermeneutics, post-colonial and autoethographic explorations through poetry, writing and visual arts, performative inquiry, which used poetry and prose, poetry and photography, and a/r/tography. They argue that these studies were, and are, significant as they sought to push the boundaries of art and research:

> Arts-based educational researchers are always seeking to understand the parameters of "good art" and "good research," and they are never satisfied with any checklist, template, or formula. Instead, each new arts-based educational research project is informed by past projects, but is always also seeking to extend the possibilities of what constitutes both research and art. This process is creative and emergent, a dynamic process of inquiry. (p. 1229)

Sinner and colleagues (2006) once again allude to the boundless nature of poetic inquiry. Where does poetic inquiry reside in the larger context of qualitative research?

Synonymous Terms and Uses

Looking not only at the field-specific uses of poetic inquiry, but also at the diverse terminology used to describe the work being done, adds greater dimension to the understanding of what it is. What is poetic inquiry? Who are poetic inquirers? These questions are not easily answered. When asked about the origins of the term poetic inquiry, Prendergast responded:

> I was using the term "research poetry" in my own graduate work, but it was never a term that "worked" that well for me, clunky sounding. I felt the same way about Richardson's "poetic representation" and "poetic transcription." As I gathered together the annotated bibliography that was the focus of my post-doc with Carl [Leggo], the term poetic inquiry popped up... So I cannot claim to have coined the term poetic inquiry but I certainly did choose to use it as an umbrella term for the array of poetry-based practices I was finding in the literature. (Prendergast, personal communication, January 27, 2017)

When asked to define poetic inquiry, Butler-Kisber (2017) remarked:

> I would define poetic inquiry as the process of using words from transcripts or field notes from our studies and transforming them into a form of poetry. This could be done as found poetry, where we use the actual words of the participant. It also can be done as generated poetry, where we use our own words to reflect upon some aspect of our research. (00:10)

Considering the umbrella term and unpacking Butler-Kisber's concise definition, where she alludes to poetic transcription, poetic field notes, poetic data analysis and poetic reflection, will assist in further dissemination of the term poetic inquiry and help to build our understanding of the methodology. For example, Prendergast offered her take on the concept of found poetry and "literature voiced research poetry" (2004) or *vox theoria* (2009), while Poindexter's more anthropological poetic data analysis used poetry to re-tell the stories of her participants coming to terms with a diagnosis of HIV (2002). Cahnmann (2003) had her own approach to ethnographic research poems, including the integration of field note and verbatim interview poems, that differed from Flores (1982) and Richardson (1992) to bring her research to life while remaining critical of her research choices. This enacts her belief that "[w]e may not all write great popular or literary poems, but we can all draw on the craft and practice of poetry to realize its potential, challenging the academic marginality of our work" (Cahnmann, 2003, p. 35). Rapport and Hartill (2012) address crossing disciplines with ethnographic poetic representation which they see as a method of "re-presenting social data and its management of language" (p. 21) in a way that demonstrates "an experiential truth that cannot be accessed in other ways" (p. 21).

Poetry is also used in studies that have social justice implications. Hartnett (2003), for example, uses poetry in the creation of a critical ethnography with elements of autobiography and political underpinnings when he looked at the treatment of prisoners in the federal prison system in the United States of America. Through his presentation of 33 poems, some about himself while others are about specific inmates, Hartnett highlights the harsh living conditions that inmates face while continuing to push for reforms to the American prison system. Similarly, a form of critical poetic inquiry has been used by Leavy (2010) who, for example, created a suite of poems reflecting on the tensions of the "artistic-scientific divide" (p. 240). In this suite, she uses poetry as a form of resistance to undermine power, to share her ideas and to allow for readers to generate their own interpretations as opposed to providing a singular and absolute truth in her text. In her article, Leavy (2010) also highlights the power of poetry as a method for finding solace, reflecting and making sense of complex ideas. She writes in "My Poem" (shared here with its original single spacing),

> unsure of my place
> I searched for a home
> a self to call my own
> like a castle far away
> the ivory tower beckoned
> but after my imagined happily ever after

> I got a chill I couldn't shake
> for ivory is cold
> so I carved myself
> a poetic path
>
> like a black hole
> surrounded by space
> I can disappear
> into my poem
> when loneliness envelopes
> graying it all
> I take it to bed
> where under the covers
> it holds me
> gives me warmth
> my poem
> protects me
> when I hide
> it seeks
> what is lost
> and becomes
> my confidant
> purveyor of truth
> and beauty
> my beauty seeker emerges (p. 243)

Through poetry, Leavy is able to process and share her experiences (autoethnographically) in academia that are at once full of depth and subtlety. This potentially makes her commentary of the system more palatable for their intended audience, while not discounting her lived experience.

Continuing the exploration of poetry and power, the work of Lahman and Richard (2014) discusses the concept of "appropriated poetry" (p. 344) derived from textual archives to create found poems in various poetic forms, including that of a *cento* or collage poem. For these researchers, poetry and power are interconnected and they see poetry as a way to amplify their participants' voices in the literature and in society. The concept of ethnographic poetics (Brady, 2004), where research occurs in the spaces between anthropology and art, supports studies like that of Carroll, Dew and Howden-Chapman (2011) who used poetry to explore the concept of homelessness. They conducted an ethnographic study with 40 research participants who lived in "informal dwellings such as sheds, vans, buses, garages and caravans" in New Zealand (p. 263). The researchers found that poetry allows the voices of the participants to be heard and broadcast across a variety of fields with the hope that their living situations would become known to policymakers, health care providers, and the public at large.

Poetic inquiry also allows for an exploration through poetic social science (Bochner, 2000) and anthropological poetics; Brady (1991) called the integration of anthropology and literature "art-ful science," a liminal space where the beauty and tragedy of the world are textually empowered by the carefully chosen constructions and subjective understandings of the author (p. 270). Prendergast, Gouzouasis, Leggo & Irwin (2009) sought greater understanding of their participants' experiences in making music through the process of creating haiku, a form of Japanese poetry, from research participants' interview responses. In the study "the haikus were written by the first author and massaged by the second author, who re-read the interview transcripts and reviewed the interviews in digital video format" (p. 312). From their interactions with the haikus, a form that they see as "an intentionally accessible art form" (p. 313), the researchers not only show that students value music and their music education, but also demonstrate that poetry "is one more way to make sense of the lived experience of the arts in our students, our teachers, ourselves and our schools" (p. 313).

Continuing the discussion around terms, we consider the work of Neilsen (2008) who posit the idea of Lyric Inquiry, which "marries lyric [poetry] with research" (p. 94). While Lyric Inquiry does not take up a significant space in the literature, it provides a different way to look at a particular facet (or approach) of poetic inquiry. Neilsen's use of the term *lyric* was chosen to avoid narrow interpretations that often accompany work done using poetry. She says, "the term lyric is a term with the roomy capacity to include the expressive, the poetic, and the phenomenological in our scholarship without returning to the false distinctions or choices our enterprises often invite" (p. 94). This form of research method, she argus, is aimed at connecting with the reader on an emotional level through criteria akin to that of poetic inquiry. Her criteria entails: "Liminality, ineffability, metaphorical thinking, embodied understanding, personal evocations, domestic and local understanding, and an embrace of the eros of language-the desire to honour and experience phenomena through words...and to communicate this experience to others" (p. 95).

Studies in poetic inquiry may not use universal terminology, but often the intentions behind the studies are the same. They seek to enliven knowledge through the use of poetry, with its unique functions to construct visceral yet subjective meaning. A review of the literature also reveals that poetic inquiry is not limited to the proverbial pen and paper ways of writing. James (2009), for example, discusses the notion of digital poetic inquiry that used cut-up texts to create found poems in order to glean more from the data. Of this process, he writes:

resonation becomes key to unlocking the intent of the text, but it is only brought into awareness through the deliberation and textual dwelling undertaken as a method of interest. Thus while other poetic inquirers using these methods may choose to work with texts gathered from information environments more savory and solidified than junk email, there is no essential difference in the process of inquiry. (p. 71)

Advancing the discussion around non-physical text-based forms of poetic inquiry, Fels (2012), describes performative inquiry not as a method "but rather a way of being in embodied inquiry with others through the arts" (p. 55). Performing poetry, like performing one's own stories (Saldaña, 2011), allows a different perspective on the research not only through the performance, but through the act of speaking the poetry/data, which becomes an embodied representation and invites others to share in the work and spurs further inquiry. Using poetry as part of performative inquiry has been done to explore curriculum (Fels & Belliveau, 2008), reflective praxis (Prendergast, 2010) and the connection between physical bodies and the notion of self (as in Snowber's, 2016, embodied inquiry). It has also been used to further explore the concept of performative inquiry as a methodology and poetic inquiry's place in qualitative research (Prendergast & Belliveau, 2013; Allsopp, 2015; Kreider, 2015).

Performative inquiry can also extend into the realm of digital poetic inquiry as demonstrated by Natasha Wiebe's (2008) online journal article where she explores the notion self in the context of organized religion which includes hyperlinks to audio files of her reading her poetry. Wiebe believes that her "poetic inquiry is performative research in that it is performed to an audience, and because it is reshaped as a result of interaction with that audience" (p. 15). Wiebe suggests that adding the multimodal level of auditory voice to her journal articles allows her an opportunity to rework her research and poems through the feedback provided by the audience and through her critical reflection of her poetic performances. In these examples, poetry, in both textual and non-textual forms, allows for unique interactions to take place between research and researcher that allow for greater insights into their topic(s) of inquiry. This idea is echoed by Prendergast who speaks of the power of poetry in her practices with performed research and in the writing of her 2006 dissertation, saying that "writing poetically was a necessity brought about by the challenge of representing the ephemeral and transitory nature of a theatre performance" (Prendergast, personal communication, January 27, 2017).

Returning once again to the notion of poetic inquiry existing and growing in liminal spaces, I turn to explore the idea of using poetry as part of a hybridized, collaged or bricolaged (Kincheloe, 2001) text. Hasebe-Ludt, Chambers and Leggo (2009) and Hasebe-Ludt and Leggo (2016) explore the idea of métissage which they explain "comes from the Latin word mixtus meaning 'mixed,' primarily referring to cloth of two fibers" (2009, p. 142), to describe their weaving of story and/or poetry with visual art in their exploratory work with ties to Indigenous ways of knowing. In their book (Hasebe-Ludt et al., 2009) describe their hybrid process as one where they "braid strands of place and space, memory and history, ancestry and (mixed) race, language and literacy; familiar and strange, with strands of tradition, ambiguity, becoming, (re)creation, and renewal into a métissage" (p. 9) in an effort to create what they call an "eco-zone" (p. 15) that will give readers a way "to better understand the pedagogical and contextual relationships—social, cultural, political, and otherwise—that are a part of their lives" (p. 15).

The literature around hybrid texts also includes the work of Christianakis (2011), who explored the process of creating hybrid texts with fifth graders using rap (music and lyrics) with its elements of rhythm and poetry. First, she explored how students interact with popular writing models and later with hybrid text creation using poetry. Seeing that students express feeling more connected to the poetry through this multi-layered writing process, she recommends that there is a need for more embedded popular writing or pop culture-focused works in classrooms. This multi-modal approach, confirmed by Christianakis (2011), uses poetry and music as ways to better reach students in ways that are similar in nature to the work being done by Morell and Duncan-Andrade (2002) who used hip-hop to support students' literacy development and their understanding of canonical texts. Another version of the hybrid text, where poetry and story are interwoven (enacting Prendergast's, 2009, idea of vox theoria), is found both in published pieces (see Quinn-Hall, 2015, who mixed text types to find greater meaning), and in unpublished dissertations and theses (such as Vincent, 2015, who created a textual métissage that explored the ties between poetry and literacy education). This weaving of text types, as indicated in the published and unpublished literature, is done with the intent to generate deeper and more meaningful understandings of concepts and to further explore the literature. Leggo (2008c) praises these liminal spaces, between art and traditional ways of knowing:

> As a language and literacy educator, I am committed to exploring the intersections between creative practice and critical pedagogy, and creative pedagogy and critical practice. I want to linger in the spaces of binary oppositions in order to build bridges like metaphors from one vertex to another, even in the midst of one vortex through another. (pp. 146-147)

The intersections, with various terms to describe researchers' interactions with poetry, re-affirm the idea of rhizomatic clusters and the metaphor of ever-growing strawberry plants that embody poetic inquiry. There is no singular set of terms or one exclusive way of enacting a study using poetic inquiry, which gives researchers greater liberty to explore their research and answer their research questions. This lack of concrete definition, which allows for emergent explorations of language and analysis through poetry, however, can also be seen as problematic. This is a problem that is taken up as part of this book.

Acknowledging Concerns With Poetic Inquiry

An understanding of poetic inquiry would not be complete without considering some opposing views, problems, or criticisms of the method that exists across the rhizomes in the literature. Richardson (2000) has argued that art and inquiry do not need to be separate, writing that "any dinosaurian beliefs that 'creative' and 'analytical' are contradictory and incompatible modes are standing in the path of a meteor; they are doomed for extinction" (p. 962). While there are few "dinosaurian" arguments in the literature, there are, however, poetic inquiry practitioners concerned with the quality of studies and who caution against grouping novice poets with those who have studied the art and craft of poetry. They believe that the study and act of writing poetry, or poiesis (from the Greek for *making*), needs to be attended prior to undertaking studies that adopt the use of poetic inquiry. Piirto (2002) wrote,

> For some thinkers in the field of qualitative research, the person using poetry in the depiction of qualitative findings need have no background in poetry, no record of having written poetry, no formal study of poetry. To write poetry one need not have studied it, seems to be the thought. (p. 435)

She cautions against the idea of novice poet-researchers and argues that researchers and readers of research should not "confuse the poetasters, [a term used to describe one who writes inferior poetry], for the poets" (p. 444). She expressed a fear that this lack of classification could dilute the reputation of the methodology and undermine the work that was being done through poetic inquiry.

This call for a form of quality control was also voiced by Barone (2001), who suggests that arts-based research must be affective or the reputation will falter (p. 27), and Faulkner (2007) who wrote, "I am tired of reading and listening to lousy poetry that masquerades as research and vice versa" (p. 222). Faulkner suggests that there is a greater need for researchers to be thoughtful when undertaking a study using poetic inquiry and contends that researchers should consider why they are using poetry, what they seek to accomplish through the medium of poetry, and how they intend to use poetry in their studies. She suggests that addressing the motivation behind the use of poetry and how the research will be undertaken could help to ensure that the research being done is able to demonstrate the balance between art and research. This idea, a need for balance between the poetry and the inquiry, is one that resides as a core tenet of poetic inquiry as a method. Perhaps not every node on the rhizome is meant for everyone.

In contrast, Lahman and colleagues (2010) suggest that if researchers are restrained in their modes of accepted communication that it limits their ability to produce effective studies. They wrote, "we must continue to ask ourselves why the field has privileged prose, and a very certain type of scripted prose, over other forms of representation and what knowledge this privilege has lost or obscured in relation to new research understanding" (p. 46). To further counteract what they see as limits put on who can and cannot use poetry, they created what they call "good enough research poetry" (Lahman et al., 2011, p. 894) during their exploration of the ways in which poetry and research can coexist. This is an obvious push against the cautionary remarks of the likes of Piirto (2002) and Faulkner (2007). They support their open exploration through poetry by citing Leggo (2008c), who writes,

> I am concerned that some researchers put poetry on a pedestal as an object for awe-inspiring reverence. I like to stress that poetry is earthy, rooted in everyday experience, connected integrally to the flow of blood in our bodies, expressed constantly in the rhythms of our speech and embodied movement. (p. 170)

Prior to this discussion of poetry, Leggo (2008c, pp. 167-9) discusses his belief that everyone who undertakes studies using poetry should study the art of writing poetry (which mirrors that of Piirto and Faulkner, who Lahman and colleagues were pushing against). Knowing the greater context of Leggo's comment, however, does not diminish Lahman and colleagues' argument that poetry should be accessible to everyone. Their fear is that if the mode or genre becomes elitist, then the world potentially misses out on important discoveries, ways of knowing and ways of expression. This is because, as Ely (1997) writes, "poetry allows for maximum input – in and between the lines" (p. 136). The question of accessibility of the method is one that remains unanswered and somewhat contested, yet use of poetry in these areas continues to grow and proliferate.

What then of the definition of poetic inquiry? It is clear that poetic inquiry lacks chronological linearity or an exclusive disciplinary home. Poetry is being used in a variety of fields/disciplines, is being discussed using synonymous terms, and is being undertaken in individual research contexts. While the studies that I have reviewed are hugely disparate, poetry functions as a vital way to inquire and express thoughts, feelings and/or knowledge derived from the creation of poetry in the inquiry/research process(es). While poetic inquiry's lifecycle is difficult to trace, especially without a singular definition, the poetic rhizomes are ever-present in the literature. With more studies being added frequently to the literature across the disciplines, it is clear that poetic inquiry is burgeoning.

Poetic Inquiry Today

As I have explored, poetic inquiry is happening in various fields, at the intersections between disciplines/fields and in emergent ways that use art and research for the purposes of understanding. Looking at some of the communities and recent published studies helps to garner an understanding of how the methodology has grown and what rhizomes exist today.

In addition to the International Symposium on Poetic Inquiry (ISPI, 2020), which has been taking place every two years since 2007, where those who practice the methodology and those who are interested in it meet to discuss their work and expand on ideas, there is an ever-growing community of arts-based researchers who are members of notable professional societies. poetic inquiry, as a form of Arts-Based Educational Research, is of particular interest to special interest groups in two of North America's largest educational research associations. The American Educational Research Association (AERA, 2020) has a special interest group centered on arts-based educational research (ABER SIG, n.d.) which includes poetic inquiry and sharing of poetic research at their annual conferences. Likewise, Canada's Canadian Society for the Study of Education (CSSE, n.d.) has the Arts Researchers and Teachers Society special interest group (ARTS, n.d.). These special interest groups facilitate workshops, presentations and discussions at their conferences and promote the work of artist-researchers through their academic journals and publications.

Looking briefly at the Canadian context for contemporary journals that publish studies that use poetic inquiry, the *Journal of the Canadian Association for Curriculum Studies* (JCACS, 2020), has been publishing the work of Canadian and international scholars since 2003. The journal published a special edition, guest-edited by Erika Hasebe-Ludt and Carl Leggo (2016), with the theme of "A Métissage of Polyphonic Textualities." It includes poetry and influences of poetic inquiry in discussions provoking thought around curriculum development and curriculum changes. There is also significant evidence of studies that employ poetic inquiry being published through one of Canada's newer academic journals, *Art/Research International: A Transdisciplinary Journal* (ARI, 2018). These are but a small sampling of the journals publishing artistic academic work in Canada.

In recent years, there have been numerous studies that employ poetic inquiry in the literature. These publications continue to push the rhizomatic growth of the methodology taking place in a multitude of fields. The practice of poetic play (Wiebe et al., 2016) aims to better understand positionality, and there is a continued call for criteria around the methodology (Faulkner, 2016b). Exploration of human experience, such as the experiences of living with physical disability (Downey, 2016), or what Görlich (2016) calls a "polyvocality of experience" (p. 525) through poetry to explore how students feel about their educational experiences in both domestic and international contexts (Wiggins & Monobe, 2017), continues to arise in the literature. The use of poetry to better understand the *Self* (Grimmett, 2016; Norton, 2017) and the experiences and voices of the *Other* (Apol, 2017) is also ever-present.

The use of poetry in social justice-focused poetic inquiry studies amplifies the voices of marginalized communities. Saunders, Usher, Tsey and Bainbridge (2016), for example, use poetry "to draw attention to the ways the endings of stories of 'Aboriginal Recovery' are currently being told and heard; particularly, by You, the reader, and by others who contribute indirectly and directly to the way these stories end" (p. 2). The authors create multilingual poetry "as a therapeutic and storytelling strategy to highlight the difference between hearing and listening, and how that difference relates to the word Recovery as a paradigm shift and story of social change" (p. 1). This use of poetic inquiry highlights the divide between how words are used and interpreted by using poetry as the vessel to share the authors' lived experiences, poetic inquiry is also being used by members of the 2SLGBTQ+ community to bring forward experiences and stories of those whose stories may not otherwise be heard. Lambert (2016) uses poetry to share the story of Scout who, through poetry, shares Scout's conflict between her acknowledging her identity as a lesbian, while being a part of a community who deems it "wrong" to be one. Lambert uses poetic inquiry

> to show how poetic inquiry and poetic modes of representation may provide an alternative way for an often silenced and marginalized 'voice' to be heard, and in that act open a space in which to challenge oppressive discourses and present a different angle and type of knowledge regarding what it is like to 'be' different (lesbian). (p. 585)

Finally, *Poetic Inquiry II* (Prendergast & Galvin, 2015) and the publication of a third anthology around poetry and place (Sameshima, Fidyk, James & Leggo, 2017) continue to amalgamate pieces from both new and more seasoned researchers who employ poetic inquiry in their work. This propagates the continuation of poetic inquiry by providing exemplars of studies that use the methodology to inspire others to explore their research through poetry. These studies are a sampling of the recent publications in the literature which use poetry or poetic inquiry, but do not reflect the exploratory work that continues in academia, both written and performed (e.g., Hume & James, 2017), that seeks to push ways of knowing and interpreting lived experience through poetry.

Recently, Sandra Faulkner, a major proponent of poetic inquiry out of the United States, noted the shift in titles from multiplicity to the umbrella term of poetic inquiry. She writes:

> In the past, I advanced the term "research poetry" to reference poems used in the research context, but I now use the label Poetic Inquiry, given the rise in popularity of the term (Faulkner, 2017a; Vincent, 2018). James (2017) traced the use and prevalence of the term in books from 1900–2008 with Google's Ngram Viewer finding a surge in 1948 after the Second World War and another in 2008, both times of political, economic, and social change. Thus, I offer the following definition of Poetic Inquiry while acknowledging that a uniform and fixed definition of Poetic Inquiry does not exist (see Vincent, 2018): "Poetic inquiry" is the use of poetry crafted from research endeavors, either before a project analysis, as a project analysis, and/ or poetry that is part of or that constitutes an entire research project. The key feature of poetic inquiry is the use of poetry as/in/for inquiry. (Faulkner, 2019, pp. 13-14)

Until recently, there were dozens, if not hundreds, of ways to describe or label how poetry was used in qualitative research studies. This, as noted in the previous sections, was anywhere from "research poetry" (Richardson, 1993), to "poetic field notes" (Flores, 1982), to "poetic rendering" (Glesne, 1997), to "poetic rumination" (Leggo, 1999), to "poetic representation" (Butler-Kisber, 2002) and so on and so forth. It is now frequently labelled, in contemporary entries in the literature, as poetic inquiry. The other terms remain, and have power, but there is now a distinct label that can provide an access point for those looking for one.

A recent search, conducted through the UBC library's database, revealed dozens of works that use the term "poetic inquiry" (in its proper and common noun forms) in their titles. Among them are works such as Faulkner (2018) who considers the power of poetic inquiry as a feminist methodology. There is also the research of Fernández-Giménez, Jennings and Wilmer (2018) who argue that poetic inquiry can further engagement in the area of natural research science. Loads, Marzetti and McCune (2019) explore the professional development experiences of university educators through poetic inquiry. The are also autoethnographic therapeutic pieces in the literature that explore the experiences of marginalized people through poetic inquiry as in Teman (2019) who specifically looks at violence against those who identify as queer and even work that uses poetic inquiry as a way to analyze teacher experiences, as Stapleton (2018) does in her participatory action research study about teacher marginalization in urban areas of the Midwestern U.S.

There is also a second edition of Faulkner's text on craft and method within poetic inquiry (2020) and further significant work done by Cutts (2019) who highlights the poetic inquiry work of Black women and pushes Faulkner's notion of *ars poetica* (2007) to include a spiritual element. Cutts (2019) suggests the addition of "ars spirituality" in poetic inquiry practices as a way to mindfully use poetry for reflexivity purposes and to merge "craft, criterion, *and* the creative spirit (p. 917). Her ars spirituality entails,

1. Writing is a critical necessity, particularly for those who have been forced to be or have chosen to be silent about their pain, oppression, and marginalization;
2. Accessing racial/cultural memory and engaging in the process of (re)membering are radical acts that facilitate much-needed awakening and healing; and
3. Spirituality is a conscious relationship with the mind, body, and spirit, for both theindividual and Community. (p. 912)

These are a small snapshot of the work being done that uses poetry in conjunction with inquiry. And yet, they show that the work active and still occurring rhizomatically across the disciplines. These studies continue to develop the approaches used through poetic inquiry by engaging students, faculty and the community in poetic exploration of research. They act as exemplars of where this work can go and grow (keeping the metaphor of fruiting alive).

Concluding Thoughts on the Literature

In this chapter, I provide an introduction to the intricacies that make up poetic inquiry. The metaphor of the rhizome supports this exploration of the area growing in different directions, yet all yielding the same general type of product (poetry) and undertaken for similar purposes by those engaging with information through poetry to learn more (to inquire). My inquiry reveals that attempting to create a working definition of a dynamic method such as poetic inquiry, while not an exercise in futility, is a near-impossible task. Through engaging with the voices in the literature who caution those with limited experience in poetry to walk gently through the proverbial strawberry field (Faulkner, 2007; Piirto, 2002) as well as those who champion open engagement (Lahman et al., 2010), I too, bring forward a reminder for critical and purposeful engagement through poetry where both elements of art and inquiry are ever-present and understood. Without an understanding of these elements, researchers risk undertaking studies and producing documents that will never reach their intended audiences, which would be an act of futility. Even strawberries, thinking back to Leggo, need favourable conditions to grow.

Exploring the Literature

This chapter provides a contemporary look at poetic inquiry in the literature from its accepted history (Prendergast, 2009; Hanauer, 2010; McCulliss, 2013; Faulkner, 2016a) to the lesser cited, yet impactful, research that has been conducted and continues to be done. Through this process, I seek to garner a greater understanding of poetic inquiry and its current uses as a generative research method or methodology. This study also affords an opportunity to contextualize the work of the participants in this study and begin to develop an understanding of how their work fits in the rhizomatic makeup of the field. Beyond this cartographic charting of poetic inquiry in the literature, each of this study's participants' corpus of work has been explored, in depth, and have been used to support the creation of the profiles that are represented in the following chapter.

Recognizing the Poetic Rhizomes
(Adam Vincent)

Labels precede
or
succeed
     poetic
          rumination
          transcription
          analysis
          ethnography
ethno-
          poetry
autoethnographic
fieldnote
field
found
          informed-research
that seek to classify
characteristics of craft,
yet they all grow out of
inquiry
and
poetry-
they are all
(really)
poetic inquiry.

We see
symbiotic

tendrils
connecting disciplines:
Education-focused p o e t r y reaches health-related

```
p                              i
o            and               n
e                              q
t                              u
r                              i
y                              r
                               y
```

connecting sociological p o e t r y to anthropological

```
    p                          i
    o        and               n
    e                          q
    t                          u
    r                          i
    y                          r
                               y
```

    creating deeper understandings
of research
and
researched,
researcher
and
reader,
method
and
methodology.

Chapter 3
Research Methodology:
Theory, Design and Methods

I never thought of myself as a poet until my graduate studies. Yes, I wrote poetry from a younger age, not much different than the participants in this study. Yet, I was not a poet. For a time, I thought of myself as a songwriter, strumming away on my acoustic guitar to songs performed by memory. I could read sheet music, but I could not write music. I could write lyrics and recall melodies, but I could not chart it. This would see me with lyrics, but no music, leaving me with lyrical poetry. Instead of focusing on music, I went out looking for poetry. I published my own poems, sold chapbooks to family and friends and sent them out for vetting, yet I was not a poet.

It was during my MA studies that poetry became more than a form of personal expression or way to bring creativity into my repetitive undergraduate essay writing processes. It was not until I had conversations with Dr. Carl Leggo, Dr. George Belliveau and peers in my graduate-level classes that I began to acknowledge myself as a poet. I had publications, sure, but I had something more I did not notice until it was brought to my attention. I had a poetic voice that emitted from within me. Others around me had heard my poetic voice before I did, and when I heard it, I knew I could not, nor should not, silence it. I am a poet.

I also see myself as an educator more than as a teacher. I have more than 10 years of post-secondary experience, ranging from support staff work to faculty work. I am an instructor, facilitator, tutor and teacher, all of which I encompass under the notion of being an educator. I use my knowledge of arts-based approaches to research and learning, student development theories, transformative learning theories and adult learning theories to support my praxis. I wish to educate, which for me is to inform, to inspire and to support the creation of bridges between students and knowledge. I am an educator.

I gravitated towards the role of researcher during my graduate studies. Beyond conducting research to write papers, I was drawn into research to expand my knowledge and understanding of concepts so that I could not only support my own development as a person and as a scholar, but to support others in their learning journeys. This role as researcher has grown exponentially during this study where I take my knowledge of writing, poetry, teaching, research methods and methodologies and enact them in purposeful ways.

The following chapter highlights the methodological approach that framed my study. It begins with me positioning myself in the research by highlighting my theoretical stance, drawing on my identity as a poet, researcher and educator who has post-modernist tendencies, to identify ways that individuals' experiences can add to our own and produce new ways of knowing. I then explain the problem that I identified, where poetic inquiry and its unique functions, will potentially continue to be overlooked in the larger sphere of qualitative research if it is seen as unverifiable or inconsequential. This would see the knowledge being produced across the disciplines through poetic inquiry left unused and therefore not making the impacts that it could (on poet-researchers or on the researched). The study shone light on poetic inquiry, its uses/functions and its potential uses in research and scholarship, but it also posits the need for closer examination of poetic inquiry products which may hold untapped knowledge.

Theoretical Stance: Where Am I Coming From?

My theoretical stance, as a poet, researcher and educator, is akin to my colleagues who identify as a/r/tographers and artist/researcher/teachers, who at once marry the three elements of their identity while existing between disciplines and/or the confines of the expectant behaviours of prescribed roles (De Cosson & Irwin, 2004). Irwin (2013) describes a/r/tography as "a form of practice-based research" that "transforms the traditional relationship between theory and practice by recognizing the movement found within a rhizome" (p. 199). Within this movement between (and with) perspectives that at times diverge and others converge, I am guided by over-arching wondering. This wondering, akin to inquiry-based model or method, leads me to want to know more about poetry, research and teaching which foregrounds this study. I am unsure where the process of wondering will take me, but I continue to ask questions and seek answers. I also approach this work with post-modern tendencies, which Richardson (2000) describes, when speaking about writing as a form of inquiry, as "the doubt that any method or theory, discourse or genre, tradition or novelty, has a universal and general claim as the 'right' or the privileged form of authoritative knowledge" (p. 928). This notion speaks to my approach in this study. I am inquiring, as a poet, teacher and educator, about what poetic inquiry is and identifying *ways* that it can inform research and teaching practices, not overtake them as an absolute epistemological or pedagogical approach.

Research Rationale

In recent decades, qualitative methods have emerged that challenge researchers to consider their research participants and data in different and more personal and aesthetic ways (Denzin & Lincoln, 2011), thereby enhancing personal insight and deeper connection to the data as a way of generating new knowledge that is otherwise unattainable through conventional scientific methods. Across the social sciences, the arts-based method known as poetic inquiry (Prendergast, 2009a) has become increasingly popular. Arts-based research methods include various forms of artistic expression as a component of the research design and analysis.

Poetic inquiry uses poetry in diverse ways, including the use of poetic form, poetic language and poetic devices, as an integral element of data gathering, data interpretation and/or data representation and dissemination. The term data is used somewhat loosely in this context as data in poetic inquiry may not necessarily have the characteristics of traditional qualitative research data sets and is a construct that not all who work in poetic inquiry resonate with. Examples of poetic inquiry as a form of data include Flores' (1982) use of poetry as field notes and Richardson's (1992) use of poetry as a way of analyzing the transcript of her participants' life stories. These studies are often cited as inspirations for those who work in/through poetic inquiry. Despite a mounting interest in poetic inquiry, as evidenced by hundreds of published studies that use these approaches to scholarly research (Prendergast, 2009; James, 2017; Vincent, 2018), very little attention has been paid to poetic inquiry's uptake and use in Canada. Even more than mainstream qualitative methods, poetic inquiry faces a challenge to gain acceptance within the larger academic community (e.g., Creswell, 2013) as it has been overlooked in notable critical discussions of arts-based research (e.g., Slattery, 2003; jagodzinski & Wallin, 2013). Without a critical assessment of the state of poetic inquiry and a clearer understanding of the unparalleled functions of poetic inquiry approaches in research, one which yokes language-based aesthetics and epistemology, there exists the possibility that ground-breaking work using poetic inquiry will go unnoticed. Poetic inquiry, as highlighted in the participant profiles (Chapters Four to Seven) and poetic analyses (Chapter Nine) of this book, creates visceral and multidimensional representations of data, in ways that are not present in other qualitative methodologies, through using language-based aesthetics and epistemology that, when combined, reveal knowledge that cannot be attained through other means. To ignore this knowledge would mean missing out on new ways of knowing and solving problems. There also is a risk that these methods, which lend themselves to curriculum development and teaching strategies, will go untapped in the classroom. If poetic inquiry appears uncritical or remains under-theorized, it will likely remain marginalized or be rejected as a viable approach to scholarly inquiry and/or as a tool for teaching. Given that knowledge claims are being made based on poetic inquiry's functions as an approach/methodology, more needs to be known about the justification and implementation of poetic inquiry in both research and scholarship.

To gain this knowledge, I have undertaken a multiple-case study that seeks to explore the impetus to employ poetry in scholarship, how it functions and to illuminate the processes and products of four leading scholars and proponents of poetic inquiry in Canada. Through exploring the practices of long-time poetic inquiry scholars, this study will not only add to what is known about poetic inquiry, but also highlight dynamic research and teaching practices that can inform approaches to scholarship across the disciplines.

Selection and Description of Participants

For this study, I purposefully selected four participants based on their active scholarship and leadership in the area of poetic inquiry in education: Dr. Carl Leggo (University of British Columbia), Dr. Pauline Sameshima (Lakehead University), Dr. John Guiney Yallop (Acadia University) and Dr. Monica Prendergast (University of Victoria). These scholars were integral to the inception of the bi-annual International Symposium on Poetic Inquiry, which began in 2007. Moreover, they continue to act as leaders for the symposium over a decade later and have edited scholarly collections associated with the symposium (Prendergast, Leggo & Sameshima, 2009; Galvin & Prendergast, 2015; Sameshima, Fidyk, James, & Leggo, 2017). They have also published journal articles, edited books, and book chapters on the topic of poetic inquiry (e.g., Prendergast, 2009; Butler-Kisber et al., 2017) and have explored poetry and its uses in a variety of disciplines (e.g., James, 2017; Leggo, 2012). These participants were selected based on my pilot study (Vincent, 2018), which undertakes the task of finding a definition of poetic inquiry in the form of a literature review, which also brought attention to the scholars' contemporary catalogue of work (i.e., the last five years). Frequent citations in the literature, affirmed through the creation of my literature review and by Google Scholar (2021) which show that these scholars have over 7000 citations between them, indicates that their work is seen by the academic community as valuable. This process helped to not only select these participants but supported the development of initial questions for the semi-structured interviews. As a poet-researcher myself, I wanted to speak with these scholars not only for their recurrent citations in the literature from around the world and praise from colleagues who had interactions with them, but I wanted to expose myself to their diverse approaches to build my own repertoire. Each scholar took a slightly different approach to poetic inquiry and had different reasons for engaging with/through it; I wanted to draw knowledge from my interactions with them and their publications in hopes of finding commonalities that could lead me to the core of this work.

Data Collection Methods

While this study has elements of more traditional social science research, it is ultimately a poetic inquiry on poetic inquiry. Poetry has been used as a form of data, poems have been created to support an understanding of data, poems have been analyzed and there are also poems that act as summaries for each chapter. This, however, does not mean that this study was conducted without an awareness of other, non-arts-based qualitative research methods. An awareness of Stake's (2006) multiple case study approach foregrounds much of the within-case and cross-case analyses which are employed to learn what similarities and differences exist between and among cases (distinguished poetic inquiry scholars). Stake's (2006) case study approach was chosen as a reference point for this study because his approach is constructivist in nature (see Vygotsky, 1978), pushing away from positivist or scientific epistemological approaches that do not fit with the purpose of this study. Further, Stake's (2006) approach also has parallels to facets of poetic inquiry as it relates to valuing the experience of unearthing knowledge and sharing information in different ways (e.g., through narrative vignettes), depending upon the case and the findings (see Stake, 2006, pp. 3, 29, 78). As a study of this nature had not been undertaken, there was a need to venture into uncharted territory yet, akin to a common tenet of poetic inquiry, that did not mean ignoring the merits of other qualitative research approaches. An awareness of Stake's (2006) guidelines for multiple case studies, which include "observation, interview, coding, data management and interpretation" (p. 29), supports the data gathering process while not dissuading diverse approaches to data management and interpretation which are necessary for this study. The data for this study was collected by way of semi-structured interviews (Creswell, 2013, p. 160) over the span of a year. Another reference to a common social sciences convention in this study, again using a working knowledge of Stake (2006, p. vi), includes using three common questions for each participant with other questions crafted specifically for each participant. This practice highlights similarities and differences in the participants' poetic inquiry approaches and purposes for using it in their research and scholarship. The questions were also used to confirm seemingly universal views found in the literature, such as those that push against a positivist philosophical view of research and those that value poetic inquiry's subjectivity as it relates to the creation and reading of this type of purposeful academic poetry. Examples of consistent questions asked during the interview process are:

- In what ways does your work with poetry (including poetic inquiry, arts informed/arts-based methods) inform your teaching practice?
- Given that artists and researchers use a number of terms to describe their work with poetry, I wonder, what do you call it?
- Does poetic inquiry have limits?

For Monica, Pauline and John, the first two interviews took place four months apart, individually with each participant, with the final interview taking the form of a group interview (with Monica in person and John and Pauline calling in from their respective provinces). As it relates to Carl, interviews one and two were individual, with the third group interview occurring after his passing (on March 7, 2019). This data is outlined in Table 3.1.

The semi-structured interviews were 60-minutes in length and began with three consistent questions, followed by questions tailored for each participant or were created *in medias res* as part of the discussion. The interviews took place from June 2018 to June 2019, in settings selected by the participants to ensure their freedom to speak openly. A follow-up three-question questionnaire asking further details about the participants' teaching practice was sent via email in July 2020. There were also ongoing close textual analyses of both the interview transcription and each participant's corpus of work in the literature. These focus on how and why they create poetry in an effort to shed light on the capacity of poetry to create and mobilize new knowledge.

I also use the findings of my pilot study, an in-depth literature review (building off Prendergast, 2009) that sought to define poetic inquiry, to identify key works in each participants' corpus of work and key words to help me identify additional pieces that link to their work surrounding poetic inquiry, research and scholarship. These documents were then analyzed as part of my data analysis processes with particular attention paid to the purpose of poetry in their studies and in the dissemination of the poet-researcher's findings (the poetic products). I also took field notes before and after each interview, making notes about settings and my own feelings in order to generate an awareness of my positionality in the study. I would also, at times, craft poetic field notes (explored in Chapter Nine) in an effort to better understand my perception of the research process and my place within it. This reflects what was gleaned about the duality of a poetic inquiry approach which marries the rigour associated with more traditional qualitative research methods with the sensibilities of a poet.

Research Methodology

Table 3.1: Interview Details.

Participant Name	Data Collection Method	Frequency	Duration	Location
Dr. Carl Leggo	Semi-structured interview	~Every 4 months over the span of one year*	60 minutes	His home, Steveston, BC *Dr. Leggo passed away prior to the final group interview
Dr. Pauline Sameshima	Semi-structured interview	~Every 4 months over the span of one year	60 minutes	Telephone
Dr. John Guiney Yallop	Semi-structured interview	~Every 4 months over the span of one year	60 minutes	Telephone
Dr. Monica Prendergast	Semi-structured interview	~Every 4 months over the span of one year	60 minutes	Her office at UVIC, her home, UBC office

Interview Settings

The interview locations and times were, for the most part, selected by the participants with the exception being the final interview, where I found quiet office space on the UBC campus to conduct the interview. Monica had been in Vancouver to attend and/or present at two different conferences and so it made sense to conduct the group interview at that time. As each participant, more often than not, selected the time and setting for the interviews, I hoped that they would feel comfortable to speak candidly without fear of interruption or indirect observers. Having the participants participate in the selection of the interview settings also made sense with my informal or semi-structured interview approach which drew from my knowledge of traditional social sciences conventions (Creswell, 2013, p. 16). I did not want the interviews to feel overly formal and scientific in nature, as I was seeking to better understand not only how poetry affects their research and scholarship, but why they (as people) were drawn to poetry in the first place. What better place to draw that out than a place where they feel comfortable?

Carl Leggo

My first interview was with Carl at his home in the small village of Steveston, BC. Steveston can be best described as a small fishing village that grew into a small community that mixed the architecture of that of the Maritimes, including buildings of vibrant yellow and pale blue, with the modern necessities of stuccoed condominiums and townhomes that were stylized to look quainter in an effort to match the character of the village. This is a far cry from its beginnings as a Japanese fishing village, whose Japanese-Canadian residents were interned during World War II, yet the original cannery remains standing today. We spoke in Carl's study, which was half homage to his academic career, with pictures of academic events, a variety of books and his computer station; the other half was an homage to his love of family and friends, with pictures of life events from decades prior. The second interview also took place at Carl's home, in his living room, surrounded by Maritime-inspired art. Unfortunately, Carl passed away before the final interview which took place on the UBC Vancouver campus.

Pauline Sameshima

I conducted my first telephone interview with Pauline from my familiar office in The Learning Centre that I once coordinated on the outskirts of the Fraser Valley in British Columbia's Lower Mainland. The corner desk was angled in such a way that you could look out the windowed door to see the tutors supporting students while having privacy if you needed it. From here, I called Pauline in Thunder Bay where she lives and works. I was not sure if I was calling her at home or at her office on campus and that information was never discussed in our interview. I had my second interview with Pauline from the same office. The final interview took place on UBC's Vancouver campus, in a glass-walled office of the Ponderosa Commons, sitting next to Monica, with Pauline and John on the phone.

John Guiney Yallop

My first interview with John took place over the phone. I had never called a scholar who I had not met before, having met some of the other participants at conferences or other educational contexts. I usually elect to use the more editable medium of the email to tailor my words. I tried to reflect on my interpretation of John's surroundings to help me to better imagine sitting next to him. I sat in a small room, in a part of my wife's friends' house that they would rent out on Airbnb. Abstract art of red and white was prominent on one wall, while the bright yellow sun shone through the sheer curtains of a window that took up most of another. I perched on the edge of the bed, afraid to sit on the brown leather chair near the window, for fear of the squeaking overtaking the sound of John's voice going into my handheld recorder. I am not sure if I spoke with John at home or at his office for this initial interview as it never came out in our conversation, though he appeared able to speak freely from a quiet space. For my second telephone interview with John, I called him from the same office that I first called Pauline from, with him making mention of being at home for our conversation. The final interview, as above, took place on UBC's Vancouver campus, with Monica in person and John and Pauline on the phone.

Monica Prendergast

My first interview with Monica took place in her office at the University of Victoria. Her office, in the MacLaurin building, a sienna-hued brick building, is situated close to the ring road that surrounds the campus. Her office walls were clad with bookshelves containing hundreds of books. The only blank space was the small window behind her desk that looked over a treed pathway that led into the building. My second interview took place in Monica's home, sitting in her living room during a windstorm. The final interview took place with Monica sitting next to me, as above, on UBC's Vancouver campus in a small office where the walls were windows, with John and Pauline conference calling in.

Role of the Researcher

As the researcher, I was a part of the dialogic exchanges that took place in the interviews. I initially created the semi-structured interview questions based on my knowledge of the participant from reading their profiles online, having known them (Carl), seen them at conferences (Pauline and Monica), or heard about them from colleagues (John). I also created my initial questions based on my knowledge of some of their more frequently referenced pieces in the literature (as above). After the first interview, I was able to draw on our previous interview(s), my reflections on our discussions and a deeper understanding of some of their published pieces in order to create more precise and personally relevant questions. There were times that my questions led to lengthy discussions and other times that my questions fell short or were, in a kind way, noted to be "the wrong" question. If the participants did not resonate with the wording of a question or understand its intent, they would critically discuss why the question may not yield clear answers. While this may appear to have sidetracked the discussion, it was in these sidebars that information would arise that would support an understanding of earlier conversations and/or support the development of new questions. These new questions not only answered the original question but lead towards further insights on the given topic. In the final interview, between Monica (in-person), and Pauline and John (on the phone), I acted more as a participant-observer. I asked questions here and there, but mostly listened to their conversations that built on one another. Further, due to my understanding of my role as an active agent in the discussions (as in the final interview), I was able to ensure that my data analysis processes were varied and critical with an awareness of my role in the creation of the interview data. This view, based on my knowledge of research approaches developed through multiple research methodology courses at UBC and Athabasca University, is also supported by my reading of methodological texts (e.g., Stake, 2006; Denzin & Lincoln, 2011; Creswell, 2013) that highlight the need for criticality and data triangulation (e.g., Stake, 2006, p. 33). This reflects the duality of the role of the researcher in a poetic inquiry study. I had to be aware of qualitative conventions, while also allowing my inquisitive nature and sensibilities as a poet to guide me towards learning more about poetic inquiry and those who practice it.

I believe that this approach of inquisitive listening and natural conversation served me well in this process as I did not come in with a lengthy set or questions or heightened expectations. I was in the role of researcher, the one who acquisitioned knowledge and formed it into diverse understandings, yet I approached the study more as an interested colleague. Then again, beyond being colleagues with the unique moniker of being "poets in the academy," I had the mentality of an apprentice, seeking knowledge from those with greater and more diverse experiences in the trade. I argue that as researchers we are always apprentices in some form; we seek to learn more from those who we are engaging with and if we do so with the humble inquisition of an apprentice, we can learn more.

Data Analysis and Coding

I took an innovative approach to data analysis in an effort to draw out intricacies not only from the interview data, but from the poetic products of the participants that exist in the literature. This saw me using a grounded, or inquiry-based, approach where I had questions that I wanted answers to. I then had to adapt previously known processes or create processes around data analysis and coding without knowing what the findings would be; I had no hypothesis or initial indicator of where my process may lead. For my first cycle of data analysis, which occurred after multiple readings of the transcripts, I processed the verbatim interview transcripts through the GTR Language Workbench (2019) which is software designed to support a generative process where language can be identified, mixed and remixed. The software developers, Klobucar and Ayer, describe the workbench as "means to explore how creative writing (and language use in general) might take advantage of digital processing applications to create new and innovative forms of literary art, electronic or otherwise" (NJIT, n.d.). I used the software to conduct analyses of the interview transcripts by creating lists of words, replacing words using parts of speech, and using a variety of experimental processes (such as homonym and hypernym replacement) to engage poetically with the data (see Figure 3.1). I initially used the workbench to create lists of parts of speech to draw my attention to specific words that I populated in Excel, with one page per participant interview and one for the final group interview.

I created lists of verbs, nouns and adjectives from the interview data that I could quickly skim through in order to identify words that did not coincide with the others in the list, or those that appeared more than once. I then returned to

Research Methodology

my interview transcript, used the find feature of Microsoft Word to find the term, read through the corresponding response(s) and put the verbatim interview quotation in a separate file for later thematic review and sorting. I also used the workbench to create lists of antonyms and to replace adjectives with adjective antonyms. These processes identified discrepancies in the lists, by showing their oppositional meaning (see Figures 3.1 and 3.2).

Figure 3.1: GTR Workbench Interface.

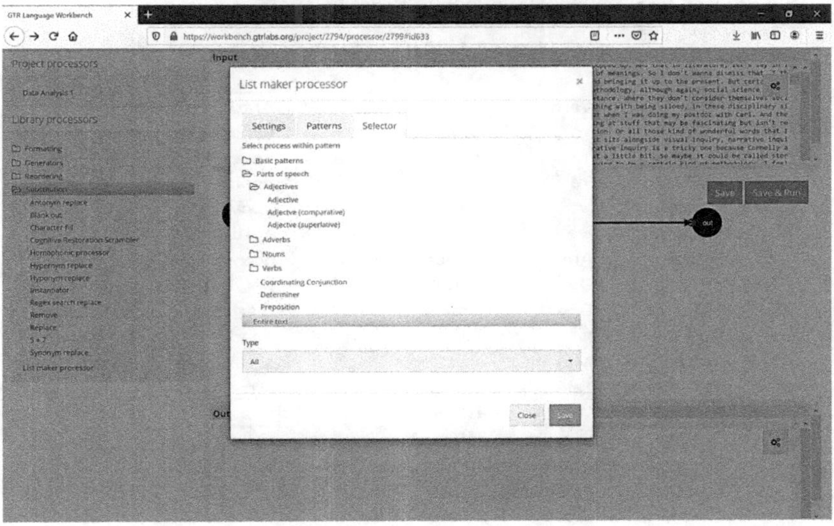

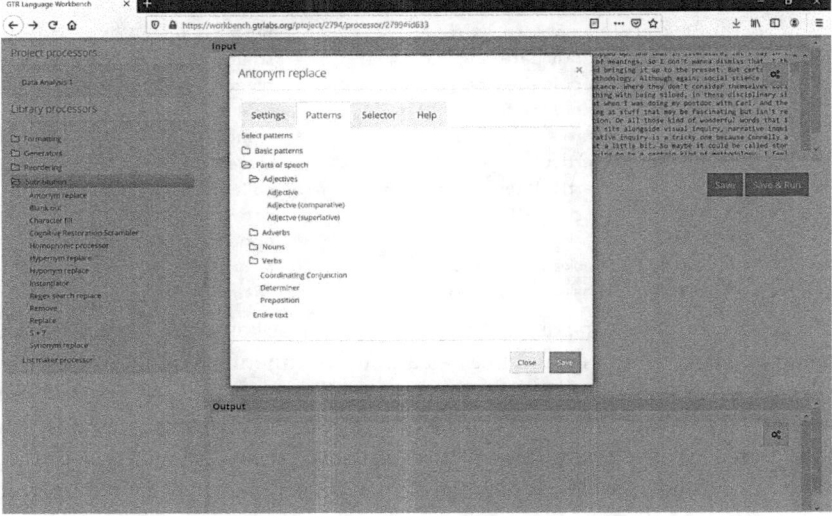

Figure 3.2: GTR Antonym Replace Function.

Given the positive nature of the conversations, these words are unusual to see on a list of antonyms. Returning to my original list of adjectives, I found the coinciding term and once again used the find function in MS Word to find the passage in my verbatim transcript data and placed the quotation in a separate file for further thematizing and sorting. Once I had concluded looking for specific parts of speech, I reviewed and sorted the quotations based on their overarching topic or theme (supported by thematic analysis in Creswell, 2013, p. 186, pp. 333-342; Stake, 2006, p.306, pp. 323-5).

Figure 3.3: GTR List Example.

	A	B	C	D	E	F
1	Noun	Verb	Adjective		Antonym Adjective	
2	Ah	'd	Canadian		Canadian	
3	Alex.	'm	Poetic		Poetic	
4	Blue	're	able		unable	
5	Brill	's	above		above	
6	Canada	've	academic		academic	
7	Carl	Are	accountable		accountable	
8	Chair	Do	actual		possible	
9	Conrad	Does	afraid		fearless	
10	Cuz	Is	alive		dead	
11	Deleuze	Making	amazing		amazing	
12	Diane	Take	arts-based		arts-based	
13	Digger	Wait	ashamed		unashamed	
14	Duff	accept	assistant		assistant	
15	Education	acknowledge	authentic		authentic	
16	Eisner	advancing	awake		asleep	
17	English	agree	awesome		awesome	
18	Faulkner	allows	bad		unregretting	
19	H-A-G-G-A-	am	beautiful		ugly	
20	Haggarty	answer	best		best	
21	Haggarty	answered	better		better	
22	Holly	anticipate	big		small	
23	Inquiry	apologize	bigger		bigger	
24	J	appreciate	bottom		side	
25	JCACS	are	clear		cloudy	
26	Jagodzinski	articulate	clever		clever	
27	Jan	articulated	collaborative		collaborative	
28	Jan.	articulating	corny		corny	
29	Jason	ask	**critical**		noncritical	
30	Kedrick	asked	deductive		inductive	
31	LAUGH	asking	deeper		shallower	

I then took the verbatim passages that included these key words or phrases and created, based on my experiences as a poet, rudimentary found poetry that allowed me to use line breaks to emphasize words and see connections between words and meaning. This helped with my data analysis as I was able to explore language on both literal and hermeneutic levels. Was I interpreting what the participant said in an authentic way? Was I interpreting their inferred meaning or was I creating my own? How does their voice, on the recorder, change the meaning of the transcript excerpt? These poems were meant to help me process the information, through a form of triangulation (akin to Stake, 2006, p. 33), and connect themes and terminologies. They were not meant as public representation of my findings but were a form of poetic processing or poetic play that helped me to clarify my interpretations and/or discover nuanced meaning that may have been missed during my multiple readings of the transcripts.

Figure 3.4: Poetic Play Example.

There's nothing new under the sun
and as the great the Hebrew preacher said,
right,
in the book of Ecclesiastes
there's is nothing new under the sun.
And I grant you he was being quite pessimistic,
hopeless, and whatever,
at least as part of his persona,
but I like that idea that there's nothing new under the sun.
Uh
that human beings are not coming up with anything
that hasn't already been hinted at,
spoken about
written about along the way
and so on
and so for all of the, ah, interesting appeal
and clarity of Jacques Derrida.
You know,
it's all his grafting his work onto the branches of other people's trees
and he knows that
like he knows that he's writing into the spaces
between the lines
of the people
that he is reading
and that's fascinating
and he did it was such vigour.
And and with Foucault
of course, Foucault

My second cycle of data analysis entailed the creation of a comparative data chart (akin to data charting methods found in Stake, 2006, p. 324) identifying five commonalities and five differences that exist between each participant based on the interview data (see Figure 3.4). I then performed close readings of each participants' relevant corpus of work, academic journals, books and/or book chapters, with an aim of further understanding how and why they create poetry. I was, again, seeking five commonalities and five differences between each participant as their views appear in the literature and supplemented my chart with quotations from the interview data.

Figure 3.5: Data Table Example.

| What does poetry do in their work | So, I would say it's a really great way to **synthesize a large amount of data**. It also allows people to integrate themselves into it. For example, if you collected a lot of data and you did analysis and then you wrote your findings. Your findings are in the voice of the researcher. And often this kind of one-way talk, when you talk back to the audience, like you're teaching them something about the findings, you're telling them something from the findings. (PS1, p.1) | Leggo, C. (2004). Living poetry: Five ruminations. *Language & Literacy (Kingston, Ont.), 6*(2)

Leggo, C. (2012). Living language: What is a poem good for? *Journal of the Canadian Association for Curriculum Studies, 10*(2), 141.

Leggo, C. (2018). Poetry in the academy: A language of possibility. *Canadian Journal of Education, 41*(1), 69-97. | Well, that, that's a really good question. I'm not quite sure if I can say it does anything that other work doesn't do for someone else. But I certainly feel for me that **poetry gets at things more succinctly**, I guess. With fewer words, more clearly, in some ways. Or more up close. I think maybe because of the language it uses, the metaphors, or the sparsity of, if that's the right word, of the language. (JGY1 p. 2) | I think it was Lawrence Ferlinghetti who I use this quote quite often who said **a poem is the shortest distance between two people**. And so, for me, it's not about the shortcut, it's about the short distance. It's about how can I say what I wanna say in the most directly effective and potentially affective way. And often the answer to that question is write a poem. (MP2 p. 15) |

I did this same practice one final time, this time focused on their views on teaching as it appears in the literature, the interview transcription, and data derived from the emailed questionnaire that contains three questions specifically about their teaching praxis. The questions are:

- In what ways does your work with poetry (including poetic inquiry, arts-informed/arts-based methods) inform your teaching practice?
- Why do you select these approaches and what do you believe the impacts are on/for students?
- Could you please provide an example of how you have applied these approaches in your own teaching practice?

My data analysis process resembles Charmaz's (2017) conception of a constructivist grounded theory. She writes that this type of theory/approach "keeps you involved with your data and emerging analysis and thus prompts you to act and progress. This method helps you define, explicate, and conceptualize what is happening in your data" (p. 299). She also describes that it entails,

> (1) assuming a relativist epistemology, (2) acknowledging you and your researchparticipants' [sic] multiple standpoints, roles, and realities, (3) adopting a reflexive stancetoward your background, values, actions, situations, relationships with researchparticipants, and representations of them, and (4) situating your research in thehistorical, social, and situational conditions of its production. Constructivist groundedtheory attends to researchers and research participants' language, meanings, and actions. (p. 299)

More than a grounded approach, my process could be described akin to an inquiry-based approach to research. Like an inquiry-based approach to learning, this approach can been seen to entail a process where one "observes the phenomena, manipulates/'tinkers with' materials, asks questions, designs investigations, conducts experiments, analyzes data, and reports results" (Brown & Melear, 2006, p. 939). This approach resonates with my data analysis process, that included language level analyses and the creation of poetry, as I did not know what I would find prior to undertaking the analysis and, therefore, had to experiment.

My analysis continued with a close reading of selected texts from the participants' corpus of publications. For this study, the four focal participants are Carl Leggo, Pauline Sameshima, John Guiney Yallop and Monica Prendergast. The selection of works from each participant's corpus is based in large part on my knowledge of their work that was derived from the writing of my 2015 MA thesis and my pilot study for my comprehensive exams that supported the creation of a recent publication (Vincent, 2018) where I explored the rhizomatic history of poetic inquiry. The findings of the pilot study are reflected in the literature review of this book. I also used keyword searches during my library and online searches that include such terms as "poetry," "poem" and "poetic" in conjunction with the participant's name that more overtly linked to their publications in academic journals and books. Further to this, I looked at the references lists of their publications to lead me to potentially uncover other previously unknown publications. Previous knowledge of recent publications in the area was helpful as some relevant texts were omitted from my library keyword searches, e.g., I knew to look closely in such areas as curriculum development to further explore such publications as Ng-A-Fook et al. (2015) whose edited collection includes chapters by notable poetic inquiry scholars. I was also able to use my previous knowledge of the participants' work to read other publications of relevance. This includes an exploration of Pauline's work with research methods (2019) and Monica's work with performance (2016) that further inform my understanding of their work and if/how poetic inquiry informs their academic practices. This allowed me to draw connections among the interview data, their publications, and their poetics which also helped to inform my understanding of their approaches to research.

I furthered my exploration to include their scholarship of teaching and learning. I sought to answer the following questions: How did they become teachers? Why did they become teachers? What are their views on the profession of teaching? In what ways is poetry a part of their teaching practice? This led to the identification of themes that link to their poetics and publications, why they went into teaching as a career, why they became a teacher or professor, their views on the profession, educational levels that they have taught and for how long, and examples of courses that they currently teach. This information, when combined with the interview data and each participants' poetic profiles, afforded me an opportunity to further explore their lives as academics, committed to living and working poetically. This process would allow me to draw further inferences around what poetry does in their research and scholarship that was lacking in other genres or approaches.

From these processes, I created participant profiles (Chapters Five to Eight) for each participant that I cross-referenced between the other participants and their individual corpses of work. This supports my critical poetic analysis (which I use a working term of close analysis) of how and why they use poetry in their research and scholarship which is the focus of Chapter Eight.

Close Analysis of Poetic Inquiry Products

I undertook a close reading of select poetic inquiry products from each of the participants in order to glean more about how and why they use poetry in their research practices and processes. My close analysis of the poetry of each participant began with a review of my comparative data chart which led to me generating questions that I wanted to know more about. I then used the questions to create a list of characteristics that I wanted to identify for further analysis. I sought:

- To identify poetic devices for unique attributes/usage
- To identify frequently used poetic forms
- To identify the poem's genre or type
- To evaluate how stanzas are created and distinguished on the page
- To evaluate line and stanza structures/units
- To explore the representation of voice/perspective
- To explore who they reference in their published academic works who use poetry and identify correlations between who they reference and how they write
- To explore similarities and differences in their poetic purposes and products and to contrast my findings with the interview data to discover characteristics that distinguish each participant's poetry from that of the other participants in the study.

From these characteristics, I then identified seven themes for closer inspection:

- Use of punctuation
- Portrayal of voice
- Frequently used poetic devices
- Appearance on the page

- Frequently used poetic forms
- Common themes/topics in their work, and
- The purpose behind the creation (or use) of poetry.

This analytical approach was hermeneutic in nature in that it sought to generate an interpretation and to understand the exegesis of the poetry. As Iivari (2018) writes, that "[r]eading involves the realization, or enactment, of the semantic possibilities of a text – it 'actualizes the meaning of the text for the present reader' (Ricoeur, 1981, p. 185)" (p. 116). To better understand the meaning of each poem, I had to analyze it on different levels (line, stanza and whole poem), consider how language creates meaning and make connections between the poem and the purpose of the study/inquiry. This approach closely resembles that of the hermeneutic circle (Heidegger, 1927) that, as described in Iivari (2018),

> emphasizes that when trying to understand a text as a whole, one needs to interpret its parts, but in order to understand the parts, one needs to grasp the whole – there is constant movement between considering the whole and its parts (e.g. Boland et al., 2010; Hansen and Rennecker, 2010; Klecun-Dabrowska and Cornford, 2000; Klein and Myers, 1999; Myers, 1995, 2004). (p. 116)

Through multiple readings, I had to closely examine and interpret the ways that each poet created meaning through language use and their application of poetic devices in order to better understand the poem and therefore better generate an understanding of the data therein. While hermeneutics are fitting for this close reading approach for it is, as Bleicher (1980) describes, "as much art as it is science; it endeavours to reconstruct the original creative act – 'how it really was'" (p. 15), there remains the need to expand the analysis to include a further examination of not only the affective impact of the poetry, but the purpose of the study/inquiry.

The close reading approach used in this study somewhat differs from more traditional literary close reading practices adopted by New Critical movement from the 1920s and 30s. Historically, "close reading" as described by Ransom (1937), meant engaging in

> technical studies of poetry [including] its metric; its inversions...; its tropes; its fictions, or inventions by which it secures 'aesthetic distance'...or any other devices, on the general understanding that any systematic usage which does not hold good for prose is a poetic device. (p. 600)

There was also a belief, as in Ransom (1937), that the close reader (the literary critic),

> knows that [their] practical interests will reduce this living object to a mere utility, and that [their] sciences will disintegrate it for their convenience into their respective abstracts. The poet wishes to defend [their] object's existence against its enemies, and the critic wishes to know what [they are] doing, and how. (p. 601)

The close reading approach used in this study, while attending to some of the fundamental elements associated with historical close reading approaches (e.g., in relation an awareness of poetic devices and forms), considers that while the poem may be a form of data, its purpose extends beyond "mere utility." The poem, as a representation of the products of the inquiry process, affects both the poet and the reader in e/affective ways that allow them to learn more about themselves and/or others. This belief could be seen more in line with the transactional theory of Rosenblatt (1994) who sees reading the poem as a dialogic meaning-making experience between the reader and the poem. Similar, however, to a New Critical approach is that this study approaches close reading as a mode of inquiry. Moreover, this approach is akin to Federico (2015) who contends that

> close reading asks for a direct encounter with a work of literature, it has the potential to restore agency to both the reader and the text, as well as reveal details of the world and of our own consciousness that we could not see without the help of the literary work. (p. 26)

Close reading, in the context of this study, has been adopted as a way to approach the poem as a literary work that can be read for aesthetic and affective purposes, while also (re)approaching the poem as a source of significant data. The analytical process used to analyze samples of this study's participants' poetry has emphasized that an understanding of the poems' functions and how they are structured does not take away from their aesthetic impact but provides further understandings of the breadth and depth of the poems and each study's findings.

Currently, poetic inquiry is predominantly generative. There is a lack of critical, close and/or hermeneutic analyses from either poets or non-poets, which may lead to knowledge being overlooked that can have significant uses in research and scholarship. Through engaging with poetic inquiry products through close analysis, as trialed in this study (Chapter Eight) as a way to examine a sample poem from each of the participants, there exists an opportunity to gain knowledge from a currently untapped data/knowledge source. Further, close analysis of poetic inquiry products can provide an analytical approach that can be used to delve into the academic rigour and realize the efficacious creativity that are integral elements of previous and current poetic inquiry studies. This is significant in that, as re-affirmed by this study, a traditional social science method for identifying trustworthiness does not readily apply to poetic inquiry, yet there remains a way to learn more about poetic inquiry studies and their effectiveness through such evaluative criterion as ars poetica (Faulkner, 2007) and, as exemplified in Chapter Eight, a close analysis of a sampling of the participants' poetic products.

Trustworthiness? Something Else?

This is a poetic inquiry study. It uses poetry as an element of the research process, yet it also resides in the realm of Social Sciences. Trustworthiness hinges on the notion of absolute truth, but this study, while seeking truths (plural), is more greatly concerned with learning about the participants approaches to poetic inquiry, exploring distinct attributes of the poetic inquiry community, understanding how poetic inquiry is currently in use and considering its potential for future functions in research and scholarship. It also entails trialing a subjective approach to reading and analyzing poetic inquiry products that were perceived in this study to reveal more about the participants' poetic products and the purposes behind creating them. To adhere to the traditions of Social Sciences, a study must exude trustworthiness, sometimes called validation. It is described by Creswell (2013) as using strategies "which include confirming or triangulating data from several sources" (p. 53) where the researcher must have an "understanding [of] one's own topic, understanding derived from other sources, and the documentation of this process in the written study" (p. 248). He goes on to add that "[u]nderstandings from previous research give substance to the inquiry" and contribute to its substantive validation (p. 248). He cites, among others, Whittemore, Chase and Mandle (2001) who have created four criteria for assessing the trustworthiness, or validity, of a study. The criteria, including Creswell's clarifying questions in parentheses, are: "credibility (Are the results an accurate interpretation of the participants' meaning?); authenticity (Are different voices heard?); criticality (Is there a critical appraisal of all aspects of the research?); and integrity (Are the investigators self-critical?)" (p. 248). Applying Whittemore, Chase and Mandle's criteria for a trustworthy and valid study would see many of their criteria met, including their requirement of member checking the interview transcription and the participants' profiles and the fact that the data was triangulated to ensure meaning was retained or interpreted in fair ways, yet this notion of trustworthiness does not take the poetic elements into account. A researcher who undertakes a poetic inquiry study must have an awareness of qualitative research practices. Yet, a researcher is also inherently subjective in their use of poetry with its poetic devices, multiple meanings and diverse forms that are extremely difficult, if not impossible, to measure. That is not, however, to say that poetic inquiry and its poetic products are without any checks and balances.

Faulkner created a criterion for reading research poetry, ars poetica (2007), that remains in use today (most recently referenced in Cutts [2020] who expands the criteria to better include Black women's research poetry writing experiences). Faulkner recently revisited her criteria (2019), further elaborating on ars poetica as "artistic concentration, embodied experience, discovery/surprise, conditional, narrative truth, and transformation" (p. 142) that she believes resides in the liminal space between scientific criteria, concerned with such areas as "trustworthiness" (p. 144), and artistic criteria, including "moral truth" (p. 144). Applying ars poetica (2019) to this study, this study has artistic concentration, with the poetry paying attention to such considerations as "rhyme, figurative language and word choice" as well as through it having feeling ("mood/tone") and sharing information in a "fresh way" (p. 145). It also highlights embodied experience, "the need for poetry to make audiences feel *with*, rather than *about* a poem, to experience emotions and feelings in situ" (p. 145), discovery, learning "something about the human condition and ourselves," conditional with its narrative truth in that "[t]he partiality of the story should...be recognized through poetry," it should "ring true," and that it should transform, "by providing new insight, giving perspective or advocating for social change" (pp. 145-6). Each element of ars poetica, in relation to research poetry, is represented to some degree in the writing of the chapter conclusion poems, through the initial identification of elements of each participant's poetry and through the close critical analysis of a poem from each participant's corpus of work, yet despite these subjectivities, there remains shades of Social Science criterion for trustworthiness.

This descriptive and exploratory study not only identifies but exemplifies the paradox of many poetic inquiry studies. They cannot be considered measurable qualitative research studies, as they have immeasurable poetry. Yet, they are also not representational of purely literary texts that adhere to centuries of literary conventions for they use facets of traditional research conventions in the inception of the poetry. This study has rhizomes of trustworthiness, artistic concentration, criticality, embodied experience, authenticity, surprise/discovery, integrity and transformation where not only the study, but the poetic inquiry products have been engaged with an aim of learning more about poetic inquiry and its functions in research and scholarship. Is it trustworthy by Social Science standards? No. Is it a literary exploration akin to graduate studies in literature? No. It is something else. It is based on a subjective epistemology, harnessed by poetry, that has fragments that exist simultaneously in multiple research traditions which allow discrete bits of knowledge to unite in unmatched ways.

Application and Contribution

The analytical methods trialed in this study potentially provide a way to critically analyze the products of poetic inquiry research studies (i.e., the poetry) that support a deeper understanding of the lived experience of the participant(s) or of the concept(s) researched. This approach, a close reading of poetic inquiry products, also potentially provides a way to generate greater understandings of the techniques being used by the poet-researchers/poetic inquirers in its crafting, thereby building on processes of data gathering, analysis and dissemination. Currently, poetic inquiry is completely divorced from approaches encountered in the humanities, such as close literary analysis, rhetorical analysis and/or literary criticism. While poetic inquiry can be seen to have a purpose that differs from solely literary poetry, marrying poetry with more traditional approaches to inquiry or research that yields new knowledge, there is a dearth of criticality around its poetic products. Faulkner (2019) suggests that "[t]he power of poetic inquiry can be realized if we ride the dialectic between aesthetic and epistemic concerns" (p. 221). In introducing and trialing the use of literary analysis methods currently void in poetic inquiry, as exemplified in this study, that examine the use of language, poetic devices, poetic structures, and poetic semiotics, there exists an opportunity to delve more deeply into poetic-research approaches and the experiences being explored in the poetry. This level of analysis acts as a device for validation for the researcher, which is described by Eisner (1991) as seeking of "confluence of evidence that breeds credibility, that allows us to feel confident about our observations, interpretations and conclusions" (p. 110), where the poetic products, the poetry, has authentically represented what the researcher would like it to represent (aligning with the aims of the study). The researched, if human, or if the data is based on another author's original texts, then may also feel fairly represented. The reader is subsequently invited to read the poem more closely in order to become confident in their interpretation(s) as they would with other forms of literature. They are also invited to derive questions about the poem and its purpose just as they would with any other form of data in any other research study. While Social Sciences criteria for truth, which do not readily apply to poetic inquiry studies, and Faulkner's (2007) notion of ars poetica for assessing the level of craft undertaken in the writing of poetry can be useful tools when creating and assessing studies, more can be done. The close reading approach outlined and trialed in this study (Chapter Eight) can potentially be used in its current form, (which proved beneficial in this study) or be adapted to garner a deeper understanding of poetic inquiry products. The approach can also potentially act as a guide in the creation or poetic products or serve as a way to accentuate poetry's functions in diverse types of research.

A final contribution from this study (outlined in Chapter Nine) is that it reveals insights into ways that poetic inquiry can act as a standalone research method or methodology or act as a co-methodological approach, with poetry as a tool for data gathering (e.g., poetic fieldnotes), analysis (exemplified in Chapter Eight) or data dissemination (explored throughout the study). It critically examines facets of poetic inquiry, its (indefinable) definition and its unparalleled functions in research. It bridges what was previously known about poetic inquiry with new knowledge that emphasizes its uses as a research method, methodology and pedagogical tool. This may add to its visibility in qualitative research and open up discussions around how poetic inquiry affects not only research approaches but also interpretive or philosophical frameworks (see Appendix 1).

Summary of the Methodology

This chapter outlined how I went about conducting my study where I sought to find answers to my research questions around poetry's purposes, functions and applications in research and scholarship through a multiple case study approach. It explains how I interviewed four leading scholars of poetic inquiry in Canada, examined their publications in the literature, analyzed their poetic approaches (through close reading) and considered how poetic inquiry influences their approaches to scholarship. I also described my data gathering and hermeneutic analytical processes in depth and highlighted ways that this study answers my research questions. Finally, I outlined how this study has added to what we know about poetic inquiry as a viable approach to qualitative research and as a valuable tool for teaching across the disciplines.

The following chapters present the profiles that were created for each participant, with a focus on the findings of the interview data, an initial characterizing of their poetic approaches and products, and an identification of how poetic inquiry influences their teaching practices.

Musings on Method and Meetings
(Adam Vincent)

> I took my stance.
> I answered my questions
> with questions
> about those questions
> which I critically analyzed
> for the imposition
> of my disposition
> around poetry

and
research as craft.

(I fear the label of post-modernist
though I tend to
break
down
    to
    find
    meaning;
reconstruction is a place of joy)

I rationalized
as a Canadian,
that I should speak
first with Canadians
about this approach
proliferated noticeably,
by Canadians,
based on the findings
of my pre-study
literature review
and
experiences
in my academic life.

I selected a short-list.
I contacted Carl
then Monica
then Pauline
and
finally John
to ask them to help me to see
what is so special about poetic inquiry
I asked,
"Would you talk with me?"

We met in-person
by car and by ferry
we "met" on the phone
in offices framed in glass.

I took what they said
and
created questions

about my questions,
took note of their language
(questioned it)
critically analyzed their disposition
(questioned it)
critically analyzed their poetry
(questioned it)
seeking a then unknown answer
a truth unseen.

Revelations revealed
unspoken regulations
in the process
of resuscitation
of representation
of lives lived
of voice
that should be considered by all.

I now present the profiles
of the prolific proponents
that support my pontification
on poetic inquiry
as method
methodology
as a way of being
in the pages
herein.

Preface to the Profiles: Crafting the Crafters
(Adam Vincent)

I tinkered at the workbench
                               no schematics in sight
not sure how to
lyricize the likes and loves of Leggo
showcase the shine of Sameshima
gregariously yammar on and on about Guiney Yallop
pontificate playfully at last on Prendergast
in ways that would accentuate their essence
and
corroborate what I learned
through the literature
through interviews

through countless hours
of working
and
reworking the data.

What facet should I focus on?
How are they similar?
How are they different?
What themes seem important?
How can I profile the poets?
How can I anthropomorphize the data
the once blank page?

Chapter 4
Profile: Dr. Carl Leggo

> *"And, see, I think Poetic Inquirers are to a significant extent performers. They're doing something, and they don't necessarily know what they are doing until they have done it. And that's a big deal. So much of my work was done because I felt called to do it a certain way. And so then I was constantly wanting to try something."* (CL2, September 18, 2018)

Dr. Carl Leggo was a poet, researcher and teacher who would openly and joyfully say that he spent his life in school. He said that he never wanted to be a teacher but did so initially to make a living. During his time in a small single-room classroom, in his early twenties, he heard his calling, which took him from teaching elementary, middle and high schools to his nearly thirty-year career as a professor at the University of British Columbia. While teaching and conducting research at UBC, Carl co-founded the International Symposium on Poetic Inquiry (ISPI) with Monica Prendergast. The bi-annual symposium, which began in 2007, celebrates and highlights academic work being done with and through poetic inquiry by long-time and early career scholars in the area.

His career ended somewhat unexpectedly before his intended retirement, due to cancer, that, after a valiant battle with it, ended his life. His life in school, as a self-identified a/r/tographer (artist, researcher, teacher), having taught thousands of students, having been published hundreds of times and having been cited thousands of times by others (Google Scholar), are the focal points of this chapter.

What is this Work? Who Can Do It?

Carl uses the term poetic inquiry, which he attributes to using more readily as a result of his advisory role during Monica Prendergast's post-doctoral work in the area, when he explores his and his family's autobiographical stories and strives to make better sense of others' theories or views. He uses poetry as a tool for teaching, as a tool for unearthing knowledge, as a way of living and as a way of tapping into the power of language. He describes poetic inquiry as a methodology, method and way of living.

Carl is a staunch believer that poetry is written by poets and therefore poetic inquiry is undertaken by poets. He likens this idea to a carpenter who works without due care for the trade of carpentry. He says, "to be a poet means that you are living poetically. That you are engaging in poetic inquiry. That you care about the world in the ways that poets care about the world" (CL2, September 18, 2018). He goes on to explain that "the poetic inquirer can certainly have any number of views [or] perspectives on poetic inquiry and I would support all of those perspectives. But I want to highlight the importance of acknowledging how poetic inquiry is, first of all, a way of being and becoming" (CL2, September 18, 2018). For Carl, being a poet and writing poetry changes how a person sees the world and how they grow within it. Attention to detail in every facet of life is significant as it may garner a deeper understanding or recognition of beauty that may otherwise go unnoticed. This includes how and why blackberry brambles grow near the water, how imagination is fostered or stunted and how words hold nuanced layers of meaning. It also, for Carl, supports generating a greater understanding of his lived experiences and the experiences of others and crafting ways to express learning.

Reasons for Poetry in his Work

Carl is known for exploring, autobiographically and autoethnographically, how his stories inform his teaching practice and self-identity. His corpus of work also shows his keen interest in the power of language for generating new understandings, particularly through the forms of poetry and narrative. Additionally, poetry functions for Carl as a way to respond to ideas and further explore levels of meaning. He says that poetic inquiry is seen as new by many educators and researchers and that it has the "possibility for revealing new perspectives on education or social work or nursing or any number of different disciplines. But, and this is the big but, poetry has been with us forever" (CL2, September 18, 2018). Carl's work uses poetry to create, expand and mobilize knowledge; he also uses it for fun. He says, "Poetic inquiry personally, for me, it's always about the fun, right? That's one of the main reasons for writing to begin with" (CL2, September 18, 2018). He goes on to talk about the process of using poetry, which can come with uncertainty. He says,

> one is caught up in the possibility of surprise. You want to be startled, you want the words to show you where you're going, right? You want to have a kind of eureka moment, when you're just laughing because, wow, look at that. I would never have thought that I was going there, right? ...I trusted the process and look where we have arrived. (CL2, September 18, 2018)

Carl believes that to be a poet is to "live poetically" (CL2). He not only writes about it (Leggo, 2002; 2005), but uses that notion to further explore what poetry can do (Leggo, 2012a; 2016). This includes such notions as "poetic rumination"

(Leggo, 2004; 2011a; 2019a) which is a way to use language to explore concepts more deeply. Additionally, Carl believes that poetry is a tool for teachers to use in the classroom (Leggo, 1997; 20012b), to support their students, and outside of the classroom, to support their praxis (Leggo, 2018).

(No) Limits of Poetic Inquiry

For Carl, poetry is limitless. He believes that it has the capacity to create diverse forms of expression or analysis that yield unlimited opportunities to know more. He does believe that those who use poetry should be able to *craft* poetry as poets. Yet, he does not see the requirement of being a poet as a limitation on the work; he instead champions that each person has the capacity to be a poet. He says "…I think we were all poets. I think some of us learn along the way to subdue, suppress, the poetry in us. Mm-hm. We stop jumping up in the air and clicking our heels. We stop dancing in public" and that "I mean for many of us we don't acknowledge it because we think that people will laugh at us if we wax poetically" but that we should find our way back to poetry (CL2, September 18, 2018). He contends that poetry, and the use of poetry for learning and expression, is not limited. It is instead our views on its legitimacy as a form of expression that become suppressed as we strive to appear more scholarly or more business-like in our dealings. We lose sight, he suggests, of its power to answer questions and to produce meaning and joy.

Unique Features of his Work

A unique element that Carl speaks of, and is evident in his corpus of work, is a focus on the interplay between poetry, language and love. Of his career, he says "what's intriguing to me is that when I go back through my CV to realize just how frequently the word love or something like it comes into play" (CL2, September 18, 2018). He not only publishes with the notion of love being prevalent (e.g., Leggo, 2011b; 2017; Sameshima & Leggo, 2010), but suggests significant changes to UBC's Bachelor of Education program at the time of the Bachelor of Arts re-revisioning process lead by then Associate Dean of Teacher Education, Rita Irwin, so that it had a focus on love. While his idea was not taken up at that time by the Faculty of Education, he continues to espouse the idea saying,

> [it] would be, then, the love of one another, the love of self but the love also of learning, of inquiry, of poetry, of reading, of writing--just the sheer love of being an a/rt/ographer, the artist, researcher, teacher. In other words, the love of being childlike. Yeah, the love of being filled with passion. (CL2, September 18, 2018)

A recent compilation of some of Carl's unique contributions to education and the poetic inquiry community (Irwin, Sinner & Hasebe-Ludt, 2019) highlights much of his work around love which he sees as the underlying foundational purpose of his life both inside and outside of the academy. He believes that if love is the motivation behind teaching and learning that it will yield deep and meaningful results for educators and students and that the world will be a better place for it. The collection also displays that Carl and the work that he creates, with love as a foundational motivation, is about learning more, knowing more and sharing with those who are interested or are open to engaging with the work. It also provides examples of Carl's voice in his work. This harkens back to his PhD dissertation on the topic of written voice, which remains an underlying (at times, overlaying) element of much of his work. Carl shares a story of having an article in review for publication where one reviewer was able to discern his voice through his writing. He proudly recalls that the reviewer said, "Well this could only be Carl Leggo's writing' and that's how strong the voice was for somebody who, you know, had heard me right or read me" which speaks to his belief that voice is unique and significant to creating meaning (CL1, June 20, 2018).

In the article "Living Love: Confessions of a Fearful Teacher," that also appears in the aforementioned compilation (2019) of his academic publications, Leggo (2011) highlights some of his views on living and teaching with love while also questioning the meaning of life in contemporary society. He begins the article by questioning his own identity and place, asking, "Who am I? Who am I in relation to the world? How should I live? What are the responsibilities of a human being in the contemporary world?" (p. 116). He ruminates throughout the article on those initial questions, adding more questions and answers, with earnest wit and even pragmatism as he progresses. He explains his position around teaching with love, discussing:

> What do I mean when I promote love as the heart of a teacher education program? I certainly don't mean that I will like all my students or colleagues equally. I certainly don't mean that I will not sometimes well up with despair and frustration and hopelessness. Of course, teaching is tough. So is living. (p. 118)

While he champions for a life lived with love in the article, he also poetically and poignantly shares a fear. In the poem "SOS," inspired by Fisher's (2010) discussions of being fearless, Carl shows vulnerability and expresses his own fear of being disconnected from the world:

SOS

I have stories
to tell
and language

for telling them
but still not enough.
I need others

who know
the language.
otherwise why

tell the stories
at all
when I can

live them,
except in telling stories
I hope to weave

my stories
with the stories
of others lining

a text together
a textile sufficiently
close woven

to warm reality
to let real light
through/in/out.

my writing is
always an SOS
fear of desertion

alone frantic
for rescue
connection human

foot prints in the sand
wanting the search(ers)
to return (pp. 125-27)

The prosaic elements of this same article, while seemingly honest and articulated clearly, do not have the same visceral imagery as his poetry. The poem accentuates Carl's desire to weave his stories and his life together with others, thereby seeing the thread of his life continuing. It also sees him never being abandoned by the world. He makes powerful statements in the article, such as "Of course, teaching is tough. So is life" (p. 118), but they are nowhere near as impactful as the images in the poem. The evocative image of tightly woven textiles, implying the closeness and interconnectivity that Carl was seeking, and the implied fear in the lines "alone frantic/for rescue/human connection/foot prints in the sand/wanting the search(ers)/to return" (p. 127) reveal the previously unspoken depths of his fear of being left behind and forgotten. This example showcases one of many ways that Carl uses poetry to express and to reach readers, sharing his story to build on what is known about a particular lived experience. Carl's contributions to poetic inquiry, with his unique voice, can also be found in his literary poetry and in his approaches to teaching which are explored in this book.

Carl Leggo's Poetics: Love, Fun and the Process of Becoming

Carl's belief in the capaciousness of poetry as a way to generate new knowledge, to explore meaning and beliefs and to express that which could not be expressed through other genres is evident in his published poetry. He uses various poetic forms and poetic devices to share his own story or respond to others. This links with his approaches to living poetically and teaching where he encourages students (often future teachers) to, in essence, become poets and use language in a variety of ways to better understand themselves and the works of others. His work also frequently includes references to other poets or theorists who inspire him and his work. His work displays an explorative characteristic where he often tries different approaches to draw out his own thoughts or to discover the meaning behind others' words or experiences. For Carl, poetry functions as a mode of inquiry, as a way to craft questions around his or others' ideas and as the vessel that holds his findings.

The following outlines my findings as they relate to Carl's poetics.

Punctuation:

Carl's poetry uses both standard and non-standard punctuation. There are examples of his poetry where he begins what would be seen as a conventional sentence with a capital on the first line and appropriate punctuation (e.g., a period, question mark or exclamation mark) to end the stanza. This, however, is not an exclusive convention of his poetry. It also does not mean that the idea, contained in what would most easily be thought of as a sentence, stops at the end of the stanza (Leggo, 2008a). Ideas, in his poetry, can move over multiple stanzas, where the new stanza is not capitalized (as it is not the start of the sentence). He also uses a mixture of standard and non-standard punctuation, for e/affect, where end punctuation is omitted (Leggo, 2018). Through his choices, he is able to either give the reader a specific complete sentence, which may represent one thought, or allow them to move across different interpretations of a thought before it either reaches a punctuated conclusion or is left without punctuation to continue.

Portrayal of Voice:

Carl's work, often autobiographical or autoethnographic in nature, is characterized by having the first-person pronoun "I" capitalized, with other's voices being shared through other narrative constructs. This includes mentioning the person by name for whom the words are attributed and using italics to show their voice as different than his as the poem's narrator. An example of this is found in his poem "SWALLOW LIGHT" in his chapter "Autobiography: Researching Our Lives and Living Our Research" in the book *Being with A/r/tography* (2008b). In the poem, he writes:

> Like the pond skater knows shadows, fissures, vibrations,
> the resonant text read hypertextually, poised between
> sun and night, I no longer know the way back, but
> Carrie's wisdom like fridge magnets might guide me still:
>
> *always remember to forget*
>   *what you don't know won't hurt you*
> *always remember somebody nice*
>   *kindness somehow stays with you*
> *be open to new ideas*
>   *we're getting older like everybody else*
> *be nice to want nothing*
> *everything is good*
>
> As a boy Carrie always bought me McGregor Happy Foot socks.
> The other day I bought a pair. I might even take up dancing (p. 19).

This convention of italics showing others' voices provides the reader with an opportunity to engage with multiple voices in Carl's stories that are written in poetic form and that use poetic devices to bring his stories to life. It allows the reader an opportunity to follow his poetic story without needing to pause to consider *who* is speaking, thereby strengthening their connection with *what* is being said. Additionally, through explicitly sharing the words of others in his poetic inquiry, he implicates his awareness that he is a limited omniscient narrator in his life and in his stories. He explores his experiences without imposing a heavy interpretation on the voices of others, trying to authentically share what they said. He tries to differentiate between his thoughts and his memory of what others said. He is also mindful to quote other's words with their punctuation choices (e.g., Leggo, 1998) so that it is his poetry that shows his interpretation of what was said and not his grammatical choices. This is a unique function of poetry in that voice is shown not only through what is written on the page, but how it is written (in relation to line breaks, stanza breaks and typography).

Frequently Used Poetic Devices:

Carl's use of poetic devices is extensive in his corpus of work, which makes sense given his focus on exploring the power of poetry. He uses such devices as alliteration, allusion, assonance, consonance, internal rhyme (more often than common rhyme), imagery, puns/wit, repetition and simile. One example of assonance, which displays his enjoyment of exploring language within academic contexts which would normally not see poetic play of this nature, comes with his play on sounds in "Loose Goose" in Living Language (2012a):

> loose goose   boost couscous   doozy foozball
>   whose noose   kazoo moose
> ruse rouse   souse tousle youse   woozy zoo (p. 154)

In addition to his more playful approach to assonance, he also uses it for affect. An example of this comes from his (2010) article with Pauline Sameshima where they share correspondence between the two of them which includes poetry. He writes:

> Joy recommends a film about
> a man who takes a mistress.
>
> *I recommend it*, she says, *because
> it's good, not because you have.*
>
> I miss my mistress: just another
> asinine line with assonance,
>
> nothing more. my mistress is lost
> in the mist, in the midst
>
> of regret and fear and silence,
> absence held in the imagination (pp. 72-3).

This particular excerpt not only shows an example of Carl's use of assonance, with its play on sounds, but is explicit with the reader that he did that on purpose to give them a unique reading experience. He is not always as overt with assonance, as in these previous examples, but instead can use the device more subtly, along with consonance and simile, to provide the reader with vivid imagery. This approach extends from his literary poetry to his poetry that is created for academic or inquiry purposes. From his literary poem, "Lynch's Lane" in his collection of poetry *A View from my Mother's House* (1999):

> shoveling snow searching for crocuses
> fallen leaves holding the sun
> and cutting shapes in ice
> everywhere the air lemon
> smell of freshly washed cotton
> the world melting splashing washing
> away like saints in the River Jordan (np)

Through his use of poetic devices, Carl either intentionally or explicitly shows his reader how the device functions, teaching them while expressing himself, or he uses it in subtle ways to further engage his reader and relay his ideas. His playfully long O's, which make the reader extend their lips should they read it out loud in "Loose Goose," draws attention to the notion that words on the page are meant to be interacted with. Moreover, his explicit naming of his own use of poetic devices shows self-awareness and levity, while his more subtle uses of poetic devices provide sensory details for his readership. This diverse use of poetic devices highlights his belief in the need for an understanding of the craft of poetry in order to convey different ideas for different purposes.

Appearance on the Page:

While some poems play with line and spacing, the bulk of his poems are left justified with traditional stanza breaks. His expression does not necessarily stop where the stanza stops. Ideas and/or sentences potentially continue from one stanza to another, culminating with end punctuation (e.g., a period or question mark). A notable attribute of his poetry is that he frequently separates stanzas using symbols or letters of the alphabet (abecedarian). An example of this attribute is in "Living Poetry: Five Ruminations" (Leggo, 2004) where he uses an ampersand (&) to separate his stanzas, keeping his discussion going without needing to use end punctuation. This sees the creation of a 16-stanza poem that begins with a capital and ends with a period only after the conclusion of the last line.

Frequently Used Poetic Forms:

Carl's work sees him engaging with/through as many different forms of poetry as he can in order to learn more about the form and its power to produce new knowledge or share knowledge. Of his experimental processes, he says,

> What happens *if* I set up a heuristic of 26 sections or 72 sections? Or what will be like if I set up to look at things from four perspectives? But then at the same time, to look at them from four opposite perspectives. Yeah, so I set myself a goal and then I tease it through, all right? To see

where it goes, and something emerges, and I'm pleased. But ah, look at that, that's fun the way that unfolded. (CL2, September 18, 2018)

Carl's corpus of academic-poetic and literary poetic works includes such forms as abecedarians, erasure poems/blackout poetry, free verse poetry, found poetry, concrete poetry, computer-generated poetry, Haiku, lyric poetry, narrative poetry and odes.

Common Themes and Purpose of Poetry in his Work

His work often focuses on family, teaching, the power of poetry, living poetically, storytelling, responding to the work of others, and ruminating on his own thoughts.

Of his diverse poetry he writes,

> I regard each of my poems as a center, etymologically related to the Greek *kentron*, or the sharp, stationary point of a pair of geometric compasses. There is no single center, but we do see and know and understand from a specific center or centers, and we need to take the measure of these centers. In this way, I regard each poem as a center that provides a location for speculation and locution, an aesthetic and imaginative stance (even an instance) for circling, spiraling, perhaps like a Spirograph. (Leggo, 2012a, pp. 156-7)

For Carl, poetry has no limits and as such, his work has diverse purposes. Poetry in his academic work supports his autobiography and is used to inspire others, to ruminate, to inquire, to generate a deeper awareness of self and others (autoethnographically), to better understand the power of language and as a way to live and to seek out the purpose of life.

Frequently Cites:

His work highlights whoever he was reading or thinking about at the time. This includes other poets (e.g., Adrienne Rich, Patrick Lane, Hélène Cixous), those interested in language or poetry (e.g., Helen Sword, Peter Elbow, Richard Miller, Gregory Orr), philosophers (e.g., Martin Heidegger, Jacques Derrida), and/or those who work in/with curriculum (e.g., Bill Pinar, Ted Aoki, Paulo Freire). These references may appear in the discussion that leads into his poetry or in the poem itself by way of direct citations or, in some instances, footnotes. There is an example of this in Chapter Nine in his poem "Pondering the Ponderosa Pine" (2016).

Carl Leggo's Teaching

Unfortunately, Dr. Carl Leggo passed away before we could further our conversations on teaching. However, his corpus of work houses a great deal of his views on the subject that can be drawn on.

How and Why Did he Become a Teacher?

He shares, through poetry, that he fell into teaching. He writes, "I never wanted to be a teacher/I am not a teacher on call/I am a called teacher/a calling teacher, a teacher calling/always calling for students" (Leggo, 2002, p. 4). He also writes (Leggo, 2008c) that he became a teacher for financial reasons; he needed a job. Only after did his job become his calling.

Carl Leggo's Views on Teaching

Carl wrote frequently about his life in school as student, teacher, teacher educator and poet in the academy. He summarizes his view on teaching by saying, "As an educator, I am committed to supporting others to learn how to live with love, how to live creatively, how to live with hope, how to live with and on the earth with heart" (University of British Columbia website, n.d.). While he took his role as a teacher educator seriously, Carl was also known to be critical of his privilege as a scholar. An example of this is evident in the video of him reading his poem, "Ring Around the Scholar," published by Joe Norris on YouTube (2014). In the video, Carl reads a lengthy poem that satirizes the complex nature of being a scholar. It begins in his office, in his normal, everyday, clothes. And As the poem continues, his attire changes, sees him wearing a graduation gown as he lists the different, often contradictory, items that scholars want including recognition from their institutions and from others. The poem and its accompanying video show Carl's deftness in using humour and language to provide a commentary on the requirements of being an academic. Readers and/or viewers are encouraged to think about the conflicts that academics face between their goals as educators and the requirements of their positions. He is using his privilege in the system to challenge and problematize it. He is able to say what may otherwise be seen as taboo or impolite about the system in a way that is seen as light-hearted and palatable. For Carl, teaching is about love (for learning, language and life) and supporting others' learning and he chafes against other elements that distract from that. Poetry serves as a way to question systems and challenge them in a way that may let more love in.

Notable Features of Leggo's Teaching Praxis that Correspond with his Views and his Poetics

Carl encourages students to play with language and poetry in order to gain an understanding of its fundamental features as a genre and of its power for expression and understanding. He writes,

> in order to expand and enlarge students' responses, their sets of expectations must beenlarged and expanded. To achieve that objective, students need exposure to a widevariety of poems. Found poems, prose poems, concrete poems, and sound poemsbroaden and develop students' expectations concerning poetry. (Leggo, 1997, p. 16)

He facilitates students' introduction to diverse forms of poetry and supports them, as a poet and teacher, as they trial expressing ideas through them. Through trialing, students learn not only how poetry functions and why authors have used the genre for centuries, but also how it can inform their own lives. This links back to Carl's notion of living poetically:

> The world obviously influences the classroom, but the classroom ought also to influence the world. The world of students cannot be locked outside the classroom door. But at the same time the students' world is too narrow and needs to be expanded by schooling. (Leggo, 1997, p. 10)

He uses poetry to expand the views of his students while being aware that the world does not necessarily see poetry as a primary means of being. He does, however, believe that it should be a place to live poetically. In his last personal profile on the UBC website, he says,

> The fundamental inquiry of my work is—how can we live well? Poetry is the heart of all my research and teaching. Poetry is a way of attending to the personal, but poetry always reminds us that we always live in relationship with others, with the vast network of all creation. (University of British Columbia, n.d.)

He teaches based on his experiences as a writer. He argues that poetry could expand critical and creative ways of thinking noting that:

> All my teaching of writing, both in school and university classrooms, is informed and generated by my practices as a writer of poetry, fiction, and scholarly texts. Hence, the way I teach writing is connected to my own experiences as a writer. In turn, I encourage my students to pay attention to their writing processes in order to understand the complex ways that writing unfolds in individual practice. When I read many influential books about teaching writing, I find myself nonplussed by the advice that is provided because I just do not see my own processes

and practices as a writer and teacher in the typical textbook advice. (Leggo, 2019b, p. 449)

Carl's consistency between his beliefs and actions around teaching are evidenced by the stories of those around him and in his published books, articles, and poetry. He often explores, ruminating or playing with/through language and guides his students along a similar journey.

Discussion

As a researcher and scholar, Carl puts value in the power of language and uses his poetry (poetic language, word choice, playing with poetic forms and styles) to explore what he refers to as the "capaciousness" of poetry (CL2, September 18, 2018). He often unapologetically writes based on his interests at that particular moment; that certain something that he thinks may uncover more knowledge about language or that could support others in becoming better educators. He explores his life through poetry and creates his own narrative/poetic voice through his stories of particular people and places that are important to him. To always gain a better understanding of the power of language, he reads frequently as a way to be exposed to and explore others' ideas. He then links their ideas to his own life, posits questions for inquiry or generates understandings through the creation of poetry.

He inspires others to think more deeply through the creation of poetry which includes an exploration of the uses and power of language. This exploration may require students to pause and evaluate what they know or do not know about poetry and language use. This effectively then pushes them to learn more purposefully in order to create poetry which can more impactfully show their understanding of a concept or more effectively explore their identity, relationships with others and/or their feelings that are often discounted in the classroom. He approaches teaching as a writer with a foundational belief that students are writers whose voices and experiences are integral to the learning process, be it learning how to write or how to teach others (e.g., Leggo, 2007; 2012).

For Carl, the poet and educator, using poetry as a way of knowing, of processing ideas and of sharing the findings makes complete sense. Teaching others how to use poetry in their own inquiry processes also makes sense. When his literary poetry, some exemplified in this chapter, is contrasted with his examples of poetry published in academic journals one gets a clearer understanding of Carl's blurring of the lines between literary poetry and poetry used in research and scholarship. Through all forms of his poetry, or his poetic products from studies, he is able to inquire and make sense of his views, reflect on how they fit in the world and use language in diverse ways to express the depths of his feelings/findings. As exemplified through his poetic-academic publications, some of which are explored in this book, he uses poetic devices, such metaphors and similes, to express complex revelations in simple yet refined terms. He uses line breaks for impact or inversion, e.g., witfully using enjambment to express otherwise unspoken views, while using poetic construction to unearth and express greater or deeper understandings about his topic of inquiry, or what I posit he would call "wonder."

Chapter 5
Profile: Dr. Pauline Sameshima

> "I call my work arts integrated research. So, what I mean by that is I'm using various arts, whether it's visual art, or literary art, to generate deeper, more meaningful data, and then to analyze the data and to disseminate that data through the medium of literary or visual art." (PS1, June 27, 2018)

Dr. Pauline Sameshima is a visual artist, poet, researcher, Canada Research Chair in Arts Integrated Studies, gallery curator and professor at Lakehead University. She taught at the elementary school level for 17 years where her interest in becoming a principal led her to complete a PhD in Curriculum Studies at UBC in 2006. Her committee, which speaks to the diversity of her ekphrastic work, was made up of Drs. Carl Leggo, Anthony Clarke, Rita Irwin and J. Gary Knowles who are well-known scholars in qualitative research, arts-based research, a/r/tography and pedagogy. Her interest in the arts and their place in research saw her co-creating the Parallaxic Praxis model (first published in Sameshima & Vandermause, 2008), which supports interdisciplinary teams as they collect, process and interpret data. This model focuses on ways to use the strengths and experiences of team members to provide multiple perspectives and ways of exploring a concept or problem, often spanning interdisciplinary or multidisciplinary areas. She currently has over 15 years of teaching experience at the higher education level. In addition to researching and teaching, Pauline is currently the editor-in-chief at the *Journal for the Canadian Association for Curriculum Studies*.

What Is this Work? Who Can Use It?

For Pauline, who also uses the term poetic inquiry in many of her publications, her work with poetry frequently extends into other art forms. She intentionally calls her work "arts integrated" research (PS1, June 27, 2018) as she does not see it "directly or purely" fitting under Eisner and Barone's arts-based research (2012), Knowles and Cole's arts-informed research (2008) or Irwin and Springgay's notion of a/r/tography (2006). Instead of only using one of those descriptors to describe her approaches, she suggests that her work follows "tenets that are drawn from all three" of those distinct methodologies (PS1, June 27, 2018).

She has been heavily involved in the publications that have been created based on the works shared at the International Symposium on Poetic Inquiry as either an editor or contributor. Her view on who can use poetic inquiry is important because she has been an active participant in the field for over a decade. When asked who she thinks can use poetic inquiry, she notes that,

> the tension is always there between when you are a poet and when you are a researcher using poetry. I think that if you are attentive to the craft of whatever it is that you do, you then become that named. So, you become a researcher when you research. You become a teacher when you teach, you become a poet when you write poetry. (PS1, June 27, 2018)

Her view on the limits of what poetic inquiry can do and who can do it will be further explored in a subsequent section.

Reasons for Poetry in her Work

Her reasons for using poetic inquiry harken back to her interest in its uses for research where she contends that poetry is "a great way to synthesize a large amount of data" (PS1, June 27, 2018). She also believes that poetry functions as a way to give agency to others, asserting that it "also allows people to integrate themselves into [the research study]" (PS1, June 27, 2018). This, she believes, is a unique attribute that poetry and poetic inquiry have that distinguishes them from other methods, methodologies or tools. Through poetry "you present the findings in a way that opens a connection for the reader, so that the audience can place themselves into the work by thinking about their connection to what the poetry means" (PS1, June 27, 2018). This, however, does not mean that the poet is without voice or agency of their own. She believes that the poet is sharing their analysis with their audience, the reader, through their poetry and through their poetic choices where "you then are able to create a stronger…impact, because you are…inviting the reader to integrate self into the findings" (PS1, June 27, 2018). Poetry functions as a way to give the poet, who is also the researcher, a way to share with the harmonized voices of the participant(s) and the researcher, while inviting the reader to also add their voice, their interpretation, to their reading of the poem. The poet makes choices around the creation of the poem (their voice), which serves as an interpretation of the data or information, while using the voice(s)/words of those who are participating in their study. The poet performs a similar process when responding, through poetry, to quotations or ideas from the literature. The poems, the products, are then available for the reader to engage with, providing an additional opportunity for meaning to be made.

(No) Limits of Poetic Inquiry

While Pauline sees poetic inquiry as a way to synthesize data and amplify the voices of others, poetic inquiry is not without notable limits. Backed by her experience working with students, her extensive experiences with research and her recurring stint as a Canada Research Chair, she says,

> sometimes students will talk about the limitations of the research methodology…[or] they would say, 'here are the limitations of the study,' but I think it might be more helpful or useful to think about, not what the research can't do, but why you do the research. Because there's always going to be stuff that it can't do, because it's not for that reason. (PS2, December 19, 2018)

She suggests that poetic inquiry must be used for purposeful reasons. Not every question is meant to be answered with poetic inquiry exclusively. It is then up to the researcher to identify if poetic inquiry can potentially work in that instance before selecting it as a methodology. Pauline's work in poetic inquiry, however, makes it evident that it is one approach among many and while it may not be useful when adopted as an overarching methodology in all studies, it can still be used to inform and enrich the research process. This is apparent by her creation of the Parallaxic Praxis model (2008), explored briefly below, where multiple approaches to research questions are used to benefit the study.

Unique Features of her Work

Pauline's focus on the power of art to inform research, through its integration, sets much of her work apart from other poetic inquiry practitioners. Her work with the Parallaxic Praxis model with Vandermause (2008), Sinner (2009), Maarhuis (2016) and Stock and Slingerland (2016) culminated in the publication of a methods book on the topic (Sameshima et al., 2019). This model focuses on the value of researching through interdisciplinary teams and posits ways for the teams to use both traditional elements of research and arts-integrated methods to expand research possibilities in such areas as teacher education, health sciences, and social justice. This sees her work pushing what arts-integrated approaches can do and highlights their importance in the realm of qualitative research.

Pauline Sameshima Poetics: Ekphrasis, Responding and the Advocacy of Voices

Her passions for research, visual art and finding ways to amplify the voices of others is evident not only in her theoretical publications but also in her published poetry and research around arts integration and well-being (Sameshima et al., 2017). As a visual artist, who uses such mediums as textile art, tile art, digital art, photography and mixed media, her poetry has an ekphrastic quality. Ekphrasis is a rhetorical practice that uses vivid description and imagery to describe art, most often through poetry, in ways that bring further dimension to the understanding of the work of art. Webb (2009) draws attention to the deeper epistemological inferences of the term:

> The study of the ancient treatments of ekphrasis shows that it was understood to be a type of speech that worked an immediate impact on the mind of the listener, sparking mental images of the subjects it 'placed before the eyes'. As an elementary exercise, ekphrasis gave practice in this type of speech, showing students how to expand the various elements of a narration to make sure their listeners not only knew what happened but felt as if they were witnesses themselves. (p. 193)

Pauline's poetry shows a deftness for using language to enliven research or artistic works, giving the reader a visceral experience that accompanies their aesthetic experience (of the visual art or poem). This differentiates her practice from others in poetic inquiry. Further, she uses poetry to create a dialogic experience with the words of research participants thereby creating diverse interpretations that lead to further questions or generate greater understandings of the experiences of others.

Of her corpus of poetry, she says, "generally the kind of poetry that I have published is a response to data. So, I use the poetry as a way to better understand my thoughts about the data" (PS1, June 27, 2018). How she goes about this process, as the following examples and discussions in this chapter and in Chapter Eight will demonstrate, is important when understanding poetic inquiry's place in Canadian research and scholarship. She often creates multilayered poems that represent the researcher and the researched simultaneously, while also providing rich description that can be both visual and visceral.

Punctuation:

Pauline uses punctuation to illustrate others' voices. She often omits punctuation when interpreting the voice of others and instead uses line breaks to separate ideas or sentences. As such, she does not provide a textual interpretation of when the participant's idea ended (with end punctuation), instead opting to use poetic forms to explicitly show her interpretation or analysis of the data. This delineation between her voice as the researcher (who uses words as a form of data) and the voice of the participant (who shares their lived experience) then serves to retain the value of the participant-voiced lived experience(s). Language is used to construct a poetic form of data but what the participant literally said (verbatim) is not stripped of its power. Further, on occasion, she has not used the capital "I" when interpreting the words or experiences of others (so as not to impose her voice over that of others). She does use the capital "I" when she is creating poetry from a direct quote as in her transcript poetry in her book *Climbing the Ladder with Gabriel: Poetic Inquiry of a*

Methamphetamine Addict in Recovery (Sameshima et al., 2009). In this book, she and her fellow artists and researchers explore, through interdisciplinary approaches, the lived experience of "Gabriel" (a pseudonym) with an aim of better understanding the lived experiences of addicts in recovery. This convention around punctuation and capitalization does not, however, extend to work that she has voiced. She uses standard punctuation when speaking as herself, where stanzas often start with a capital and end with a period (see Sameshima & Leggo, 2010; 2013).

An example of her interpretation of a participant's experience comes from her poem "WAITING THROUGH SUNDAYS" in her chapter "Materializing the Punctum" (Maarhuis & Sameshima, 2016). This poem will be looked at again, more closely, later in the study encompassed within this book, however it exemplifies a way that Pauline uses capitalization, punctuation and line breaks to represent the experiences of others:

> i stayed through high school and college
> he said he loved me, always sorry
> please he pleaded
> god, please forgive me
> he prayed
> i forgave him, merciful me
> the sunday school teacher
> because i had it all
> love beyond compare
> family, friends, sports, grades
> even clothes, to hide the perfect couple (p. 279)

Portrayal of Voice:

When interpreting the experiences of others, she does not use the capital "I" (as above). However, when quoting a singular participant verbatim, as in "Climbing the Ladder with Gabriel" (2009), where she creates transcript poetry that is generated from interviews and discussions, she uses the convention of italics to represent other voices within the poem. This use of italics is a convention that is also shared by Carl in some of his poetry. The researcher explicitly shows their participation in the research process while showing respect for the participants who are willing to share their lives with others. Here is an example of Pauline's use of italics to show multiple voices:

> Kids (1:122-127)
> I feel bad about the kids
> I thought I was being there for them
> they said
> *even when you were there*

> *you weren't there*
> I guess I wasn't
> but that wasn't my intention
> I thought I was being a
> stay-at-home mom
> which I'd always promised
> myself that I would do (p. 53)

This separation of voice differs from Pauline's frequently used technique of merging multiple voices. Examples of this technique (i.e., the merging of the voice of the participant [verbatim] and Pauline's voice as the researcher [in poetic choices/forms and in the selection of verbatim quotes]) appear in subsequent sections and in Chapter Eight.

Frequent Poetic Devices:

Pauline's work uses a number of poetic devices including alliteration, allusion, assonance, enjambment, metaphor and onomatopoeia. A unique attribute that much of her poetry holds is a form of synesthesia. Synesthesia as a poetic device, as in the neurological condition of the same name, creates a blending of different senses where the reader can, for example, see sounds or hear colours. It gives the reader a fully immersive and visceral reading experience where their senses are simultaneously active. As in the example below, where the words "sleet screeches" gives the reader an auditory experience using onomatopoeia, the reader may still be actively experiencing the previously mentioned "iron stench" of blood which can lead to the sound having a scent attributed to it (p. 279). She uses synesthesia along with simile and consonance as in "WAITING THROUGH SUNDAYS" (2016), which is full of powerful sensory experiences, of "select data-inspired author-created poetry resulting from the study" (p. 282):

> the blood slowly pooling in my hands
> cupped tight under my chin, full control
> no drips on his cherished cloth car seats
> not a spot on his sunday shirt
> nose numb, cheeks throbbing
> quiet liquid, wet iron stench
> filling the passenger side

> sleet screeches at the wipers so i stay in the car
> i'm suddenly in front of my glass house
> he leans over and roughly pulls open the door latch
> i stumble out to the grass
> the ground is close as i open my hands
> and the stickiness runs down with the rain

> like i'm gently putting a broken bird onto the ground
> then i wipe my palms on the sweet softness
> like a defecating dog
> rude in this manicured neighborhood (p. 279)

By way of her carefully selected words and use of poetic devices, she highlights the severity of participants' lived experiences, while also providing her own interpretation of the data. She uses sensory descriptions of cupping hands full of blood (later drained onto the ground), the smell of the blood, the numb and throbbing facial impacts and the sound of the wipers to bring the reality of domestic abuse to the forefront of the reader's mind. This highlights a function of poetry where it is used to bring the reality of that which is being researched to its intended audience in visceral ways. It also shows that scholars are using poetic inquiry to push academic boundaries as these relate to ensuring that participants and their experiences are expressed as genuinely as possible even as experiences and stories are sewn together to create a narrative arc.

Purpose of Poetry:

Poetry, for Pauline, is often a form that can be used when responding, analyzing, disseminating and opening data for interpretation and sharing others' voices. Her work often has elements of ekphrastic poetry. She uses language to provide the reader with a visceral experience, or uses poetry as a form of response, either responding to data, analyzing data or responding to others dialogically (as in Sameshima and Leggo, 2013). She routinely uses poetry to share the voices of others. Further, her corpus shows an interest in not only looking outward but inward, with instances of autobiographical poetry (as in Sameshima and Leggo, 2010) where she explores her own identity, values and beliefs which serve as valuable counterparts to her poetics that frequently focus on others.

She also uses poetry to discuss lived experiences fictitiously. One such example, from her poetic-epistolary article with Leggo (2010), is her poem "WRITTEN IN THE DARK HEART (for Luke)." Using the narrator Julia from her book *Seeing Red* (2007), Pauline writes a poem about the complexity of a decades-long relationship between the speaker and her partner. Highlighted below (with original formatting) is an excerpt of three lines, one stanza, from the poem that exemplifies how Pauline uses language to evoke a visceral response in the reader:

> The unbearable memories, physical pain, unstoppable, powerless, defenselessness
> My dark red blood, his crisply ironed Sunday shirts, hands around my neck
> Scabs on my wrists, guilty as charged, accepted (p. 79)

Through her choices around language and poetic construction, Pauline describes layers of violence, implied self-harm and guilt. As a form of inquiry, this poem asks the reader to consider why people stay in relationships where violence is present and provides a way of beginning to process an understanding of the complexities of domestic violence. Writing poetry as a different person effectively brings a voice to countless people who have endured domestic violence in silence while also informing the reader about some of the realities of domestic violence.

Pauline Sameshima's Teaching

How and Why Did She Become a Teacher?

Pauline was a teacher in Burnaby, BC. She recalls that she wanted to become a principal and run her own school but that she lacked seniority. That led her to want to do her PhD in order to "jump the line ethically" with the intent of returning to the elementary school system. Her PhD research and dissertation, entitled *Seeing Red* (2006), which used the form of a novel with instances of poetry and photographs of her artwork, ultimately inspired her to continue to engage in multi-modal research and use poetry at the post-secondary level. Of this event she says, "I wanted to write something that people would read, and then I ended up writing *Seeing Red* which has poetry in it, and that's how it all began" (PS1, June 27, 2018).

Pauline Sameshima's Views on Teaching

Of her approach to teaching, she shares, "I make as a way to create meaning and teach these methodologies. My pedagogy is based on making and assignments involve student-making for meaning-creation" (Emailed questionnaire, July 2020). Of this focus, alongside Sinner (2009), she writes:

1. Learning is transformative when it is meaningful, making static curriculums unsustainable. By changing the role of teachers, and enabling more creative social constructivist approaches, a sort of 'potluck' pedagogy may emerge, where students and teachers come together in-formally and make discretionary decisions that facilitate aesthetic learning experiences. 'Potluck' pedagogy describes a deep acknowledgement for what students bring to the table and offers choice in the possibilities for learning.

2. The presentation and representation of learning reiterated in various pedagogic forms evokes and invokes imaginative thinking possibilities. The lesson shifts to become a forum for inventive possibilities for students to enter and engage. (p. 180)

She believes that teaching is impactful when there is an experiential element that asks students to become active participants in their learning. She values that students can bring their knowledge and experience into the learning process and that the teacher is the facilitator of learning. The teacher's purpose is to expand ways to learn and not to limit them.

What Are Notable Features of her Teaching Praxis that Correspond with her Views and her Poetics?

Her approach to teaching links back to her poetics where she is sure to delineate voice (using capitalization) and show what her participants said (transcript poetry) when adding her own voice (or making it explicit); the voice of the other is important. She describes why she uses the act of making as a primary element of her teaching:

> making materializes conceptual thought and loose ideas. When something is created, it holds agency. Material objects can also be reaggregated in new ways. Poem words can be moved around and new organizations create new revelations. Students involved in embodied learning are more engaged. (Emailed questionnaire, July 2020)

Her interest in the power of art, research and cooperation (as in the dialogic elements of the Parallaxic Praxis model) are reflected in how she approaches elements of her teaching praxis. In one example of how she uses poetry in her work as an educator, she describes how she guides students through the process of taking an interview transcript and creating poetry with it:

> [t]hey are each given a page and asked to write a few lines of poetry or a stanza from the page—it can be found poetry or key themes from the page. The interview pages are kept in order and the group presents the poem in the order of the pages. The students end up with a summary essence of the transcript and an opportunity to code and analyze a data set. Generally, the finished poem is very powerful and generative for discussion. (emailed questionnaire, July 20, 2020)

The creation of poetry from the transcript data, akin to her own work, keeps the integrity of the participants' words while allowing students the opportunity to layer their voices and interpretations through their poetic choices.

Discussion

Pauline's multifaceted work is most easily distilled into, or defined as, a practice of making as a form of response or interpretation. She uses poetry to respond to the data (sharing it verbatim or distilled), to art, to others' conceptual ideas or to others' direct statements. Through her poetic practice, she ensures that respect is given to the voice of others by using such techniques as modified capitalization to denote her voice, a distilled voice of her participants or a verbatim quote from her participants. In addition to her work with poetry, Pauline also creates art in various media. This is all represented in her approach to teaching in that she creates opportunities for students to engage with concepts, share their voices (responses or interpretations) and highlight the value of the voices of others.

Pauline's use of poetic inquiry, as part of her arts-integrated processes, serves as an example of how some scholars in Canada are using poetry to better represent lived experience and amplify the voice(s) of others. Other examples from the literature include poetic inquiry being used as a way to share the voices of incarcerated women (e.g., Fels et al., 2014), individuals living with disabilities (e.g., Downey, 2016) and those whose voices are marginalized from the 2SLGBTQ+ community (e.g., Lambert, 2016; Teman, 2019) and BIPOC (Black, Indigenous, People of Colour) communities (e.g., Saunders et al., 2016; Cutts, 2020). There is also mention of poetic inquiry being used as a tool in art therapy (e.g., Schreibman & Chilton, 2012) and to explore art therapy studio practices (Wallace, 2015).

Yet Pauline's approach is distinctive. She e/affectively uses poetry to compel the reader to not only read about others' experiences, but to *feel* what it is like to live their lives. She does this through such poetic devices as synesthesia and metaphor that allow her to viscerally make what she is describing, her findings, tangible. She also uses *how* a poem is constructed, from line lengths to stanza formation, to draw attention to specific terms or ideas that further demonstrate the content or theme of the poem. As a form of affective data, her poetry (or what has been referred to in this book as a poetic inquiry product) functions as a way to showcase layers of meaning, requiring that the reader not only absorb the poem aesthetically, but consider and assess the greater knowledge illustrated therein.

Chapter 6
Profile: Dr. John Guiney Yallop

> *"I see myself as a poet, researcher, as a poetic inquirer because they're both the same for me. I started research certainly through story, but stories, they lead back to poetry, which is really how I tell my stories. So that's ... how I [got] where I am."* (JGY1, June 22, 2018)

Dr. John J. Guiney Yallop is a poet, storyteller and professor at Acadia University. A self-identified Two-Spirited person, John's research and scholarship explores his own lived experiences and identity while encouraging others to do the same. His journey towards becoming a professor started in Ireland, in a Roman Catholic seminary, where he came to realize that the priesthood was not his calling. He then moved to Toronto where he worked as an education assistant and classroom teacher. He ultimately completed his Ph.D. at Western University where he solidified his calling as an educator.

What Is this Work? Who Can Do It?

John, while hesitant to label his work, says that he was doing poetic inquiry before he knew it had a more commonly used descriptor. He reflects, "I was a bit older when I started writing, doing poetic inquiry anyway. I was very young when I started writing poetry, but I was in my 40s when I was doing poetic inquiry" (JGY2, January 18, 2019). He argues that there is no right or wrong way to engage through poetic inquiry and he pushes against the view of art as elitist. He contends, "to me it's *fash* [referring to the notion of being 'in fashion' or elitist] and because I think it closes doors" and that it is ultimately a close-minded view that prevents connection to occur (JGY2, January 18, 2019). He believes, like Carl and Pauline, that it is poets who engage in knowledge-making and mobilization through poetic inquiry. He paraphrases Norman Denzin's statement about sociologists saying, "If a poet does it, it's poetry. And I'm a poet, so if I do it, it's poetry." He also believes, "Now, it might not be poetry that you like or that you think is any good that somebody else might love it. I think it's wonderful [LAUGH] and life changing" which shows his humour and continues his push against an elitist view of art (JGY2, January 18, 2019). Akin to Carl's video about what scholars want, John uses his humour to share a strong sentiment about his work and its place in the larger scheme of poetry and academia. A statement like this could be seen as flippant, as he puts little regard in the systemic view of ranking or rating work, but it emphasizes his belief that the process of writing poetry holds value that extends beyond measurable products. He sees the value in his work and the work of others and believes that if the poet gets something from creating the poem that is what matters and not necessarily if others see a high level of value in it.

Reasons for Poetry in his Work

John's work reflects a strong focus on storytelling and an awareness of the importance of identity. He shares that poetry became integral in his academic work because it strengthened his voice. He says, "I rediscovered it, or reawakened it, if you will; reawakened my own poetry voice, or the poet in me started reawakening" (JGY1, June 22, 2018). It is in this voice that he can express himself in different ways. He says, "I certainly feel, for me, that poetry gets at things more succinctly…with fewer words, more clearly in some ways…or more up close" (JGY1, June 22, 2018). He goes on to explain his idea saying, "I think maybe because of the language it uses, the metaphors, or the sparsity of, if that's the right word, of the language. I think it's going to let people up close to the experience" (JGY1, June 22, 2018). He also values poetry as a way of sharing multi-layered meaning saying that "a poem can be reread several times, depending on the length of the poem, of course, in one sitting" and that "because you can go back through it so much [you are] getting up very, very close. And that lingering and sort of spending time with [it] doesn't seem to happen in other genres" (JGY1, June 22, 2018). Further, he contends that poetry functions not only as a way to zoom in, but to shorten the distance between the poet and the reader which makes poetic inquiry an impactful process. Of his own poetry, John reflects:

> whenever I've edited my poetry, it has always gotten shorter; it has never gotten longer. In some ways, I think poetry has humbled me because I realize that a lot of what I thought I needed to say, I don't need to say at all. (Final Interview, June 3, 2019)

He likens this editing to a dialogic experience with the poem itself saying, "…the poem was saying 'no I don't need that, I don't need that, just listen to me.' Not to me, John, but 'listen to me' is what the poem is saying to me sometimes" (Final Interview, June 3, 2019). Through this condensed way of conveying information, John also believes that poetry can be a way of "reclaiming identity" and that through the practice of writing poetry and using poetic inquiry that he has become "a better person" (Final Interview, June 3, 2019).

John's purpose for poetry is ultimately to support others' development of self by way of, to use a cliched adage and pun on his past in the seminary, practicing what he preaches as it relates to inquiring about self and society.

His academic-poetic and literary work shows an ongoing strengthening of his own voice. He then uses his voice in a way that also makes room for others' voices to be heard. He recalls attending the first ISPI, where he shared his view that he did not want poetic inquiry to be defined. He recalls, "I remember I resisted that. I spoke that I don't want to define because it made definitions, [and that] although they're really useful, they can also strangle" (Final Interview, June 3, 2019). He was both surprised and pleased that his voice could be heard in that forum recalling,

> there was openness to that [sharing], and I felt like, wow, that's really, that's really exciting. Like, I can say something that goes against what was even in the plan, and there's space made for me. That, to me, was like, 'oh my goodness. I can grow here.' (Final Interview, June 3, 2019)

He values individual voices, his and others, as exemplified in his poetic exchanges with others as in Wiebe and Guiney Yallop (2010) and Wiebe et al. (2016), and says that he has "no interest in being like someone else" and that he wants to "keep making more space" for others (Final Interview, June 3, 2019).

(No) Limits of Poetic Inquiry

For John, poetry has the power to lessen the distance between people and ideas and support the development or reclaiming of identity. As such, he is hesitant to diminish what poetic inquiry can do in relation to research. When asked about its constraints, he says, "It's not a question I can answer for you and so, if I say a poetic inquiry has limits for me, it doesn't mean that those limits have to be yours" (JGY2, January 18, 2019). He discusses that human beings have limits, but that does not mean that poetic inquiry does. He continues with joviality in his voice,

> And that's wonderful. [LAUGH] Isn't it?... What I can do with poetry perhaps Carl Leggo could do something else, you know?... Monica can do something else and Pauline can do something else. So, maybe it's also [that] it doesn't have any limits for me. (JGY2, January 18, 2019)

He pushes back on the idea of limits one last time, saying, "If someone was to say that has limits and here are the limits [then] I would just do something outside that just to show that, well, there you go" (JGY2, January 18, 2019). He believes, like Carl, that poetry has vast potential and focusing on its deficits does not interest him. He says with warmth and placidity in his voice, "…I'm at a point where I don't really care. And if it has limits, well yeah, that's fine, but if it doesn't it's fine too…I guess my response as such, it doesn't matter" (JGY2, January 18, 2019). For John, poetry's power to question, to strengthen identity, to give or amplify voice(s) and to support others' development is what matters to him in his research and scholarship, not its limits.

Unique Features of his Work

John's work frequently links back to stories and questions around identity. He explores his identity as a father and as a Two-Spirit man. A number of his stories focus on his upbringing in Newfoundland (as part of a close-knit community) and highlight his family's hardships. He also delves into how these experiences affect who he has become as a person and as an educator. John is an active member of the poetic inquiry community who has participated in every International Symposium on Poetic Inquiry (ISPI). He recently (2019) co-hosted it with Dr. Natalie Honein at the Art Gallery of Nova Scotia in Halifax, NS. He has also co-edited a volume inspired by ISPI presentations (Butler-Kisber et al., 2017). John brings his belief in the power of poetry as an inquiry method for creating and sharing stories to poetic inquiry. His work reflects the importance of poetic inquiry's function in the realm of identity work, in particular in its ability to give agency and voice. This is important to understanding poetic inquiry in Canadian research and scholarship as it highlights how poetic inquiry is and can be used for social justice purposes by providing a way for the voices of marginalized people to be heard (e.g., members of the 2SLGBTQ+ and BIPOC communities).

While much of North American society is becoming more accepting and welcoming of queer voices in academia, it remains, arguably, a heteronormative society (with its accompanying socio-historical biases). From Goffman's (1963) writing of the stigma associated with being an out, queer teacher to contemporary examples of ongoing struggles facing pre-service teachers (Mayo, 2020), there remains a marginalization that John's work both explicitly and implicitly pushes against. In his unpublished dissertation (2008), he explores his identity in relation to his previously active participation in the Roman Catholic community, as well as his identity as an out, gay schoolteacher. A poetic example of John's voice, as a member of the 2SLGBTQ+ community, is found in his chapter with Shields (2016) where the authors inquire about the connections between identity and pedagogy. In the chapter, John shares his poem "Remembering My Adolescent Crush" (p. 50), shared here with original formatting, where he recalls his teenage crush on Bobby Sherman, a teen idol of the late 1960s and early 1970s:

> Bobby was in my heart
> and in my head.
> He was also
> on the wall
> beside my bed.

My early teenage fantasy life included
being in Bobby's arms,
going for walks with Bobby,
talking with Bobby,
looking at Bobby,

  and Bobby
    looking
      at me,

flying with Bobby,
driving with Bobby,
doing anything
  anything
    with Bobby.

I *loved* Bobby Sherman.
B. O. B. B. Y.
S. H. E. R. M. A. N.

I wrote a love song
for Bobby Sherman
in the style of an acrostic poem.

B.
O.
B.
B.
Y.
S.
H.
E.
R.
M.
A.
N.

B is for Beautiful Bobby.

I can't recall any of the lyrics;
even that first line feels like a transplant
from now.
Still, the emotions are a part of me as I write,
and they all begin with a dreamy
sigh. (pp. 50-51)

John's poetic declaration of love for Bobby Sherman, where he uses language and poetic forms to highlight the common experience of infatuation with first crushes, serves as an example for others to inquire into how their lived experiences have shaped their identities. Had this been written prosaically, with John simply noting that he had a teenage crush on Bobby Sherman, we would have lost the buoyant repetition of "Bobby" which acts as a device that highlights that innocent, yet almost obsessive, repetition of a first crush in our thoughts. Moreover, through poetry, John brings the reader into his experience of remembering which highlights the power of reflection to, as he writes in the final stanza, "transplant" us into a re-living of experience with new perspectives. By using poetry as a method of inquiry about the ways that his identity as a gay man has informed his identity as a teacher, John brings forth a story that is not always heard in academia, while informing what is known about the power of reflection and defining one's identity. While sharing his voice is significant, especially as a member of a marginalized community, it is ultimately John's crafting of poetry, with multiple dimensions of meaning, that yield greater understandings of the power of poetic inquiry in research and scholarship.

John Guiney Yallop's Poetics: Stories, Identity and the Act of Making Space for Others

Frequently Used Poetic Devices:

His poems use poetic devices such as alliteration, allusion, imagery, simile and repetition. An example of this use of imagery and repetition comes from his chapter *The Poetics of Relationship* where John describes his father breaking down his youngest brother's cot (Guiney Yallop & Shields, 2015):

> From around the corner of our house
> I looked at Daddy
> swinging the hatchet
> ripping apart the frame with his hands
> breaking the board of the cot over his knees.
>
> Sometimes
> he would stop,
> he would just stop,
> and look
> at the broken cot.
>
> There was snow on the ground,
> and we needed wood for the fire (p. 47)

Through his use of imagery and repetition, John reveals multiple layers of his experience. He uses the perspective of being away from his father to show that he was removed from the process. There is also a comparison made between John's father's physical strength with his emotional struggle, as evidenced by him frequently stopping to look at the broken cot. John also uses the images of snow and fire to highlight his family's inability to heat their home through other means (i.e., purchase firewood or cut down their own trees). The repetition of "stop" as the last word on the line causes the reader to stop with John's father and join him in looking at the broken cot, thereby recognizing the implication of the depths of their financial troubles. This poem will be looked at more closely in a subsequent chapter (Chapter Eight) with further analysis of John's use of poetic devices.

Purpose of Poetry:

John uses poetry to lead by example as it relates to engaging in identity work. This includes better understanding his own stories and how his stories have impacted who he is as a person and as an educator. His poems function as a mode of inquiry and act as vessels for his stories. In his poetry, he references and evaluates the influences of such lived experiences as growing up poor in Newfoundland, his experiences with and within the church and his ongoing identity development (including how he views himself an educator, as a man, and as a gay person). He uses his poetic-academic work, often a form of autoethnographic research, to inspire others to engage in similar explorations and to find and strengthen their own voices within their communities. John's poetry also functions as a way to lessen the distance between the poet and the reader by providing an effective tool for generating mutual understandings of a concept, experience or feeling and thereby strengthen each parties' voice and draw them closer on an emotional and/or cognitive level. Poetry, he contends, can provide a sensory or visceral experience that brings the poet and reader to a common ground. This practice also closes the gap between the poet and themself, using the poem to generate greater understanding of self and the reasons behind their feelings, actions or beliefs. It provides a method of questioning and catharsis or expression that does not require external validation that can also give opportunities for voices of marginalized people to be heard. This is because the poet is not necessarily constrained by complex prosaic conventions, grammar and/or punctuation. Lines need not be long, and words can have multiple meanings to the poet; meanings that they may not have been able to fully express through other genres due to inexperience with writing conventions.

John Guiney Yallop's Teaching

How and Why Did He Become a Teacher?

John began his journey towards becoming a teacher in an Irish Roman Catholic seminary where he had aspirations of being a priest. It did not take long, less than a year, for him to recognize that he instead wanted to be around "a more diverse group of people" and he left the seminary shortly after (JGY1, June 22, 2018). He then went to Memorial University, where he studied philosophy and religious studies. After his degree, he moved to Toronto to work as a healthcare attendant and fell into the role of an educational assistant after he hurt his back and could no longer do the heavy lifting necessary for his job as an attendant. He ended up loving teaching, became a classroom teacher, and after nine years of teaching, decided to do a MEd and focused on homophobia in the school system. Of this decision he recalls,

> when I entered the profession, I naively thought that I was entering, you know, the most liberal and cutting-edge profession, because education I thought was where everything happened. But I soon discovered that the profession I entered was actually very conservative, and is probably one of the more conservative professions. (JGY1, June 22, 2018)

It was during his Masters' degree that he engaged in his studies around narrative inquiry which he says spoke to his upbringing in Newfoundland where stories were a prominent part of his life. In his study he "...looked at how gays experience school" by way of his own stories in academia and the study's participants. This study then led him to a different path in his career. He says,

> As I say, I wasn't really interested in teaching, so then I ended up teaching... I wasn't really interested in doing a graduate degree, but I did a graduate degree. And I certainly was not interested in doing any further graduate studies after my MEd., but I really liked graduate studies, so I decided to apply for a PhD and got accepted to a few places. And I decided to go to Western; University of Western Ontario. (JGY1, June 22, 2018)

This led to his career at Acadia University, where he has both taught as a professor and worked on an administerial level as the Director of the School of Education.

John Guiney Yallop's Views on Teaching

While John loves teaching, he is also cognizant of some prevailing issues in the field. Of his experiences in the academy, from his chapter "From Edges of Lateness" (Guiney Yallop & Binder, 2017), he writes of an ageist view that some have in the field of teaching. In the chapter, he says, "I found myself, in my fifties, being referred to as a junior scholar. One colleague even told me that I would come to see things his way once I gained more understanding by learning from my senior colleagues" (p. 155). That, however, was not his only experience and he met many more colleagues who appreciated his diverse years of experience. Yet, he continues to push back against the notion that he was late to his career. He asks, "What is it I might have to explain when someone says, 'So, you've come late to the professoriate?'" (p. 155). Akin to his poetry and publications, John's view of teaching is that more space needs to be made for diverse voices and that those who answer the calling to teach should be able to do so without prejudice.

What Are Notable Features of his Teaching Praxis that Correspond with his Views and his Poetics?

John's focus on identity in much of his work is also reflected in his teaching. He shares that when he was an elementary school teacher he would use "poetry to help students explore language, and their abilities to express themselves in language" (Emailed questionnaire, July 20, 2020). He found that poetry is "particularly helpful for students who are dealing with a lot of (usually difficult) emotions. Poetry has been a way to explore and express and to find/feel confidence in one's expression of self" (Emailed questionnaire, July 20, 2020). This focus extends to his current university-level teaching experiences where he uses poetry "…to teach about conducting research, analyzing or digging into research, and for writing up research; those approaches have usually (or always) been at the graduate level" (Emailed questionnaire, July 20, 2020). He also uses poetry to support pre-service teachers in the Bachelor of Education program as they get "in touch with their identities as teachers and…access and increase their confidence in their teaching abilities, even with the understanding that teaching is an extremely challenging (and extremely rewarding) practice" (Emailed questionnaire, July 20, 2020). As in his corpus of published works, John not only asks others to use poetry but does so himself. He says,

> I have also, when I felt it needed to be done, used poetry to let the students get to know me, as a way into my world…my lived experience. This serves two purposes; it builds trust in me and it shows/models a way to explore one's own vulnerability with confidence and care. (Emailed questionnaire, July 20, 2020)

Discussion

John's work focuses on identity and how stories support/define a greater realization of self. He values having an individual voice that is distinguishable.

His poetic voice is displayed through stanzas, as uniquely constructed sentences, which reflect his storytelling and narrative inquiry background. His work is unique in that he uses few artificially crafted metaphors, instead focusing on the observed or informed view of events and using elements of the real world as metaphors. This includes the multi-leveled metaphor of his family's struggles represented by his father destroying his brother's cot with a small, handheld axe (which will be explored in more depth in the subsequent chapter). His work often focuses on personal stories or references to growing up in Newfoundland, his sexuality, his identity (self) and his experiences as a teacher. His corpus in the literature also often has allusions to his upbringing in and around the church (which is often used as an oppositional image which furthers his understanding of his own stories). He uses poetry as a way to question and express himself and to ultimately make room for others' voices (e.g., Guiney Yallop & Shields, 2015). John's work highlights the power of poetic inquiry to not only support individuals in their identity development, but to provide ways of enacting social justice including providing avenues for marginalized people to express themselves and share their experiences (e.g., Butler-Kisber et al., 2017).

His poetic storytelling provides a further richness to the research being done in Canada around identity, equality and the power of autoethnography. Often, metaphors are artificially created to support the understanding of a complex experience or concept for a reader, but John's poetry exemplifies how real-world, observable or tangible elements of stories can hold layers of meaning that may hold the key to understanding experience as data. His poetry also accentuates how line breaks can draw immediate and more visceral attention to lived experience or require the reader to revisit the poem multiple times. This is also done through his line-level language choices, where the last word on the line will either coax the reader to pause in order to process what they have read on that line or move rapidly to the next line or stanza to further their understanding. This is a function that exists in poetry that does not readily exist in prose as each individual line risks being deemed a sentence fragment. John's individual lines of poetry that evoke meaning as part of the complete stanza (that are often the equivalent of one sentence in prose) would be seen as problematic if expressed in prose. Poetry, therefore, gives him multiple ways to question self and social norms, to express ideas, amplify voice or highlight findings within an academic-poetic research framework of poetic inquiry.

Chapter 7
Profile: Dr. Monica Prendergast

> "And so for me [it] is about lived experience, affective language, metaphoric, imagistic language, that if you want to craft poems out of interview data, you've got to find ways to make sure that what you're eliciting from your participants gives you the raw material to potentially create effective poems." (MP1, June 22, 2018)

Dr. Monica Prendergast is an actor, poet and professor at the University of Victoria. She says that she became an academic in large part thanks to arts-based approaches to research and scholarship. A teacher for over 30 years, in both high school and university, Monica values learning and developing understanding by way of the performative. With much of her teaching focused on drama and theatre education, Monica's work brings the voices of others to the forefront. She is credited with the creation of the first International Symposium on Poetic Inquiry, alongside Dr. Carl Leggo in 2007, and continues her involvement to this day, including co-editing publications inspired by the event (2009; 2016).

What Is this Work? Who Can Do It?

Monica is often credited (e.g., James, 2009; McCulliss, 2013; Vincent, 2018; Faulkner, 2019) with the contemporary use of the term poetic inquiry (proper or common noun form) (Prendergast, 2009a). Of her labeling the work, she shares that she was calling it research poetry but that the term did not articulate all that she wanted it to. She says,

> I mean you've got to find some kind of umbrella term that works for you, which was always something that Carl and I have tried to be very mindful of and to communicate to people, that just because we chose poetic inquiry as sort of the umbrella term…we never intended for that to be kind of an edict. (MP1, June 22, 2018)

She notes that she did not coin the term but that she read it in the work of Lyn Butler-Kisber before deciding to use the term in her post-doctoral work.

During her post-doctoral work, she began creating a bibliography of articles that appeared in social science journals that included poetry. She has now expanded her bibliography, as of 2018, into the form of a compendium of over 2000 pages of examples of published studies that include poetry. This gives her a well-rounded view of the work that is being accepted and published by the poetic inquiry community. When asked who can use poetry in their work, she draws on her bibliography, noting that she focuses more on quality than any other element. She notes that her bibliography contains "really bad poems" (MP1, June 22, 2018). She refers to these poems as a form of "Hallmark poetry, [the non-specific, often clichéd verses found in greeting cards],…that don't have what Anne McCrary Sullivan so beautifully identified in our first book as the poetic occasion" (MP1, June 22, 2018). For her, poetic inquiry that responds to the poetic occasion "is about lived experience, affective language, metaphoric, imagistic language" (MP1, June 22, 2018). She elaborates that "if you want to craft poems out of interview data, you've got to find ways to make sure that what you're eliciting from your participants gives you the raw material to potentially create effective poems" (MP1, June 22, 2018) and that the use of poetry is purposeful. She summarizes her view on who can use poetic inquiry by saying, "My short answer to that [question] is, like, write a good poem. Do a good job and qualify yourself over time" (MP2, December 10, 2019).

She does not wish to see poetic inquiry as exclusionary, but instead as a community of scholars who value quality and purpose over quantity. She, however, is not an idealist who believes that all works published are/will be of a high caliber. She instead is pleased that journals, including those who have little to no history of publishing poetry or works that include poetry, are now more readily accepting works that have poetic elements.

Reasons for Poetry in her Work

When asked what poetry does in her academic-poetic work that sees her returning to it frequently in her corpus of work, she responds,

> For me, it's been an unexpected tool that has allowed me to talk about my topics of interest and/or my lived experience, more recently, in a writing style that feels to me authentic. Which is something that is there and then not there, something that is transitory and ephemeral by its very nature. (MP1, June 22, 2018)

She further explains the reason behind using poetic inquiry in her own research and scholarship saying,

> I think it was Lawrence Ferlinghetti who, I use this quote quite often, who said a poem is the shortest distance between two people. And so for me, it's not about the shortcut, it's about the short distance. It's about how can I say what I want to say in the most directly effective and potentially affective way. And often the answer to that question is write a poem. (MP2, December 10, 2019)

She notes that she often creates poems through the words or texts of others. Of this practice, which she began in her doctoral work, she says that it initially helped her to work through "dense, post-modern texts [and] deconstructive theory" and that "crafting found poems out of [those texts] was sense making" (MP1, June 22, 2018).

As much of her poetry takes the form of found poetry, she continues to shorten the distance between the author, with their complex ideas, and the reader, while using diverse and distinctive techniques around punctuation, line breaks and the appearance on the page to ensure that the original author's voice is not compromised. This, however, does not limit poetic inquiry to poetry on the page. For Monica, poetic inquiry "has a very high performative aspect to it" where more can be learned and the voices of the author and reader can be heard (MP2, December 10, 2019). While she values that poetry can be written to be shared, she is hesitant to say that poetic inquiry *should* have a performative aspect to it. She says that "not every poet is comfortable with public reading" and that "many poets probably are terrified to have to read their poetry out loud because poetry writing is a very solo venture [that can be] very private [and] very intimate [where] voicing that can be a challenge" (MP2, December 10, 2019).

She appreciates that "the way of the poet is not about producing something on a production line; it's unpredictable, it's ephemeral" and is, for her, a way to say something that she could not say through any other medium or genre (Interview, June 3, 2019). Ultimately, she believes that the purpose of poetry in research and scholarship is that it "does the same thing as any other art form, which is that it helps us deal with the complexity and ambiguity of life" (Interview, June 3, 2019). An example of her polyphonic voiced found poetry comes from her (2006) article where she exemplifies a way that found poetry can be used as a literature review. Of her process and intent, she writes,

> I have played with line breaks, patterns on the page, parentheses, and the occasional use of repetition for emphasis [meant to] to capture a number of different, and valuable, voices and theoretical perspectives through the crystallizing and creative process of found poetry. (p. 372)

Her poem, with footnotes to indicate the original source material, is separated into thematic segments that function as a way to accentuate key quotations from her literature review. She also uses her stanzas to organize the poem in a way that intentionally mirrors that of a play in performance (she refers to them in the same article as "acts" [p. 375]). Through poetry, as demonstrated below, she is able to share/amplify the voice of the original author (their verbatim text) while simultaneously sharing her voice through her choices around the crafting of the poem and its appearance on the page (e.g., through line breaks and offsetting phrases through spacing). Poetry, in some of Monica's work, effectively functions as a textually polyphonic learning experience. In the following example, in its original formatting, Monica uses footnotes to reference Scruton (2004, p. 454) and highlight his discussions on the theatregoing experience. (Prendergast, 2006, p. 387)

> **theatre and religion**[14]
>
> in each case
> the same story:
>
> the ideal community;
>
> the act that separates
> (error or sin);
>
> the ultimate restoration
> (the living, the dead, the unborn);
>
> the tragic hero (who)
>   passes over . . .
>
> **the audience dances**[15]
>
> the audience dances
> (by proxy) through the chorus
> of the play, the play.

Had this content been written prosaically, the chosen quotation(s) would appear as either a longer line of text or potentially as a list written in the context of a paragraph. In using poetry, Monica is able to draw the readers' attention to very specific parts of the original text that she believes are paramount in understanding the greater concept(s) (i.e., the links between theatre and religion and the audience's part in the live theatre experience). The reader is able to read and receive the information quickly, building what they know about theatre based on her literature review, while also having an opportunity to pause and consider why these specific elements are highlighted.

(No) Limits of Poetic Inquiry

Monica, similar to Pauline, believes that the use of poetry in research and scholarship must be purposeful. She says, "I really do feel like that's so important for the conditions to be right for the use of poetry" and notes that some studies that she has seen have not had data that is "not aesthetic enough, not affective enough, not metaphorical enough to lend itself well to poetic transcription" which made the study less successful (MP2, December 10, 2019). She believes that a study that uses poetry or poetic inquiry approaches must be designed as such or it risks limiting the findings in ways that will prevent the poet from being able to fully adopt poetry as a method or tool. Of this notion she says,

> how can I then design my study so as to potentially gather the most aestheticallyaffective, metaphoric, symbolic language if I'm gathering data from participants so that I have the richest possible material to work with. (MP2, December 10, 2019)

This is significant in that she believes that the design of the study and the questions asked by the researcher have a greater impact on the ability for the poet-researcher to work with poetry, instead of the genre having limits. This draws back to sentiments shared by Carl and John surrounding the limitless capacity of poetry in research. It also directly connects to Pauline's ideas around methodology and the Parallaxic Praxis model where there is the possibility of addressing concepts through multiple viewpoints and methodological approaches to find answers to research questions.

Unique Features of her Work

With her extensive background in theatre, as both a trained actor and experienced director, her corpus of work shows a direct or indirect focus on voice. Of her poetic processes she says,

> I experience the voices I read and translate into research poems as heard, as spoken, as expressed, as soliloquies/monologues/dialogues, as character driven. I am always interested in the clearest possible voice being heard, whether it is the researcher's, the participant's, or the literature's voice(s). (2006, pp. 371-2)

Her found poetry, as in the previous example, functions as a way to amplify the voice of the original author in conjunction with her poetic voice (present through her choices around how the poem is constructed). Her use of punctuation and capitalization also supports the impact of her work on how voice is shown in research. These concepts are further illustrated in Chapter Eight of this book.

Monica Prendergast's Poetics: Vox, Performance and the Propagation of Knowledge

Punctuation:

In her poetry, Monica omits standard punctuation when interpreting the voice of others and herself. She will, however, include punctuation when highlighting a direct quote if it impacts the poem.

Portrayal of Voice:

She uses the first person "I" only when using direct quotes for impact. She otherwise uses a lower case "i." She also uses either in-text citations or footnotes to attribute the original source. An example of how she shows her own voice in her poetry comes from her poem "anecdotal" (2020). She writes:

> i confess
> this story
> is anecdotal
>
> i cannot
> offer evidence
> of impact
>
> of the power
> of theatre
>   to redeem
>   and renew
>
> beyond the
> telling of it
>   here (p. 676)

Poetry, in this sense, functions as a way for her to share her first-person experience while still offering the reader an opportunity to put themselves in her proverbial shoes. She does not use "I" to claim power over her experience, thereby asking the reader to empathize with her experience. She instead uses "i," without ownership, to invite the reader to experience the event with her in real time.

An example of how she uses the voices of others in her poetry can be found in her piece "Poetic Inquiry, 2007-2012: A surrender and catch found poem" (2015) where she cites the original author, in this case Faulkner (2007), by way of a discrete footnote (which was the ninth footnote in the original document).

> Writing like it matters
> means we
> sure as hell better
> live within the words
> and breathe within the spaces9 (p. 679)

The poetic form in this example functions as a way for Monica to provide her interpretation of what Faulkner said without claiming ownership of Faulkner's original words or assimilating them as her own.

In other instances, such as in "Education and/as Art: A found poetry suite" (2012), Monica chooses to use in-text citations after the concluding line of the poem (exemplified in Chapter Eight). Through these techniques, she shows attribution of the original author's voice while claiming her poetic interpretation as her own. This simultaneously gives voice to the author of the source text and herself, as the poet, which gives the reader a unique reading experience of texts that they may or may not have been familiar with.

Frequently Used Poetic Devices:

Her work tends to have, but is not limited to, alliteration, allusion and imagery as primary devices that support her creation of meaning. She uses poetic devices with line breaks and spacing to put emphasis on key words or terms. This is significant, especially as it relates to her found poetry practices, as she is able to emphasize concepts and create inferences in her poetry while using limited poetic devices.

Appearance on the Page:

Her poems generally have shorter line lengths that begin left aligned and are spaced across the page or on different lines for e/affect. An example of this approach, which also shows her use of capitalization and voice, comes from her article "the scholar dances" (2009b) where she writes a response poem to a speech from Donald Blumenfeld-Jones from the 2006 meeting of AERA. In its original formatting:

>   iii.
>   the scholar dances
>   his struggles
>   his joys
>   fills space
>   intensely
>   immersed
>   inside
>   the shape
>   of art
>   /
>   the art
>   of shape
>   fills space
>   touches loss
>   (the cracks
>   grief creates)
>
>   dangerous mosaics
>   caught in
>   broken memories

life
(breath
death
breath)
life (p. 1375)

Frequently Used Poetic Forms:

Her corpus of work includes frequent use of acrostic poetry, found poetry, free verse poetry, and haiku. Her frequent use of found poetry distinguishes her corpus of poetry from the other participants in this study and draws attention to her ability to craft language in impactful ways that generate greater understandings, even if the language was not originally written by her.

Purpose of Poetry:

Monica's work shows her interest in poetry as literature review, as a way of analyzing and responding to data and sharing the voice of others. Her work often shows her use of poetry as a tool. She often creates found poetry from the literature, what she would call *vox theoria* (Prendergast, 2009a), to generate deeper and/or different understandings of texts. Through vox theoria, the original text is analyzed and specific verbatim passages are used to highlight a specific concept or idea that may have been missed in its original prose format. For Monica, poetry also functions as a way to consider the power of performance or to reflect on her lived experiences with her theatre projects (Prendergast, 2020). An example of this is in her poetic-academic exploration of her creative work with inmates. This project saw her using theatre to support inmates' self-expression and rehabilitation (Prendergast, 2016).

Frequently Cites:

In her academic work that uses poetry, Monica at times cites other poets (e.g., Lawrence Ferlinghetti), theatre scholars (e.g., Blau and Belliveau) and arts-based theorists/scholars (e.g., Barone & Eisner, Butler-Kisber, Laurel Richardson, Leggo, and Cole) either in the discussions leading to her poetry or in the poems themselves. This is significant in that it shows her emphasis on sharing the voices of others that inspire or help to support her journey towards creating new knowledge.

Monica Prendergast's Teaching

How and Why Did She Become a Teacher?

Monica notes that her teaching career extends over a 30-year period as she has taught at both the secondary and post-secondary levels. Of her work in secondary schools, she believes that teaching poetry was "the most rewarding unit" that she taught (MP1, June 22, 2018). She attributes her work in arts-based research with her current role as a professor and that, without her engagement with it, she would not have become an academic. She says,

> if it hadn't been for arts-based research in general, and the flourishing that it was having in the early 2000s when I was doing my graduate studies, then of poetic inquiry in particular, I don't know if I could have become an academic. And so, for me, it was about finding this poetic voice, quite by accident, and then just letting that voice emerge. (Interview, June 3, 2019)

Monica Prendergast's Views on Teaching?

Monica appreciates the mentoring and apprenticeship elements of teaching. She attributes her use of mentorship, in part, to her positive experiences with Carl during her post-doctoral work. She says that she tries "to always be very positive and supportive and open" to those who she teaches (MP2, December 10, 2019). This potentially also comes from not only her decades of experience but from her own push against certain systemic elements of teaching. She notes that she struggled with the 50-minute blocks allotted for teaching high school theatre, as it complicated an already intensive process. She says, "I found it very difficult when I became a teacher to have to constrain the way I worked into these like 50-minute sound bites. It was tough; it was very hard. And I still struggle with that" (MP1, June 22, 2018). As it relates to the post-secondary level, she continues to struggle with the limited time to engage with students. This, perhaps, is why she appreciates Ferlinghetti's quote on poetry creating less space between people; more work can then be done to lessen the distance between knowledge and learners. Of teaching, now as a professor, she rhetorically asks, "I mean what did I get after seven years and earning a PhD?" Her response, "I got 80-minute periods....I gained 30 minutes in my life with my students. Except for grad courses where I have three-hour chunks, but that's even not enough time" (MP1, June 22, 2018). While she appreciates the dialogic experience included in teaching and mentoring, where she can hear voices and consider ideas shared by others, she would prefer to have more time. Further, her work in teaching theatre, akin to her work with writing and performing poetry, requires time to consider the nuances of language in order to generate understanding and convey that understanding to others. Poetry can lessen the distance, but the words must be selected carefully; performance can show multiple levels of meaning through voice and physical movement, but it again requires a deeper understanding of language which cannot be as richly considered with limited time.

What Are Notable Features of her Teaching Praxis that Correspond with her Views and her Poetics?

She values the performative nature of poetry and teaching but cautions against those using either approach without the appropriate knowledge/experience to do so (Prendergast, 2008). She reflects,

> but I think also the performer in me, because I have obviously a theatre degree and I was trained as an actor. I also really enjoy being able to read the poetry to students, to remind them that it is an oral tradition and that it needs to be heard, not just read on a page or analyzed that way. (MP1, June 22, 2018)

This links to the creation of her poetry in that it intentionally gives or recognizes the voice of others. In her textual work, this is done by not capitalizing the pronoun 'I.' She does this as way to keep the voice of the original author while simultaneously sharing her own voice. She is present in the poem through its crafting, that is through her choices of how the poem is presented on the page. She also frequently does not end other's quotations/statements with punctuation and instead uses line breaks, tabs and stanzas to denote shifts or areas that she wants to highlight. This technique incorporates her voice, be it as a form of commentary or content analysis, into the poem through how it is constructed. She does not alter the voice of the other as it appears in the construction of their sentence, that is as it relates to word choice and word order, but instead presents her interpretation of where the end of the thought or statement should be linguistically through her poetic line. There is then a dialogic exchange between the author of the source text, Monica as the poet, and the reader an interpreter. This exchange is elevated when Monica reads/performs her poetry in that she embodies, through her choices around voice, intonation and physicality, how much of her voice is present versus how much she highlights the voice of the other represented in her poem. Her choices impact how the reader receives and interprets the information which puts a great deal of onus on her as poet and performer. Her theatre experience allows her to make informed decisions around her poetic performances and her willingness to be vulnerable in these exchanges highlights unique attributes of her work that are not shared by all members of the poetic inquiry community.

Discussion

Monica's work that uses poetry often focuses on making sense of the literature or others' experiences through found poetry. She values the voice of the other and does not punctuate her poetry, thereby not formally beginning or ending the line/phrases of others. She instead uses poetry to draw attention to particular words or phrases, often through short lines. This literally reflects her reference to Ferlinghetti who suggests that poetry lessens the space or distance between people. This, however, does not mean that the content of each line is limited; each line is full of meaning and inference. Her choices keep the integrity of the voice of the original author while also integrating her interpretation. She acts as silent yet impactful voice that is present through her choices around the composition of the poem. She says, "the one thing that poetry has always been able to do is give voice" and her work reflects her desire to hear the voices of others and make them known (Final Interview, June 3, 2019). She does not repackage them as her own insights. Moreover, she values the performative nature of poetry for further interpretation and learning. Yet, when source material is written on the page (i.e., a direct quote from another author), she refuses to impose her linguistic interpretation of voices that are not her own. This focus on voice is seen in her autobiographical poetry (Prendergast, 2019) which also has limited standard punctuation and shorter lines which creates space (literally and figuratively as it relates to the page) for others to interpret her work more freely.

Her work is important when understanding what is happening in poetic inquiry in Canada as she uses it to express and create understanding through both her written choices and her choices when poetry is performed/vocalized. This provides another layer to academic research, linking it to performative inquiry (Fels & Belliveau, 2008; Fels, 2012, Prendergast, 2016; Saldaña, 2016), and supports the need for teachers to teach beyond the written texts (as in Morrell & Duncan-Andrade, 2002; Christianakis, 2011) in order to equip students with the ability to better interpret meaning. In using found poetry as part of her inquiry process, Monica showcases multiple voices simultaneously and does in different ways than she would have through prose or scriptwriting. Her found poetry does not override or assimilate the voice of the original author. She instead uses her poetic choices as a simultaneous voice that is often, paradoxically, unspoken textually. That is, she does not add additional words to the original text that has been converted into poetry. Poetry has an unmatched function in research, as exemplified in Monica's poetic-academic work, in that it can amplify the authentic voices and original knowledge of others while simultaneously providing a further echelon of depth and understanding from the poet/researcher.

Where Does this Lead Us?

These chapters explore why and how each participant uses poetic inquiry to create knowledge. They identify how academic and poetic conventions are used in various facets of their work and highlight each participant's beliefs around the unique benefits of working through/with poetic inquiry in their educational research and scholarship. Through undertaking an extensive study of each participant's work, I was able to create a profile of their particular attributes as they relate to research and scholarship. They focus on three key areas: an identification of characteristics of each participant's beliefs about their own work, stemming from the interview data; analysis of features of their poetry from across each participant's corpus of work and comparison of how each participant's views of teaching coincide with what they say and what they have published. These unique profiles serve to not only put a greater focus on who they are as scholars but help to support a greater understanding of poetic inquiry as a whole.

To further ascertain an even broader purview of what is happening in poetic inquiry, its distinctive functions, and chart its trajectory in the academy, these profiles will now be cross-referenced with an aim to better understand how poetry is being used in research and scholarship from a Canadian perspective. It will also provide context for how each participant's unique attributes contribute to the rhizomatic connections that make up poetic inquiry.

Profiling Prolific Poetic Practitioners
(Adam Vincent)

> This field is inscribed with love, fun,
> becoming
> ekphrastically responsive
> while
> advocating for others'
> stories
> and
> identities
> in a place where space is made
>   for voices
>   to perform
> and
>   craft knowledge
>   to share with those who need it."

Suited for poets
or
those with a penchant
for words,
it is limitless in scope
when used
when it is needed,
limited by design
questions
or the reaches of the researcher's abilities
to craft knowledge.

These poetic scholars
inquirers
researchers
artists
embody
and
embolden the diverse hues
of poetic inquiry
and
invite
students of the world
regardless of systemic leveling
to join them in their praxis
of poesis.

Chapter 8
Analyzing Poetics, Purposes and Teaching Praxis

I undertook this research, creating cases of this sub-set of the poetic inquiry community, with an aim to better understand the composition of the poetic inquiry community in Canada and learn more about the functions of poetic inquiry. I wanted to know more about those who engage in this form of research and how that research informs their teaching praxis. This meant that I could not stop at individual profiles; I had to explore further.

With an aim of better understanding poetic inquiry and poetic scholarship, the following chapter explores the findings of my cross-case analyses. It begins with an illustration and discussion of significant commonalities and differences derived from the analysis of my interview data and my findings as they relate to the participants' approaches and views on teaching. It then builds extensively on their poetics, taking a poem from each participant and performing a literary critical analysis to highlight the diversity and distinctive style of each participants' poetics. This analysis not only furthers an understanding of the diverse nature of poetic inquiry and its functions, but ultimately illustrates the correlation between the participants, a subset of the larger poetic inquiry community, and the interconnectivity of each participants' individual academic research interests, academic publications and teaching practices.

The charts in this chapter draw attention to key elements discovered in the data analysis processes. The purpose behind this is to readily see the similarities and differences that exist between the participants of the study and provide support for further discussion around how these characteristics support a greater understanding of poetic inquiry and its uses in research and scholarship. These are broken down, as in the previous chapter, by major themes ascertained from the interview data and supported through an exploration of each participant's corpus of work in the literature.

Commonalities, Paradoxes and Differences in Views
(From the Interview Data)

Overarching Commonalities

Through my initial thematic analysis, drawing strongly from the interview data, I was able to identify key similarities in the participants' beliefs around poetic inquiry (see Figure 8.1). The participants agree that it is a poet who engages through poetic inquiry. The participants also agree that there is no singular way to do poetic inquiry. All are opposed to purely prescriptive ways of engaging through poetic inquiry. As such, creating a how-to book, that outlines the ideal way of engaging with poetic inquiry as a methodology or method, would be more of an expression of different ways to use the approach. Pauline, John and Monica make reference to Sandra Faulkner's publication on poetic inquiry (2019) that provides multiple ways to use it, dynamic exercises for crafting research-based poetry and discussions that support the need for balance between the aesthetic and epistemological elements of the poetic products. This, as the participants of this study suggest, is more conducive to teaching poetic inquiry than articulating a singular way to do it. This is reflective of the findings in my literature review and my findings in this study that poetic inquiry is primarily generative. Poetic inquiry is being used in diverse ways and for various purposes, yet scholars do not dictate that they have found or are using an ideal version of poetic inquiry in their academic work. Monica says that poetry and the creation processes undertaken by poets are unpredictable and not necessarily reproducible due to the contexts in which the poems are written. The creation of poetry is often context-specific, situational and, as explored in this study, can be a highly dialogic experience between the poet and the research participant and/or the poet and the literature. These characteristics, understandably, see proponents of poetic inquiry pushing against the dogmatic nature of most how-to books as the poetry and its purpose would lose its virtues. Carl notes that he is more focused on using poetry to challenge, explore and make sense of things instead of creating a text that is dedicated to prescriptive approaches to poetic inquiry. He highlights that the diversity of poetic inquiry is one of its important attributes. He says, "the big issue for me around all of this has to do with the idea [that] the leaders of poetic inquiry do not have a system, a formula, a manual, a how-to guidebook. And so I would suggest that each of us, you know [with our] various ways, has been following our own passions. Getting into plenty of trouble along the way" (CL1, June 20, 2018). It is in this *trouble* that poetic inquiry is simultaneously focused yet expanding. Those who use it as a primary element of their praxis have specific research, artistic or academic backgrounds and/or interests, as in the case of the participants in this study, which help to refine poetic inquiry's uses in that area. At the same time, they are strengthening the rhizomatic net of poetic inquiry by showing its diverse and valuable uses in research and scholarship. They are effectively creating space for others to use it in their own academic and/or expressive practices.

There is also consensus among the participants that poetic inquiry is both a method (tool and procedure) and methodology (theory and rationale). For Carl, however, poetic inquiry is not only a method and methodology, but "a way of being and becoming in the world" (CL2, September 17, 2018) which is a foundational tenet of his academic and personal engagement with/in poetry. For Monica, it is an arts-based research method and methodology that "sits alongside visual inquiry, narrative inquiry, music-based inquiry, all the different arts-based approaches to research" (MP2, December 10, 2019). John appreciates that the work can sit on its own without a label but acknowledges that for some, a title helps them to generate a deeper understanding of the work. Pauline builds on these ideas, arguing that "it is more than just going through the procedure of doing a method of research" (PS1, June 27, 2018). She notes that methods outline steps, and that a methodology is when "you're actually thinking about the art of methodology, or the art of research, and the art of something is moving your work to a space that is really noticing the nuances of detail" (PS1, June 27, 2018). A methodology is not a checklist of practice but is instead a critical underpinning of the research study. It encompasses the way that the research process is undertaken, with attention paid to the ways in which meaning was derived and why it was undertaken in that particular way. Poetic inquiry is then a method that includes potential ways of using poetry. It is also the binding methodology that holds the study together on an epistemological level.

Its functions on a linguistic level also set poetic inquiry apart from other methods or methodologies. The participants all contend that poetry, with its diverse forms and devices, allows the poet/writer a medium to tap into a different voice and create meaning through the use of discourse and language in atypical ways that other academic discourses or genre cannot do. This links back to the *trouble* that Carl was speaking of; the creation of poetry requires that the poet/writer simultaneously use language in evocative ways that are both appealing artistically and academically (as exemplified in the participant profiles in Chapters Four to Seven). Rarely have I heard someone describe the beauty of an expository essay in the same ways that they describe the evocative nature of writing that includes poetry, be it standalone poetry or poetry integrated into another genre.

Figure 8.1: Commonality: Overarching View of Poetic Inquiry.

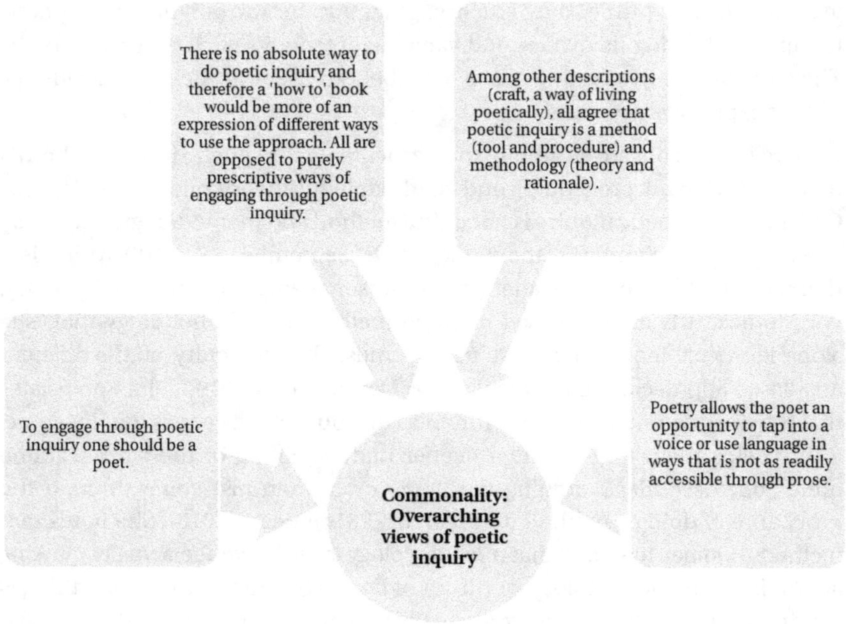

- There is no absolute way to do poetic inquiry and therefore a 'how to' book would be more of an expression of different ways to use the approach. All are opposed to purely prescriptive ways of engaging through poetic inquiry.
- Among other descriptions (craft, a way of living poetically), all agree that poetic inquiry is a method (tool and procedure) and methodology (theory and rationale).
- To engage through poetic inquiry one should be a poet.
- Poetry allows the poet an opportunity to tap into a voice or use language in ways that is not as readily accessible through prose.

Commonality: Overarching views of poetic inquiry

These similarities demonstrate overarching themes that are not only found with this unique subset of poetic inquirers, but also reflect some of the findings of my literature review (Chapter Two). This does not, however, mean that they are homogeneous. There are key themes from the interviews that show explicit differences between the participants. These differences are important when crafting an understanding of what poetry is doing, and can do, in relation to research and scholarship.

The Poetic Inquiry Paradox

Carl, Pauline, John and Monica all believe that to engage through poetic inquiry, the researcher needs to be or is a poet; they are one and the same. This then leads to considerations of what constitutes being a poet and what constitutes a quality engagement through poetic inquiry. This accentuates a common paradoxical tension that exists within the participants and within poetic inquiry.

There is a case made for quality and craft from the participants. Carl notes that he believes that "we are all poets" (CL2, September 18, 2018) who have had to suppress our expressive tendencies. Yet, Carl also believes that one must attend to the craft of poetry in order to use it effectively. This belief is comparable to Monica's view that poetry must be created based on the poetic occasion and that it must be "a good poem" (MP2, December 10, 2019) to be impactful. This then requires the poet to have the linguistic, academic and creative prowess necessary to meet the poetic occasion. Pauline contends that you are a poet if you write poetry. She states, "If you are attentive to the craft...you then become [so] named...You become a poet when you write poetry" (PS1, June 27, 2018). This is comparable to John who says, "[i]f a poet does it, it's poetry. And I'm a poet, so if I do it, it's poetry" (JGY2, January 18, 2019).

The participants share a common tension between wanting poetic inquiry to be accessible yet wanting to ensure that the poets who engage through poetic inquiry are producing high-caliber work. This stresses the paradox of poetic inquiry that makes it both accessible and inaccessible. As revealed in this study, some practitioners of poetic inquiry believe that anyone can be a poet if they avail themselves to writing poetry. Yet, not everyone who engages through poetic inquiry is suitable to be a poet. Not every person can, or desires to, write the academically purposeful poetry of poetic inquiry studies. This lack of consensus around who can use poetic inquiry may be a contributing factor in poetic inquiry's current marginalization in qualitative research. There is a discrepancy between the welcoming nature of its practitioners, the evocative nature of the work being produced and the high-level of knowledge and experience necessary to become a member of the poetic inquiry community.

Overarching Differences

The interview data shows that there are distinct differences with how each participant views the limits of poetic inquiry and their specific purposes for engaging through poetry (see Figure 8.2). These characteristics are important when trying to understand the dynamic nature of poetic inquiry.

As it relates to the argument that poetic inquiry has limits, the participants had differing opinions. Carl believes that poetry is capacious and capable of innumerable things. Of limits, he says "I haven't been able to find them in my lifetime. And I don't expect to find it." (CL2, September 18, 2018). Relatedly, John's view re-directs from the limits of poetic inquiry to the limits of the researcher. He states that he is not sure if poetry has limits, but that he is sure that a researcher or poet has limits, as they are limited by their human capacity. Both Pauline and Monica agree that poetic inquiry needs to be used in the right context and/or for the right purpose for it to make sense. This is not seen by either as a fault of the method/methodology but goes back to the research purpose and questions. Not every research study or all research questions can be answered through poetic inquiry.

Figure 8.2: Difference: Limits of Poetic Inquiry.

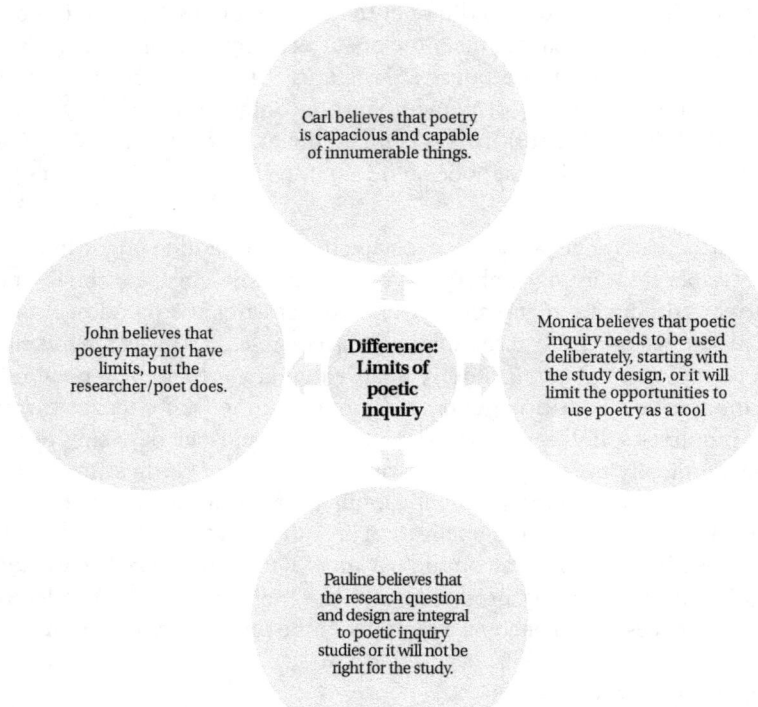

The discrepancy around poetic inquiry's limits allows for healthy disagreement as it shows the criticality that the participants use when engaging in studies that use poetry. Even Carl, who espouses the merits of living poetically (Leggo, 2005), does not always use poetry in his studies. This is evidenced by his dynamic corpus of work in the literature, which use poetry alongside more traditional academic formats/genre like the journal article and book chapter. Further, he writes prose in a poetic or lyrical fashion with his voice being ever-present in his texts. He did not believe that poetry was always the best genre for the task at hand as it relates to its forms, but he would continue to write poetically. Poetic inquiry has distinctive capabilities not found in other genre or research approaches but that does not mean, as the participants note, it is a universal approach to research and scholarship.

Analyzing Poetics, Purposes and Teaching Praxis 115

Figure 8.3: Difference: Reasons for Poetry.

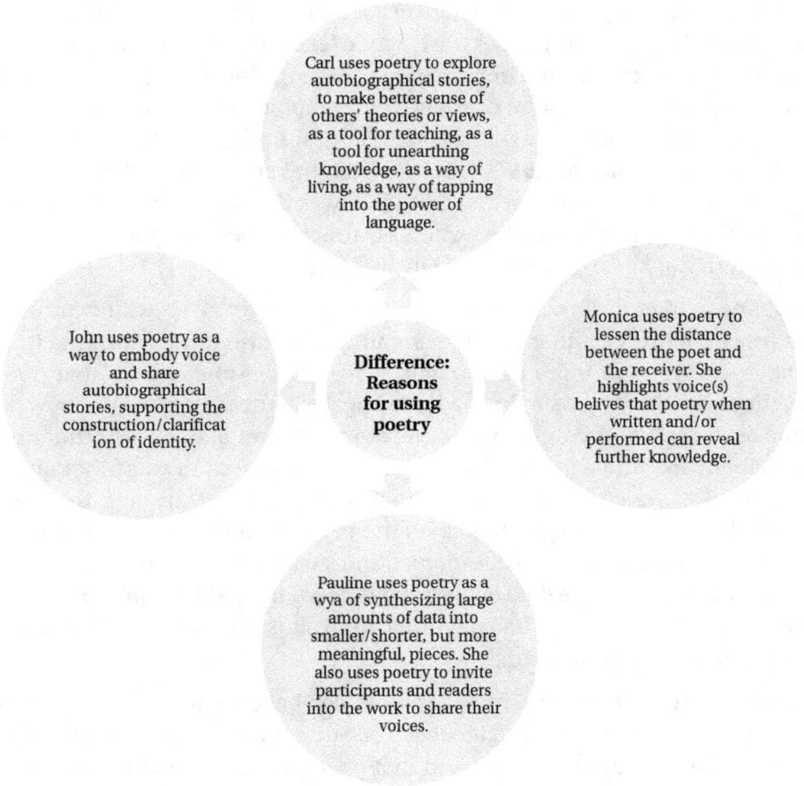

- Carl uses poetry to explore autobiographical stories, to make better sense of others' theories or views, as a tool for teaching, as a tool for unearthing knowledge, as a way of living, as a way of tapping into the power of language.
- John uses poetry as a way to embody voice and share autobiographical stories, supporting the construction/clarification of identity.
- **Difference: Reasons for using poetry**
- Monica uses poetry to lessen the distance between the poet and the receiver. She highlights voice(s) belives that poetry when written and/or performed can reveal further knowledge.
- Pauline uses poetry as a wya of synthesizing large amounts of data into smaller/shorter, but more meaningful, pieces. She also uses poetry to invite participants and readers into the work to share their voices.

The participants frequent reasons for using poetry in their work also differ (see Figure 8.3). Discussions with Carl demonstrate that he values the diverse functionalities of poetry in conjunction with academia, in particular its uses as an approach to explore autobiographical stories, to make better sense of others' theories or views, as a tool for teaching, as a tool for unearthing knowledge, as a way of living and as a way of tapping into the power of language. He writes,

> I write poetry as a creative way to lay down words in shapes, designs, and structures that encourage me to know the cosmos in chaos and the chaos in cosmos, a chiasmus of turning and returning, like furrows in a farm field, a process of verse and re-verse that exposes the chimeric chasm between chaos and cosmos. (Leggo, 2012, p. 156)

Carl believes that poetry is a way of living. Through it he can seek a greater understanding of the meaning of life that he can then share with others, thereby supporting their life's journey with love and care (2005).

John's interviews and publications reveal that he believes that poetry functions as a way to embody voice and share autobiographical stories and that it is a valuable tool for supporting the construction/clarification of identity. He is also a believer in poetry as a tool for creating space for others. This is shown in his writing, which includes poetry, around homophobia in schools (Guiney Yallop, 2002) and his push against ageism that exists in some higher education settings (Guiney Yallop & Binder, 2017). He writes that he did not begin "claiming [his] identity as an Aboriginal person…until [he] was fifty years old" which he sees as "a gift" (2017, p. 161) that he explores through stories and poetry. He shares these stories to know himself and to inspire others.

Pauline frequently links her discussion back to poetry's uses with data, where the researcher can synthesize large amounts of information by turning it into smaller/shorter, but more meaningful, pieces. She also contends that poetry functions as a way to invite the reader to engage in the texts by way of how they choose to read and subjectively interpret it. It can also allow others (i.e., participants of studies) a platform to share their voices in ways that enliven their lived experiences. This is accomplished primarily through the use of poetic devices and the appearance on the page. Pauline has described poetry in research as a way to "distill, depict and creatively articulate 'truths' and 'universals' found in the data analysis with heartfelt imagination" (Maarhuis & Sameshima, 2016, p. 297) that can impactfully illustrate both lived experience and researcher interpretation.

Through the interviews, Monica reveals her belief that poetry lessens the distance between the poet and the receiver. She contends that poetry allows for voices to be present in the work and that poetry is also something that, when written or performed, can reveal further knowledge. She says, "[t]he use of performative writing strategies, such as narrative and poetry, by those of us who live, teach and research in theatre offers a welcome resonance between method and topic" that can impactfully "communicate emotionally charged moments in our professional and personal lives" (Prendergast, 2010, p. 82). She contends that a key function of poetry is that it lessens not only the distance between what is understood, as it relates to the content of what is being relayed, but that it also provides a way for more rapid emotional connections to occur. The meaning created through poetic language, poetic devices and choices around how the poem is constructed on the page can add layers of implicit or explicit meaning. Monica notes that narratives also hold the power to communicate affectively, which is not without consequence to this study, as poetry has also been shown to be a conduit for storytelling and sharing the lived experiences of others. It is evident that poetry (as shown in this study) functions differently.

Analyzing Poetics, Purposes and Teaching Praxis 117

Teaching Commonalities and Differences: Purpose and Praxis

There are overarching commonalities between the participants (see Figure 8.4). Carl, Pauline, John and Monica have all been organizers and hosts of the International Symposium on Poetic Inquiry (ISPI). This indicates a strong value in the learning that can occur in symposia or conferences between members of the burgeoning poetic inquiry community. They are all also associated with ISPI-related publications, as chapter contributors and editors of collections, created in large part from the symposia. This highlights their belief that this knowledge is not meant to be exclusive and that it should be made available for those not fully engrained in the poetic inquiry community.

Figure 8.4: Commonality: Scholarship/Teaching.

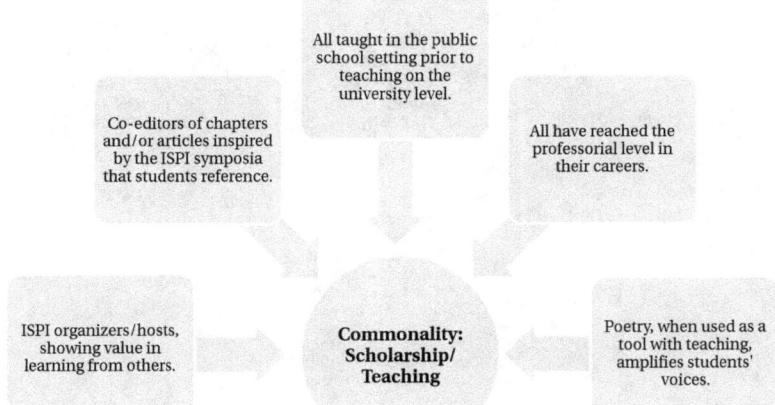

These books and journal articles are used by students to learn more about poetic inquiry and its power in research and scholarship. The participants' steadfastness around the power of learning may also be attributed to their unique experiences teaching public-school settings prior to teaching at the university level (all now reaching the professorial level in their respective institutions). Ultimately, this element of the study has highlighted that each participant values education and creating ways to share knowledge through facilitating events (as in the ISPI) and creating more readily accessible materials in the literature.

A major area where the participants differ around teaching comes from their underlying areas of interest or expertise that underpin and influence their teaching praxis. This is an integral piece in understanding how poetic inquiry both influences and is used in each participant's teaching praxis. It also provides further insights into poetic inquiry, not only as a research method and methodology, but as a tool for teaching.

Figure 8.5: Difference: Research Influences on Teaching.

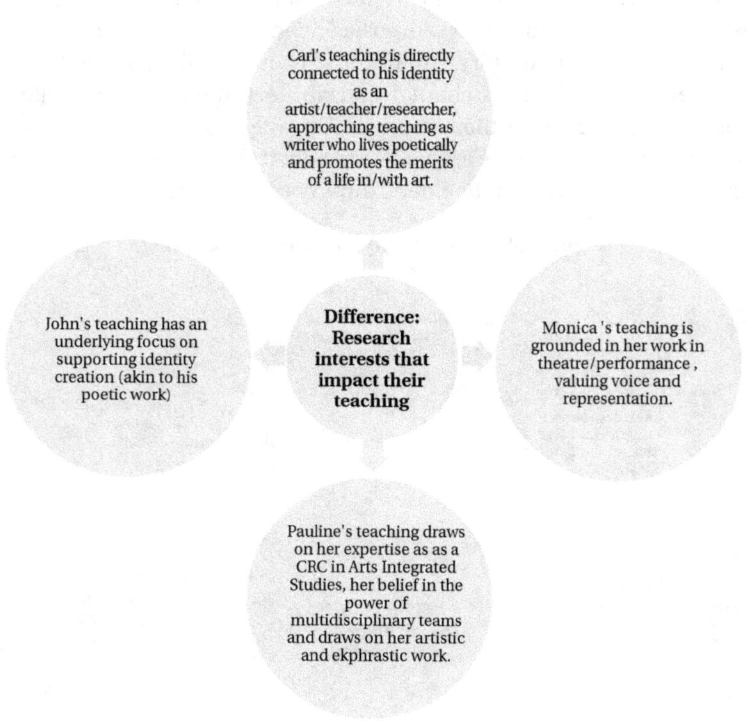

- Carl's teaching is directly connected to his identity as an artist/teacher/researcher, approaching teaching as writer who lives poetically and promotes the merits of a life in/with art.
- John's teaching has an underlying focus on supporting identity creation (akin to his poetic work).
- **Difference: Research interests that impact their teaching**
- Monica's teaching is grounded in her work in theatre/performance, valuing voice and representation.
- Pauline's teaching draws on her expertise as as a CRC in Arts Integrated Studies, her belief in the power of multidisciplinary teams and draws on her artistic and ekphrastic work.

As outlined in Chapter Three (and in Figure 8.5), Carl approaches teaching as a part of his life as a poet, living poetically (Leggo, 2005), who encourages students to experience writing poetry instead of only reading it (see Leggo, 1997; Leggo, 2012). Pauline approaches teaching with a staunch awareness of art's power to inform students' engagement with materials, to amplify voice and to support agency. She, too, encourages students to use the materials in practical ways. John keeps identity and the notion of self near the forefront of his approaches as he creates a curriculum that allows space for students to be present in their learning (through poetry and other mediums). Monica's background in the theatre sees her understanding the importance of representation and voice while seeking to generate deeper and ephemeral meaning in the classroom. She believes in mentorship and apprenticeship as valuable approaches where poetry can be a useful tool in bridging diverse understandings.

While these attributes, ways that poetic inquiry functions in each participants' poetry, were made explicit in the previous chapter, they will be reconsidered following the next section where I perform a critical poetic analysis of one poem from each participant's corpus of work. Are there connections between their research, teaching and poetic practices? If so, how?

Probing Poesis

The following section represents my approach to a close poetic analysis of one poem from each of the participants. This is an area that was revealed to be missing in the literature that proved beneficial in this study. My analytical approach is based on my experiences of interpreting literature and crafting my own poetry for over twenty years. This process focuses on how each poet uses language and poetic devices to create meaning and the impacts that their choices have on the reader. Poems were selected based on my intent to highlight as many unique characteristics of each poet's work, or functions of poetry, as was uncovered in the creation of their profiles (Chapters Four to Seven). They were also selected based on my own enjoyment of reading and interpreting the poems. Some of the poems more closely fit the perceived notion of poetic inquiry (i.e., poetry created as a result of a research study that had participants or data sets), while others (i.e., autobiographical or autoethnographic poetry) may appear more on the outskirts of poetic inquiry. As explored in Chapter Two, poetic inquiry is made up of rhizomes that link poetry with inquiry with the self and others, and therefore there was a need to explore diverse types of poetic products. While the poetic inquiry community traditionally does not provide critical voice about the poetry or poetics of its members, focusing instead almost exclusively on generative poetic processes, I am doing so with an aim to critically analyze and highlight why poetry is used, how it functions and how poetry can further inform research and scholarship practices. How is/can poetry be used to combine art and knowledge?

Currently, one of the conventions in use in academic journals and book chapters is to frame poetic inquiry products contextually at the start of the text to support the reader. Of this practice, Pauline (the current editor-in-chief of the Journal of the Canadian Association for Curriculum Studies) says,

> If you don't know how to read a poem, if you get an introduction on how this is related to the research—I think it helps people in. As a curator of the journal, I would be asking people to have a preface before the poem, or after the poem have a discussion of how this connects to the work. I wouldn't feel comfortable with publishing a stand-alone poem in the journal. (PS1 June 27, 2018)

This inclusion of guidance, while beneficial, lacks support for how to delve deeply into the content or how to identify nuanced meaning in/from the poem.

As a poem of this nature (a poetic product of the study) is both an aesthetic art form and a product of research, it needs a different treatment. In addition to an introduction, there is also a common practice of elucidating more around the construction of the poem when asked. This form of apprenticeship, expressing how a poem was crafted to support the skills of others, is described by John as a "duty," reflecting,

> It's interesting—if I feel a need to. I'm not sure if I've ever felt a need to, but I sometimes say these words that I feel a duty to. This is from my Catholic background, the word duty. To serve, to be of service. When I feel it will help someone if I explain my process, even if I haven't thought about it, even if I didn't even know I had one, then I'll do it because it feels like—And I don't mean duty in the sense of like... It's not a negative term. It's a very positive term for me. I do see it as a duty to explain my process. Especially when someone asks me, or when I think it will be helpful to someone...sometimes what needs to be done is to explain how I do this. (JGY1, June 22, 2018)

While providing initial context or explaining the process when asked contributes to overall understanding, there remains a lack of close analysis in relation to the poetic inquiry products from these studies. The following pages exemplify a potential way to analyze poetic inquiry products. This method of analysis is intended to draw out further information from the poem (as a form of aesthetic data) and support a better understanding of the craft and function of poetry in research.

The first close analysis is applied to a poem from Carl's corpus that accentuates his approach to autoethnographic poetic inquiry and draws attention to his uses of diverse poetic devices, wit and humour while providing insightful commentaries into the politics of academia and his position therein. This is followed by a close analysis of one of Pauline's poems that highlights her ability to use a poetic form of synesthesia to empathically and viscerally (re)present lived experience. John's poem is then closely analyzed to draw attention to the ways that he uses what is initially seemingly straightforward language to describe a deeply profound autobiographical/autoethnographic experience that speaks to grief and ways that societal and familial expectations impact our identities. Finally, Monica's found poem is analyzed in order to draw attention to ways that her poetic choices allow the findings of her inquiry to be shared through a simultaneous representation of polyphonic voices (i.e., the voice of author of the source text and the voice of Monica as the poet and researcher). Each participant's poetry highlights facets and functions of poetic inquiry that, when analyzed, reveal more about what poetic inquiry does in research and scholarship that no other genre can do. More is unearthed around how poetic inquiry simultaneously unites art and knowledge.

Analyzing Poetics, Purposes and Teaching Praxis

Carl's Poem

Pondering the Ponderosa Pine

My work is rooted in silence.
It grows out of deep beds
of contemplation, where words,
which are living things,
can form and re-form
into new wholes.
(Jeanette Winterson)

> Here, Carl shares a quote that spoke to him as either a part of his impetus for writing the poem, a quote that may have inspired him, or a quote that he feels compliments his discussion and adds to on-going discussions.

for more than twenty-five years you have greeted me
on treks to Scarfe for meetings and more meetings,
or seeking coffee, the high-octane fuel of scholars,
or sitting in your shade, sipping coffee, pondering
if I really need to attend another meeting

> This stanza, with its repetition of "meetings," highlights their coffee-fueled monotony. He uses wit to highlight the longstanding relationship between Carl and the tree, and Carl and his consistency and devotion to his career.

I will not render you a metaphor
    in this poem
I will not anthropomorphize you
    like a Disney cartoon
I will not sentimentalize your saga of survival
    from weather, pests, and chainsaws
I will not pretend hermeneutically
    I know your essence

> This stanza is filled with intentional irony. The pine is a metaphor for Carl and his career. He is anthropomorphizing it by speaking to it as if it were a person. Their twenty-five year relationship is sentimentalized in the poem and he knows something of its existence.

I will not claim I can name
    your existence in

    post-structuralist
        post-materialist
            post-human
                post-modern
                    post-feminist
                        post-colonialist

> Here, he uses spacing to play on the notion of 'post' where each philosophy is farther, or post, the one before it. He then juxtaposes the serious nature of his list by playing on the idea of wooden posts and making a pop culture reference to the TV show Bonanza, a western-themed program that ran from 1959-1973.

discourses, enough posts to build a fence around Ben Cartwright's Ponderosa

your wildness cannot be contained in my poem
any more than I can hold the moon's fullness in a pail

ever green, ever rooted, ever patient,
ever willing to teach us if we are willing to learn

> The repetition of 'ever' links to the longevity of the tree's lifespan and also to the enduring nature of education.

teach us to remember we are guests
on an ancient land with countless stories

> Here he draws on his knowledge of Indigenous ways of knowing, with references to learning from the land, while acknowledging his place of privilege to be on the land.

teach us to walk tenderly with one another,
filled with memories and hopes for others, too

teach us to know this place of mind
is also a place of mindfulness

in these last years I have at UBC
I will loiter often with you, and even if
I write fewer poems or papers, I might
yet learn to live like a scholar who knows
learning always begins with lingering

> He uses his simile and humour to mask a commentary that those who worked in the annex were afterthoughts.

we no longer dwell in an annex
like an appendix or supplement

we will not pine for the Ponderosa Annexes
as we settle into the Ponderosa Commons

> An obvious play on to pine, to yearn, while speaking to the pine. This pun is here is used to, once again, offset the serious and somewhat taboo commentary from the previous couplet that the educators in the annex were less visible or valued than others.

let us now dance an Argentinian tango
with light and shadow, with the rhythms
of the seasons, with the ebb and flow
of students and colleagues as we compose
new stories with the alphabet's possibilities,
new stories rooted in memory and imagination

(Leggo, 2016 pp. 362-4)

> This stanza holds references to some of his other published works and areas of interest. He has poetry and articles that discuss light, life's rhythms and imagination. He also has published abecedarians and makes reference to memory as it relates to his life's story.
>
> The repetition of roots and rooting also draws back to the opening quotation from Winterson, bringing the poem full circle.

Analyzing Poetics, Purposes and Teaching Praxis

Pauline's Poem

WAITING THROUGH SUNDAYS
(Poetry by Pauline Sameshima)

i stayed through high school and college
he said he loved me, always sorry
please he pleaded
god, please forgive me
he prayed

i forgave him, merciful me
the sunday school teacher
because i had it all
love beyond compare
family, friends, sports, grades
even clothes, to hide the perfect couple

the blood slowly pooling in my hands
cupped tight under my chin, full control
no drips on his cherished cloth car seats
not a spot on his sunday shirt
nose numb, cheeks throbbing
quiet liquid, wet iron stench
filling the passenger side

sleet screeches at the wipers so i stay in the car
i'm suddenly in front of my glass house
he leans over and roughly pulls open the door latch
i stumble out to the grass
the ground is close as i open my hands
and the stickiness runs down with the rain
like i'm gently putting a broken bird onto the ground
then i wipe my palms on the sweet softness
like a defecating dog
rude in this manicured neighborhood

somewhere far off, he is saying something
i look up and hear the whizzing sound
turn away as the car keys hit my right shoulder
a strangely satisfying sound
no pain, i fall to a knee, head still low
unafraid and wait
a thick sole in the ribs and now
I feel the rain on my face
transparent body feels nothing

Annotations:

- Lower case 'i' is used to show that it is not Pauline writing this, but instead she adopts the story from her participant.

- This stanza uses synesthesia to emote the visceral experience that is being shared. The description of the speaker's nose and cheeks have adjectives that gives the reader accessible ways to understand what they are feeling. Even if you have not been hit, you understand the feelings of a numbness and throbbing.

- The smell of blood, akin to the smell of iron, is also recognizable and allows the reader to more fully understand the trauma that is being inflicted.

- There is also a repetition in references to God, church, Sundays and the notion of forgiveness. This links to the speaker's literal role as a Sunday school teacher or to a metaphor for their faith and innocence.

- Synesthesia continues here with the sound of the wipers accompanied by the use of onomatopoeia and assonance of the "sleet screech[ing]" and the feeling of sticky blood filling cupped hands being released onto the grass. Her imagery of the blood falling gently like that of setting down broken bird is quickly juxtaposed with the vision of a defecating dog, bringing the reader back to the ghastly reality that the speaker is bleeding heavily.

- The use of simile (like) in describing the bird and the dog highlight specific meanings and images instead of using metaphors which are open for layers of interpretation. She wants the images to be clear and accessible for the reader.

a balcony door opens with a loud sucking slide
the neighbor shouts—he's calling the police
if Trey doesn't leave right now
i feel the rush of his foot fall
still unafraid and wait
but he's just reaching for the keys

muffler booms from his souped up car
as he tears away
giving me another profanity by
chirping into 2nd down the street

sliding door closes, no words
alone, i look up glad for the dark windows

steel grinds as the metal key turns
the stairs behave in their quiet outer edges
up toward my room and sleeping family
in a warm house that smells like vegetable soup and love

that was the end of the 1st year
six more years and still
i could not leave by myself

(Maarhuis & Sameshima, 2016, p. 280)

> The continued use of onomatopoeia to describe sound provides another level of synesthesia. The sounds of the door, the muffler booming and the sound of the steel grinding in the lock all bring the reader into the lived experience of the speaker. Synesthesia continues with the contrasting smell of home and vegetable soup that seeks to offset the smell of blood. The word "soup" refers to "his" car and to the speaker's home, drawing connections between the two facets of their existence.

> The use of the stairs as a metaphor is layered with meaning. The stairs serve as the threshold between the abuse that the speaker is facing and their façade of being a part of a "perfect couple." Yet, climbing the stairs is also a metaphor. It represents the concerted effort that is needed to go from being beaten to acting like nothing is wrong.
>
> It also links to the last stanza where the speaker cannot, despite years of wanting to, climb out of their abusive relationship.

Analyzing Poetics, Purposes and Teaching Praxis 125

John's Poem

When Men Say Good-bye

A hatchet
and the strength of Daddy's hands
broke apart
my baby brother's cot.

As his youngest son,
the only child after me,
crawled or toddled out of infancy,
his oldest,
strode into adolescence—into manhood;
with four living children between the new
man and me,
one also a boy,
another son,
the one who would be forever
the youngest and the oldest,
lay inside the earth
and our memories.

From around the corner of our house
I looked at Daddy
swinging the hatchet
ripping apart the frame with his hands
breaking the board of the cot over his knees.

Sometimes
he would stop,
he would just stop,
and look
at the broken cot.

There was snow on the ground,
and we needed wood for the fire.

(Guiney Yallop & Shields, 2016, p. 47)

The title serves as a commentary on how men display their emotions or are meant to stereotypically display their emotions. This ties to John's overarching interest in exploring identity and events that create identity.

The hatchet, a handheld tool, shows the direct connection between the father, who we know is John's father, and the act of destroying the cot.

When unpacking the seemingly paradoxical description of his brother who passed as forever the youngest and oldest is layered with muted melancholy. He will always be the first born, the eldest, yet in dying he will never age. This is a key characteristic in much of John's work. A seemingly simple line runs much deeper.

The image of his farther breaking the cot, somewhat hidden around a corner, with John peering on in the distance, shows that he is not meant to be a participant in its destruction or privy to it happening. The idea that men deal with their emotions in private links back to the title of the poem.

Again, there is the connection of the father's body to the action taking place; he is the one who is responsible for breaking down the cot and he is using his strength, physical and mental, to do so.

This stanza, with its repetition of "stop" as the last line asks the reader to pause their image and join his father in looking at the cot. This asks the reader to also pause and reflect on the metaphor embodied in the cot. Its destruction highlights the depths of their financial despair, the abrupt end of his parents' childbearing years, and suggests that every member of their family would have to sacrifice for the betterment of their family.

It also shows that his father is conflicted in what he has to do. He can only pause for a moment to reflect and feel his emotions, without outwardly showing them. He must then carry on with what must be done. What men must do.

Monica's Poem

imagination

we live in lands
of what might be
    and
what might have been

> Monica uses capitalization, or lack thereof, as a construct to demonstrate that she is not changing the voice of the original author or their grammatical choices. She strips them of their original syntax and uses formatting to show her interpretation or discussion of the original text.

worlds
far greater
of more import
than the world
        of what is

imagination
turns lust
        into love
the need for shelter
        into construction
        and industry
converts food-taking
        into dining
(but turns some
        into gluttons)

> The juxtaposition of line lengths shows Monica's interpretation of the text. The left aligned text shows where the idea or process began and the consistently offset words highlight the after (the cause and effect of imagination). Offsetting the products of imagination highlight them as important concepts to focus on and think about.

by virtue
of imagination
human life oscillates
        a vague median line

> The word "oscillates" cues another change in spacing and alignment where the text itself oscillates. Also, the notion of a vague line is left detached from the previous line, rendering it more vague.

(what we might call
natural animality)
it soars above
        in ideals, science,
            art, religion
it drops below
        in crimes, cruelties,
            injustices, perversions
the work of actuality
is imagination's legacy

> The oscillation continues with art, and religion, and injustices and perversions now aligning with the notion of the vague median line. This acts as an interpretation or commentary on the vague line that exists between art, religion, injustices and perversion.

> She uses spacing, playing off the words "above" and "below," to highlight the hierarchy being described in the text. That is with "natural animality" above science, etcetera and below crimes, cruelties, etcetera.

it is only
with imagination
we get away
from everything
but the bloom of the rose
early in the morning

> The word "free" is aligned with the changes that imagination brings in stanza three (e.g., love, construction) which again highlights the product of using or engaging with imagination. It brings freedom.

it takes imagination
to think of
    being free

(Broudy, 1972/1994, pp. 12-14)

> Here she cites her source material for the poem, ensuring that the reader is aware that the construction is her interpretation, but the original text is not her own.

(Prendergast, 2012, pp. 2-3)

Pondering the Poetic Analysis Process

By conducting a close reading of a poem from each participant, I was able to more closely identify the ways that they craft poems. Highlighting poetic devices, line construction and the inference behind their compositional choices give greater insight into each participant's distinctive poetics. Additionally, beyond identifying characteristics of each participant's poetics, I was able to better understand the subject matter of each of their poems. In Carl's poem, he uses repetition to provide a commentary on the longevity of his career, his wit to highlight his distaste for elements of internal politics as it relates to the perceived value of different departments and puts forward a call to remember to slow down and enjoy nature all while not losing sight of one's privilege. Pauline's poem reminds us of the grotesque and violent realities of domestic violence. Her language use, with description and vivid sensory cues, forces the reader to empathically feel, or in the very least to understand more deeply, aspects of the speaker's lived experience. Through her poetic choices and selection of words, Pauline draws attention away from her as the poet and emphasizes the importance of engaging with the content of the poem. John's seemingly straightforward story of his father breaking down his brother's crib/cot for firewood is rich with meaning and insights into the human experience. His poem reminds us that our childhood experiences often shape who we are and influence our expectations around gender norms and emotionality. Further, he is able to craft metaphors from real-world elements that appear in his poem, as in the case of the hatchet and crib, and use language to subtly, yet impactfully, touch the reader. This subtlety is evident in his paradoxical mention of his deceased brother which I found especially profound as a parent myself. Monica's poem is constructed with purposeful decisions that highlight key notions from the original text that may have otherwise gone unnoticed. She uses the poetic line to guide the reader through her interpretation by drawing comparisons or showing contrasts depending upon where, on the page, words reside. She creates meaning through words but does not claim the words as her own. She instead showcases the voice of original author, making evident her voice as the poet (through her poetic choices around construction) and, through a removal of punctuation, invites the reader to read and re-read the poem as they see fit.

These deeper revelations, discovered through my exemplified critical analyses of these poems, highlights the need for this practice to continue. Poetic products from poetic inquiry studies currently sit dormant in the literature, which leaves opportunities to understand craft and content from studies captive within their respective pages. There is more to discover. Further, future studies that use poetic inquiry could be crafted with a greater degree of purpose, knowing that the poetry could and should be looked at more closely on an analytical level by those both inside and outside of the arts-based research community. This practice could potentially add to the visibility of poetic inquiry and showcase its credence in qualitative research, potentially silencing sceptics (e.g., jagodzinski & Wallin, 2013) and seeing poetic inquiry as a greater part of relevant discussions of qualitative methods (e.g., Creswell, 2013).

Discussion of the Findings of this Process

This chapter demonstrates ways that each participant represents a unique element of the larger field of arts-based research, where poetic inquiry resides, while still maintaining connections to each other's work. They all have similar views around the underlying power of poetry, channeled through the poet, to produce and mobilize knowledge in research. They also see the value of using poetry to support students' development as learners and to provide them with diverse tools for analyzing texts.

It is, however, their differences that reveal a greater understanding of what poetry is doing, and can do, in Canadian research and scholarship. Carl's life's work with poetry displays the power of poetic inquiry to (implicitly or explicitly) use language in diverse ways to tease out further understandings of life, including notions of self and relationship with others, or larger concepts around philosophy and teaching. He does this through a willingness to explore every facet of language and experiment with its construction, poetically, to create meaning. Through his work, notions of poetic rumination and living poetically endure. There are also, undoubtedly, countless teachers who have been personally impacted by his experiential approaches to teaching or indirectly influenced by his published works. The uniqueness of Pauline's contribution lays not only in her work with ekphrastic responses, visual art, and the Parallaxic Praxis model, but also in her impactful uses of poetry and her accompanying theories, that demonstrate ways that poetry can bring participants' voices and lived experiences to life. Her work uses poetic inquiry to create new and more meaningful ways of understanding and disseminating what was learned from participants which pushes other qualitative researchers to consider if they are doing enough in that area. John's focus on using poetry as a way to better understand who he is, individually and as a part of diverse communities, and strengthen his voice exemplifies ways that poetry can also be used to amplify voices of marginalized people. He has created space for his voice to be heard and welcomes others to join him in sharing their thoughts, views and experiences. This includes modeling the power of poetry for his students, many of which are future educators. Monica's approaches to creating and performing poetry show her value in polyphonic exchanges, where the voice of the author of the original text and the voice of the poet-researcher are simultaneously present. This highlights the critical level at which qualitative researchers who use poetic inquiry must operate in order to share the stories of their participants in authentic and meaningful ways while not ignoring the crucial role of the researcher. The researcher must make sense of what they are learning and find ways to e/affectively share it with their audience. It is then up to the audience to further interpret what they have read, seen and/or heard in hopes that a greater understanding will spur change in their lives and the lives of those around them.

My discussions and a close examination of the work of the participants, a subset of the larger poetic inquiry community in Canada, demonstrate that those who use poetic inquiry impactfully in their research also embody its tenets in their scholarship and poetry. Undoubtedly, there is a correlation between each participant's expressed views on how and why they use poetic inquiry in their academic and creative endeavours with their approaches to teaching and their poetic products. They are "living poetically" (Leggo, 2005), with poetry permeating all facets of their academic endeavours. Poetry, as explored in this chapter, is not a gimmick used to make their work appear more aesthetically pleasing but is a way that allows for deeper and diverse ways of understanding, analyzing and expressing thoughts, concepts and/or emotions. It is also a way to bring knowledge to the reader in what has been described in this study as a shorter distance. Monica does this through her choices when crafting her found poetry, Carl and John do this through metaphors and Pauline does this through synesthesia that brings years of lived experiences into a few lines. With further examples of what poetic inquiry is and what it can do, the question remains: How can this knowledge further impact approaches to research and scholarship?

Critical Cartography of Purposes and Poetics
(Adam Vincent)

I have discovered...

Carl's poetry congregates
with his capacious view
of poetry
crafted
by poets
who
like carpenters
have trained to
nail
down
the correct verb
in the right place
to give meaning
and
structure
with room   to expand
the minds of others.

Parts of speech
meet
poetic devices
meet
passion and purpose
meet
others' views that need exploration
to learn more
to be added autobiographically
while living poetically
more than qualitatively
teaching others
that data need not be data
education need not be prescriptive
yet
is a part of learning the language of life-
his, a life well lived.

I see Pauline
beyond the chair
where

there
resides gritty poetry
contrasting imagery with data
synthesized
to give greater meaning
and
amplify voices of others
capital 'I'
not owned by the researcher
but by those who lived
the 'I'
unpunctuated, unless quoted
credited to a life lived
and
shared
to learn more

I see her
facilitating agency
that acts as clemency
as learning from the past
where she presents full stops
only when
permission is granted
not imposed
by her roles
as artist
as researcher
as interpreter of knowledge

She is present;
ekphrastically creating
new meaning through
portraiture
of layers
of highlighting others' voices
accentuated focally
for she values their impact
and
seeks to highlight lived learning
therein the frame

John shares his stories,
piece by piece,

building
image by image
that appear as
purposefully picked parts of speech,
practiced prose
presented poetically,
yet
when you stop
when you look closer
you see that
you have been deceived,
not maliciously
but
meticulously by meaning
below the surface
where metaphors
are molded by the literal
not the implied,
where turns of phrase
expose depths
of pain
of wit
of life
that lets you know
you are not alone
that your voice matters
and
should be heard.

He invites:
tell me a story about who you are
about your identity
about who you thought you would be
about who you want to be
tell me poetically
with your unique voice
that cannot be emulated
or
assimilated
due to it being authentically you.

Monica,
i found your poetic choices interesting

though they are not in my voice to claim
as my own
nor are the lines
    mine to
        break
yet
i chose to share this poem
with you in hopes
that you will be inspired by it
    we can talk about it
    together
    learning more
i caught it yesterday
and will need to return it
        to you
its rightful owner
        by way of my citations
but
i will keep the inspirations

that jump   off   of   the   page

I have mapped,
following their voices, polyphonically,
on my path towards my
understanding of poetic inquiry;
their poetry unpacked along the way
where I can now pontificate
on their purposeful practices
that can pragmatically be used to posit
possible changes
to be presented hereafter
that can lead to greater knowledge
yet to be discovered
somewhere down the road.

Chapter 9
Implications, Applications and Conclusion

Implications

Sitting outside of a coffeeshop, sharing my writing from a chair parallel to Dr. Leggo, I did not realize what all that poetry was doing outside of my microcosmic view of the world. My MA gave me further perspective on poetry's uses in teaching writing but I wanted to know more, especially around its uses for research purposes. I set out in this study to understand what poetic inquiry is, what it does and what it can do. Through this study, I have unearthed and examined the rhizomatic roots of poetic inquiry across multiple fields. To make sense of this complexity, I also sought out experts in the field, distinguished by their records of publication and teaching in the area. Through speaking with Dr. Leggo, Dr. Sameshima, Dr. Guiney Yallop and Dr. Prendergast, or as I grew to know them simply as Carl, Pauline, John and Monica, I came to understand the nuanced elements of poetic inquiry as a method, methodology, craft, tool and way of living. I have now been able to identify and analyze ways that I see poetic inquiry informing and supporting current research and teaching practices, from a Canadian perspective, and where I believe it is going, or growing if we extend that metaphor, in those areas.

Implications for Qualitative Research

I have come to a greater understanding of poetic inquiry's diverse uses in qualitative research that are currently in use and others that I believe can, and will, be expanded further. My literature review yields a wide array of examples of ways that poetry, and the fundamental tenets of poetic inquiry, have been used in recent decades. In speaking with the participants of the study, I was able to delve more deeply into the mind of the researchers who use poetic inquiry in their academic work. These scholars exemplify ways that poetic inquiry is currently being used to implicitly or explicitly use language in diverse ways that further explore and analyze the self and ideas. Poetry, as a function in their work, is either a naturally occurring form of expression from the poet/author who uses it to discern more about their research, or it is used as part of a carefully crafted plan to create findings that appeal to a different readership and/or to draw out understandings that were unattainable through other genre or methods.

Further, I learned through this study that poetry, by way of poetic inquiry, affords the researcher a unique opportunity to use highly descriptive and e/affective language in ways that bring participants' stories and lived experiences to life. Beyond simple description, poetry and the use of poetic language and devices can emote, often in fewer words, that which could take pages to describe or, perhaps, not be able to be described in impactful ways at all. This is a significant characteristic when considering the representation and translation of voice (verbal) to literary voice (written). More traditional approaches to academic writing, such as expository essays, can limit the voice of the speaker as, students especially, try to adhere to a skewed perspective of academic writing. By incorporating diverse ways to represent the nuance of spoken voice on the page, poetry functions as a way to give the researcher options for representing the lived experiences of their study's participants and of their role as researcher. This is evidenced by some the poetic-academic publications of the participants in this study, especially in Pauline and Monica's corpuses of work. Pauline, as exemplified in Chapter Five, merges her voice with those of the participants to create meaning. That, however, is not her only technique. An example of her use of verbatim interview transcription to create poetry, "Feeling Good (1:262-268)," from her study around the lived experience and recovering addict exemplify how poetic inquiry can be used to amplify the voice(s) of others,

> it was easy to start
> it felt so good
> I didn't feel inhibited
> I've always had it browbeat
> into my brain how worthless
> I am
> all my life
> and for the first time
> I actually felt good
> I could go out
> and be sociable
> confident at the pool table
> I have a problem with men
> I've been raped more than once
> so I have these men issues
> but meth made me
> feel good
> I could banter with the best
> of them at the pool table (Sameshima et al., 2009, p. 56)

Pauline does not explicitly merge her voice with the voice of the participant, Gabriel. She instead shares, verbatim, what they discussed in their interviews. Pauline, however, remains present through her choices around which aspect of the transcription she uses, line length and line breaks. These choices show her interpretation of the data and draw attention to specific words or phrases. Yet, she does not alter what was said or add, through additional text, her textual interpretation. If Pauline had only summarized what Gabriel shared, she would have risked minimizing the vulnerability present in how Gabriel's words were spoken. For example, in the excerpt shared from "Feeling Good (1:262-268)," Pauline shows how plainly Gabriel expressed that "meth made [her]/feel good" (p. 56) and that it allowed her to deal with her "problem[s] with men" (p. 56). Moreover, had Pauline shared excerpts from the transcript in prose form, her interpretation of key themes in the data would have been more overt, potentially taking away from Gabriel's words. In using poetry in this way, the reader has an opportunity to first read what Gabriel said, interpreting her words and potentially pausing with each line break to reflect on what was said. This is comparable to reading a literary poem. The reader then, as this is a poetic inquiry product, has room to read the poem again with the intent of consciously identifying what more can be gleaned from the poem as a form of data.

Similarly, Monica's poetry has displayed a way to represent and amplify the voices of others. This is evident in her examination of Blau's (1990) *The Audience* where her found poetry uses verbatim passages from the text and splices them with reviews of the original text and parenthetical additions of her voice for effect. With its original formatting:

listening

the audience (endless)
                    sees
                                if it does
                                  at all

in the labyrinth
of the ear

(the telltale mark
of audience)

losing itself thus
in the circuits
of the ear

somewhere between
dreams and events
listening speaks

> through the very tears/fractures/punctures/debilities
>
> of language
>
> as the plot thickens
> in emblooded thought
> in the silence at its centre
>
> (pp. 136-138)
> (Prendergast, 2004, pp. 80-1)

Monica's poem highlights a unique function of poetry in research studies. That is that poetic inquiry can, and is, used to share multiple voices; the voice of the original author and the voice of the poet/researcher (through poetic construction and interpretation). Instead of writing something to the effect of "Blau contends that the audience is impacted by what is spoken or not spoken on stage," Monica is able to add her interpretation for clarity and effect. She does this while accentuating the importance of Blau's metaphor in relation to the importance of what and how lines are spoken on stage and how silence also adds to the audience's interpretation of what they are witnessing on stage. Poetry, as her poetry exemplifies, has a unique function in that a form of textual polyphony can occur, giving layers of explicit and implicit meaning.

Important, as it relates to voice in poetic inquiry, is the realization that marginalized individuals, including those who may not have access to higher education due to socioeconomic or cultural reasons, have an opportunity to use language in diverse ways, through the use of poetry. This gives them a way to share their stories or to reclaim their expropriated stories (e.g., De Vito & Johnston, 2017; Cutts, 2019; Elbelazi & Alharbi, 2020; van Rooyen et al., 2020) and links them to autobiographical or autoethnographic poetic inquiry (see Rothenberg, 1994; Smith, 2002). Autoethnographic poetic inquiry, as in some of Carl and John's academic-poetic publications, allows for a greater understanding of self in the context of society and highlights varying degrees of (mis)representation therein. An example of this comes from Carl's (2016) poem "Thirteen Meditations in the Dentist's Chair" in his academic article "A Poem Can: Poetic Encounters" where he enquires about the capaciousness of poetry. In the following excerpt, Carl uses poetry to explore his views on prayer and question how they relate to others in his life (i.e., family, as represented by Carrie, and other colleagues in academia):

> 6
> Carrie claims nothing means
>   anything anymore
> but doesn't everything mean
> something, perhaps
> we have forgotten how to be

> 7
> what if my prayers are
> foolish and futile,
> offered into the stratosphere
> like an expulsion of air?
>
> what if there is no God?
>
> 8
> prayer is a way of breathing
> oxygen spirit pneuma
>
> prayer is a way of leaning into
> the world, refusing to surrender
>
> 9
> I don't know what prayer is
> but in the moments of each day
> something won't let me go,
> something tantalizing,
> desire's constant goad
>
> 10
> perhaps prayer is a message
> tapped in Morse code
> on the stone walls of our cells
>
> 11
> at a conference in San Francisco
> with thousands of other educators
> one colleague said, I am
> suspicious of anyone
> who talks about hope (p. 354-55)

This excerpt shows one way that Carl uses language autobiographically and autoethnographically to explore larger ideas and questions around life, while also using poetry to provide a tongue-in-cheek commentary on academia. To do this, he uses enjambment. First the prayers are a form of Morse code on cell walls (presumably asking a higher for help or forgiveness), followed by the next stanza which inverts the imagery from somewhat positive to somewhat negative where he insinuates that the cells are located at an academic conference. This highlights Carl's disparity between how he views the world and learning with hope while others appear more pessimistic.

John's autoethnographic poetry, as in the following example, accentuates an element of his lived experience as a member of a marginalized community (the

2SLGBTQ+ community). From his 2010 article on writing poetry in academia, "Through the Words of a Poet: Experiencing a Writing Journey," he shares the poem "What Hate Is" about the discrimination he faced as an out, gay schoolteacher:

> Hate is a mad guard dog
> biting at my heels.
>
> Hate is an unwelcome elbow
> in my back.
>
> Hate is spit on my desk
> and *This teacher sucks cock.*
> on the chalkboard.
>
> Hate is letters and telephone calls
> to administrators
> to express concern about me wearing *that* t-shirt,
> or kissing a man in the parking lot,
> or looking at construction workers outside the school, hate is
>
> long fingers around my neck
> not being able to speak,
> words jamming my throat
> like an apocalyptic rush hour.
>
> Hate is a well-oiled apparatus
> that contours the body;
>
>   we get used to it. (pp. 204-5)

John is able to use imagery in his poem to draw the reader in and highlight the mental and physical pain associated with hate and discrimination (in this case, homophobia). He is also able to provide a commentary about how, despite the obvious instances of hate, there is little to no support to stop it from occurring as in the last line "we get used to it." Each stanza highlights a different facet of his experiences with hate with line breaks and stanza breaks asking the reader to pause for a moment to reflect on what has been said. Poetry, used autoethnographically, affords the poet/researcher an opportunity to use language, imagery and the form on the page to tell their stories in more evocative ways than if they were written in paragraph form. If, for example, the line breaks and stanza breaks are removed, the impact of each statement becomes lessened, e.g., "Hate is a mad guard dog biting at my heels. Hate is an unwelcome elbow in my back. Hate is spot on my desk and *This teacher sucks cock.* on the chalkboard." This is because, despite the use of periods, the instances of hate become list-like and are no longer individual snapshots of lived experience. Poetry, when used to inquire about facets of lived experience and how those experiences adhere to the norms of society, provides the poet/researcher a way to enliven and add depth to textual accounts, making them more visceral and meaningful for the reader.

I initially understood, tacitly, that poetry (including poetic language and devices) was a way that I could tap into my own thoughts and feelings. It was not until this study that I came to understand the capaciousness, as Carl would say, of this medium to empower myself and others. Through a close reading, I paid closer attention to vivid imagery and uses of such poetic devices as assonance, rhyme and synesthesia. As such, I came to not only affectively but cognitively comprehend the level in which poetry can bring others' lived experiences to life through text (using art for epistemological purposes). This holds significant weight when it comes to social justice and movements that support equality and diversity. Not only is the researcher able to share their findings, through their poetic choices, but poetry can allow their participants' verbatim words to be shared simultaneously. This allows unique data sets to be created, or captured, analyzed and disseminated. These can take multiple forms, including researcher-voiced poetry, participant-voiced poetry, found poetry and transcript poetry. This analytical approach to the poetic products of poetic inquiry studies asks the reader to engage with the poem on both cognitive and affective levels that ultimately reveal deeper understandings of the study as a whole.

Future Research Applications

Chapter Three introduces the notion of poetic inquiry's validity or trustworthiness in relation to this study and to poetic inquiry as a whole which do not readily apply to this study. While this study has elements of social sciences criterion and has some relevance to Faulkner's notion of ars poetica (2007), this study ultimately identifies a gap as it relates to being able to use standardized measurements in relation to poetic inquiry studies and, in the case of this booked based on my doctoral dissertation, studies about poetic inquiry studies. Future research could explore equitable ways of evaluating studies that do not take away from the creative/poetic elements but give guidance for understanding their potential power for additional knowledge creation. Further, generating a greater understanding of poetic inquiry's uses with philosophical/interpretive frameworks and how data is analyzed and represented in diverse qualitative research approaches would be beneficial. These concepts were considered (see Appendix 1), but lacked direct relevance to this study beyond a confirmation that poetic inquiry has innumerable possibilities in research and that close literary analysis of poetic inquiry products may prove beneficial in these studies as well.

Implications for Data Gathering

I further discovered, through my own research practices during this study, that poetry can be used to add depth and richness to fieldnotes (Vincent, 2020a) which gives the researcher yet another way to engage with their data and evaluate their place within the context of the research (Vincent, 2020b). Of the practice of creating fieldnotes through poetry, I posit that there are typologies that have informed my research practice:

> i) autoethnographic poetic fieldnotes, ii) found poetic fieldnotes (for use with observations in the field), and iii) reflective/reflexive poetic fieldnotes (as a tool for analyzing interview data and for positioning the researcher within the interview/research context). (Vincent, 2020a, p. 144)

Autoethnographic poetic fieldnotes function as a way to critically reflect on your place in the context of your research, field and/or society. Keeping ongoing fieldnotes, whether created or processed through the crafting of poems, can help one to evaluate their place in their larger socio-cultural context and generate a reflexive understanding of positionality within the research study. In order to craft meaningful poetry, the researcher/poet must draw their attention to their intentions, feelings and/or experiences and find ways to express complex notions through their language choices. This adds an additional layer above reporting their observations, one that then combines data processing alongside initial observations. This approach, which I use in this study, is derived from my initial trialling of this practice in my unpublished Masters' thesis (2015) where I created a narrative-poetic métissage that sought to better understand the use of poetry in the teaching of writing. In my thesis, I combined observations of my research processes and my engagement with the literature with my own interpretations of the work and how it coincides with my research. This process enabled me to generate a greater understanding of the materials that I was reading by giving them deeper meaning and allowing me an opportunity to process my thoughts by engaging with the concepts through poetry. The second approach that I posit is the creation of found poetic fieldnotes. This is done by taking artefacts, in the form of direct quotes from texts of relevance to the study, and using poetic choices, such as line breaks and appearance on the page, to declutter the prose and add emphasis to important terms or ideas. This process allows for a greater focus on the word choices of the original author and relevant meaning to the researcher. It also, however, offers an opportunity to expand an understanding of meaning through the creation of poems that focus on specific concepts by grouping lines of text or juxtaposing them in side-by-side stanzas. There is also the possibility of creating inverse meaning through poetic choices that highlight potential discrepancies in the original text. These poetic reconstructive processes function as a way to reveal deeper levels of meaning when the original text is brought back into view. A word that may have appeared benign in an initial reading of the text may now prove integral to an understanding of what the author/text is saying. These greater understandings then give the researcher/poet further information as it relates to the context or finite details of the study which can have a major impact on the process and findings of the study.

The third approach is reflective/reflexive poetic fieldnotes. In a recent publication on this process, I describe ways that I make further sense of my positionality in the research process through the creation of poetry. The following paragraphs, which comprise an excerpt from my chapter entitled "The Poetry of Fieldnotes" (2020a) provides a closer look at this type of fieldnote practice that, I believe, is highly beneficial in the research process.

I use poems in my research practice, including in this study, to help me to reflect on who I am as a poet-researcher and how my notions of self can influence the research process. Who am I as a researcher? How do my background, biases, values and beliefs influence my interactions with my participants and affect my interpretation of stories or events? I wrote the following poems in conjunction with a few short fieldnotes during an interview with Carl. While drafting my poem, I reflected on the interview using my audio recording of the interview and my interview transcript. This triangulation—my memory, the audio, and written transcript—gave me different ways to reflect on my lived research experience as I wrote the poem(s). During this interview, I noted physical, auditory, and sensual items, but did not want my focus to be only on my notes (as I knew I would have time to reflect and write after the interview). I jotted short fieldnotes on paper, which includes: the call of seagulls, a brown futon, many photographs over the decades, small room, computer, sea breeze. From these jottings, I wrote the following poem:

> The seagulls call to him
> in the distance
> as his voice bounces
> rhythmic
> like the poetry that he writes
> soft as the sea breeze
> that blows the blinds behind him
> next to the photos of a long career
> next to the books of a long career
> in his humble study
> designed for writing, marking
> and guests to stay on the pull-out couch.

I formulated my understanding of the interview through the writing of the poem. My interpretation needs to be made explicit when I consider the meaning behind his words. I asked myself: "How did I interpret the interview?" I quickly likened Carl's literary voice, his poetic voice, to his spoken voice. During the writing of my poem, I tried to be aware that I may unintentionally slant what was said so that it fit my perception of Carl's literary voice and not his verbal voice. I felt that it was important that my transcription reflect the dialogic experience of the verbal interview. I must be explicit about my syntactic choices so that I do not unconsciously create an inauthentic version of his voice; the voice that I heard during the interview. My interpretation, I contended, should be based on the interview event rather than an intertextual knowledge of Carl's work and his literary voice. Making my experience and my perception explicit is integral in ensuring that I do not void any of my participants' voices in lieu of my voice (see Prendergast & Galvin, 2015).

My short fieldnote observations did not include much more than the physical space and immediate surroundings. It was not until I engaged in poetic forms of inquiry, after the interview, that I was able to delve further into the meaning of our exchange and of my interpretation of our exchange. This line of thinking led me to write another poem about the same interview event:

> I am nervous
> fiddling with my recorder
> fearful that the fabric of the couch
> will rustle with the interpretation
> of our voices
> as they reach the microphone
> I wonder if he hears the cadence of his voice
> akin
> no
> the same as the voice I have read
> in text
> in medias res
> of a debate that I have only began to consider.
> The couch squeaked.
> Do I harness the voice I read
> in text
> in my text
> or do I listen for a change?

Through poetic reflection, drawing from Flores' (1982) work, I was able to place myself in the research in a way that was not intrusive but instrumental (acting simultaneously as an active voice, as part of research itself, and as the interpreter of the exchange). I was also able to analyze what I did as a researcher

Implications, Applications and Conclusion 145

and how these choices may have had an effect on the research outcome. For example, I was so focused on my recorder that I did not clearly hear something that could have changed the line of questioning or changed my interpretation of what was said. In feeling like my fieldnote process helped me to reflect on my interviews with Carl, I created fieldnote poems after my meetings with Monica, John and Pauline. I used the poems to position myself prior to engaging in my transcription and data analysis processes. From my first interview with Monica, with notes of "ring road, brick building, slick pebbled stairs, office like a living book, jovial knowledge sharing," I wrote the following poem after our interview:

> Monica, where are you?
> I parked.
> I found the brick building.
> I scampered through the empty foyers
> trying to find my way
> up.
> Monica, how are you
> floors above me?
> Where is the elevator?
> Monica, I found the stairs.
> They are slick like river rocks.
> I am grateful for a lack of rain.
> I am not late yet.
> I have not fallen down them.
>
> Monica, I am here.
> I feel as if I am living
> downstage right
> privy to your soliloquy
> of knowledge
> drawn into your office
> a living book
> where you somehow breathe with it
> making sense of it all
> and
> give your knowledge away
> to those who visit
> to those who can find it
> and
> somehow take it with you
> as you travel the world
> inciting meaning.

Based on my first interview with John, with the notes "red painting, windows, sneezing from the dander, squeaky leather chair, balancing the recorder, quiet" I wrote the following poem:

> They say red is the colour of anger
> that enrages colour-blind bulls
> that will keep you awake
> should you paint your walls as such
> yet this is a painting
> with swirls of reds
> is hued differently when hit by the sun
> through the wall of windows.
> Recorder perched
> on my knees
> parallel to the phone
> paper with lefty scrawl
> crinkled from my pocket
> that must not fall
> or
> draw my attention
> from John
> who graciously agreed
> to talk to me
> time zones away.
>
> His voice is not red
> more golden
> like the light now filling the room.
> He speaks with conviction
> he speaks with care
> yet I hear no apologies
> in his assuredness that he is where he belongs.
> I wonder how can I share his tones
> when I make sense of what I will learn
> balancing the recorder
> on my knees.

Following my first interview with Pauline, with notes "my old office, small windows, cheap MDF (medium-density fibreboard) desk, wrong number, hard to read pages of notes and questions, sticky note on the door," I wrote the subsequent poem:

I met her once
(sort of)
in the halls of the University of Calgary
where I stumbled on my words
to say hello
having read her work along my way
to presenting at the conference
taking place that week.

I am in familiar territory
where I supported students
for years
yet I am calling to liminal spaces
where the bay thunders
where Pauline
the chair
sits
with information
willing to share
with me
no longer stumbling for words.

I ask with conviction
she replies the same.
I listen to understand
what lays before me
knowing I will
chart deeper
with conviction
into the uncharted.

Using poetry in my fieldnotes gave me the opportunity to explore using metaphor, line breaks, simile, and other poetic devices that are not often employed in academic prose. This approach to reflection helped me to recognize important information that I would not have taken much note of if not for my poetic practice(s) (Vincent, 2020a, pp. 144-45). These are three potential approaches to using poetry in conjunction with new or pre-existent fieldnote practices that can support the researcher/poet in understanding their positionality as it relates to the research, their research setting and research context. These processes provide ways for researchers to begin to discern and differentiate between their voice, interpretation of language and lived events, and their participants' voice(s) with their intended meaning(s).

This study affirms that poetic inquiry is an ideal method or methodology for those who identify as poets or have a keen interest in the study of poetry and/or those who have experience exploring the connections between language and meaning (e.g., semiotics, hermeneutics and critical literary studies). It is, however, as described in my section on the poetic inquiry paradox (Chapter Eight), not for every research study or for every researcher or poet. I have learned that to e/affectively use poetic inquiry, the researcher must not only have a strong grasp on language and poetic forms, they must also have at least a working knowledge of diverse qualitative research methods and their purposes. This is because poetic inquiry is often used in conjunction with other theoretical or methodological frameworks with their own functions and norms. The use of poetry, as the participants of this study note, needs to be purposeful or it puts the whole study at risk. This is because the researcher will not be able to draw out the information that they need, through the functions of poetry, to answer their research questions.

Additionally, the poetic inquiry researcher must have a level of self-awareness as it relates to their values, ethics and abilities as a writer. This is because, as accentuated in the poetry of the participants, there is a vulnerability required of poet-researchers when they share their academic-poetic work. Their poetic choices are open for scrutiny from other poets, researchers and the research participants themselves. This sees something as superficially benign as a line break, to some outside of the field, as a technique that holds a great deal of power that can impact the study or its findings. Additionally, the power of poetry to share the words and experiences of others can lead to multiple interpretations which may misconstrue the purpose behind its creation. The poet-researcher, the poetic inquirer, requires a grasp on language, meaning and aesthetics (by way of an understanding of poetic devices and poetic language) in order to deftly create research-based poetry and find impactful ways to share it with others. If they fail to do so, there is a great risk that this work will remain marginalized and that the voices and experiences of their participants will not be recognized thereby not adding to what is known about the problem(s) and/or not resolving the problem(s) that they sought to address in the first place.

Implications for Scholarship

Poetic inquiry, while potentially an impactful method or methodology for conducting research, also houses techniques that can be useful in teaching. In addition to these theories and techniques being present in the literature (e.g., Leggo, 2007), this study has shown what a life lived poetically (Leggo, 2005) can look from the perspective of the participants where poetry permeates through all facets of their academic praxis. As poetry is an essential element of who they are, it makes sense that it also influences their approaches to teaching. In the following section, which highlights ways that poetic inquiry can support pedagogy,

I not only highlight what was learned from the participants of this study but draw on my own experiences as a university instructor.

In my own teaching practice, I have experienced that multimodality, akin to Monica's use of performance and Pauline's use of visual art as elements of their teaching practice, in conjunction with poetic inquiry is especially impactful when teaching writing. Students are not only invited to write in diverse poetic forms (e.g., free verse, prose poems, haiku, sonnets) but they are encouraged to speak their poetry and/or share it through visual methods such as drawings, paintings or videos. For students who are musically inclined, they can also use their poetry (with such elements as meter and rhyme) to create musical representations of what they have learned. While these processes appear divergent to standard academic assignment formats (e.g., paragraphs, essays, personal responses in prosaic form), poetic inquiry functions as a way to give students the opportunity to engage in course concepts in different ways that ultimately increase retention and understanding. This multifaceted approach to working with concepts is akin to the theories behind active and experiential learning (e.g., Kolb, 2015) which is in use in classrooms ranging from elementary/primary level to graduate-level studies.

The findings of this study also affirm that poetic inquiry supports the processes of rumination (Leggo, 2004) and personal self-reflection which can support researcher and student identity development. It also, as in elements of John's teaching practice, encourages the creation of identity for pre-service teachers. Additionally, it gives teachers a way to engage with students in ways that promote individual learning over an immediate need for an adherence to prescription. While some students are comfortable writing based on a template, and a clear step by step process for writing, not all are able to express what they need to express which leaves their assignments lacking in content. Through poetic inquiry, students are able to first focus on what they know, make efforts to fill in any deficits in their understanding, and then work towards the creation and completion of their standard assignment (based on its criteria). This is not far from the widely accepted approach to the writing process that we see in school settings. This process, as contemporarily outlined in a common university textbook used in the fields of Business and Communications, "Communicating for Results" by Carolyn Meyer (2017; 2020), suggests that the writing process entails pre-writing, organizing and outlining, drafting, revising and editing and proofreading (p. 84). This builds on the notions first introduced in the Process Writing method (or Process Writing approach) in the 1970s and 1980s by the likes of Applebee (1986) who promotes the approach as it "provided a way to think about writing in terms of what the writer does (planning, revising, and the like) instead of in terms of what the final product looks like (patterns of organization, spelling and grammar" instead of focusing solely on the merits of students' prescriptive written products (p. 96).

In place of standard notions of pre-writing and outlining, students can use poetry to put their ideas on the page and cluster them into stanzas, which can then be transposed into a more traditional outline. This requires that the teacher or instructor supports students more actively in the early stages of this adaptation process. Ultimately, poetry provides students with tools for generating deeper understandings of concepts and diverse ways to use language to construct their ideas before they move into drafting of what will ultimately be their final product (that adheres to more traditional forms, such as the expository essay).

As Pauline discusses, in her example of a way that poetry is a useful tool in her teaching praxis, and John alludes to when he works with graduate students, poetic inquiry also gives a unique way for students to further their understanding of data analysis, coding and data dissemination. Students can convert transcripts into verbatim poems to accentuate specific terms or themes. They can also create response poetry to affirm their understanding of what has been said. While some students are resistant to reading academic journal articles or texts, they are often open to the notion of reading poetry. The perception of shorter lines equating to less complexity appears to draw students in; the text superficially appears more accessible. Ultimately, poetry is, for some, a more palatable way to be exposed to ideas and/or ask questions than prosaic forms. Poetry, with its potential lyricism, may also speak to students who enjoy making or listening to music. While this study highlights that poetry holds the power to lessen the distance between the poet and the receiver, it also accentuates the significance of each word and each poetic choice that goes into the crafting of the poem (through a close reading and analysis).

Poetry's Unparalleled Purposefulness
(Adam Vincent)

It functions fruitfully
with fragments   (grammatically speaking)
enlivening experience
and
knowing on each
line   (of varying lengths)
polyphonically synchronizing the
synesthesia of senses
and
voices
succinctly
in a stanza

or
                        across the stanzic expanse
linking immediate
or
implied images of self
to
society
to
the spiteful spit on the desk
to
the blood-cupped hands
to
the fading footprints in the sand
to
the actively engaged audience
with
potentially witty inversion
of a tongue-in-cheek
movement towards making marginalization
of the visceral nature
of humanity
of human experience(s)
more than a mark on a page
in a prosaic literature review
of a complex concept or idea.

Application and Contribution

Application of this Study

The application of this exploratory study extends from qualitative research to pedagogy. This study can be used to further an understanding of poetic inquiry as a valuable part of qualitative research most frequently found under the sub-categories of arts-based research and arts-based educational research (ABER). Specifically, this study impacts the definition of poetic inquiry (i.e., as a method, methodology and tool) through identifying its current and potential functions as it relates to gathering data (e.g., poet-researcher or participant created research poetry and/or field note poetry). The study also highlights how poetic inquiry can act as a method for analyzing data (e.g., using such techniques as the creation of found poetry or using poetic devices to highlight and make sense of language and meaning) and shows how poetic inquiry can facilitate the sharing of data/findings in diverse ways (e.g., sharing transcript poetry or co-constructed poetry). This is but a fraction of the approaches and practices accessible through the tenets of poetic inquiry that are discussed and illustrated in this study.

Poetic inquiry functions not only as a set of methods for approaching research, but also as a methodology (that is the rationale behind the research and the perspective that the study is undertaken from). Through the use of poetic inquiry, the poet/researcher is able to make purposeful choices that highlight participants' voices and exemplify their lived experiences in the most authentic and visceral ways possible. Data (written accounts, recordings of interviews, field notes, relevant information or knowledge that supports the study) is collected with an understanding that poetry will be used in the study in some capacity, be it in the data/information gathering, analysis and/or dissemination. This changes the perspective of the researcher in that they must also see through the lens of a poet, noting detail and nuance that may have gone unnoticed. This changes the perspective of the poet in that they must attend to rigour by ensuring that the research has purpose and merit.

As a standalone methodology, poetic inquiry simultaneously applies the sensibilities, creativity and linguistic capabilities of a poet with the criticality and rigour of a researcher. This sees each element of the research considered through dual lenses and influences the choices that are made before, during and after the study. As a co-methodological approach, poetic inquiry can also support studies that adopt phenomenological approaches that are focused on particular phenomena or lived experiences, because they provide a way to more viscerally explore and analyze data. It is useful when using an ethnographic research approach to explore culture, society and belief systems as the creation of poetry can draw out meaning in diverse ways while not requiring that the researcher assimilate the voice(s) of their participants in their findings. Poetic inquiry is also useful in studies that adopt a grounded theory or an inquiry-based methodology, where the researcher nimbly adapts facets of the study as more is revealed and creates new ways to generate knowledge. Poetry functions as a reflective and reflexive outlet for the researcher to make sense of events and/or data which can support their decision making as it relates to the direction of the study. This opens the door for adapted qualitative methods that will no doubt enhance studies and provide richer findings that can solve problems and add to what we know about topics across the disciplines.

In relation to teaching, this study highlights ways that poetic inquiry can be used in curriculum development and in the delivery of lessons. Poetry can be used to highlight terms or concepts in readings that can be broken down into manageable chunks for analysis. It can also support the writing process by way of providing students an outlet for idea generation and concept mapping. Moreover, poetic inquiry has a focus on experiential writing that can be adopted in the classroom where students are encouraged to explore their ideas through poetic forms prior to writing to specific academic forms, e.g., the expository essay. This again draws on the notion of using art for meaning-making purposes.

Contribution to Knowledge

This research contributes to the naming and framing of poetic inquiry as a valuable research method and qualitative methodology within the larger framework of arts-based research methods. It furthers the use of the umbrella term "poetic inquiry" (common noun) to describe all research that uses poetry as an integral part of the research or inquiry processes undertaken by scholars. This was done by first highlighting the groundwork done by Prendergast's (2009), whose vox categories highlight the diverse ways that scholars had and were using poetry in their studies, and the subsequent work of James (2017) who seeks to chart the dynamic ways that the term has appeared and been used across the disciplines over the last many decades. This study builds on their contributions by further exploring and drawing attention to publications, across the disciplines, that employ poetic practices that contribute to the rhizomatic network of poetic inquiry. These publications, I argue, should include the terminology "poetic inquiry" in order to provide greater access to the knowledge that was unearthed using poetry in the research process. Using diverse terminology to explore specific approaches is valuable, however, I believe that it is integral to use the common noun form of "poetic inquiry" akin to how researchers connect their unique studies to larger constructs (e.g., case studies, ethnographies, narrative studies). In addition to propagating the use of poetic inquiry to connect the innumerable poetic approaches within it, this study contributes to understanding what poetic inquiry is and how it functions in qualitative research studies. It highlights that it is both a method and methodology that is purposefully used to add depth and meaning to studies. This finding was ascertained by undertaking an in-depth study that includes close textual analyses and interviews of four major poetic inquiry scholars in Canada. This provides first-hand reports of poetic inquiry applications in their research and scholarship that, when compared to the knowledge in the literature and analyses, reveals further insights into their poetic-academic approaches and products that, despite the notable careers and publications of these impactful scholars, did not fully exist in the literature.

This study has also drawn attention to ways that poetic inquiry uses aesthetics for epistemological purposes. Through poetry, meaning is created and/or revealed to the researcher and to the reader. It may also appeal to the research participant as they craft poetry or explore the researcher's subjective interpretations of the knowledge that was shared during the research process. This can yield multiple understandings that, when combined, create an even clearer understanding of the topic or lived experience. The poetry is at once literary, appealing to emotions and visceral senses as a form of art, while simultaneously remaining cognitive and epistemological as the poem creates or deciphers meaning for the poet and audience/readership. A reader may at first grasp the artistic intentions of the poet (through their linguistic and aesthetic choices), they may understand the epistemological purposes therein (using those same choices) or they may tacitly experience both at the same time. They may also have to revisit the poem with purposefulness, aiming to affectively experience the art or they may endeavour to unearth the levels of meaning that exist in its carefully crafted lines. This affords the reader multiple ways of experiencing the poem and diverse ways of drawing from the knowledge therein.

This study has also increased the visibility and accessibility of poetic inquiry as a methodology by presenting it as a critical approach to research that at once merges the sensibilities of a poet with those of a researcher. It highlights ways that scholars e/affectively use the methodology for research to yield new understandings while accentuating a variety of entry points for those who may have an interest in using it as part of their research practices. This, I believe, will be especially helpful for undergraduate and graduate students who do not feel that they can answer their research questions by engaging solely and squarely through other qualitative methods. Poetic inquiry offers them diverse ways to use creativity as part of their studies to elevate how they go about their research practices and provides a richness to their findings that new researchers would not have accessed due to their perceived limits of other methodologies.

This study also provides a unique contribution to our knowledge of poetic inquiry and its functions by trialing close analyses of the poetic approaches and products of poetic inquiry scholars. Through close reading, this study exemplifies a way to acquire further knowledge from poetic inquiry products. It supports an understanding of poetics on a structural level and how using poetry for academic purposes functions as a way to generate a greater understanding of the lived experience of the participant(s) or concept(s) explored in the poetry on an epistemological level. This knowledge may have remained untapped without a close analysis of the participants' poetry. This trialed analysis yields a deeper understanding that may also serve as a call to the poetic inquiry community to begin analyzing the poetic products found historically in the literature, as well as analyzing new products that are seeking publication. This practice could potentially exhume hidden knowledge that can further poetic inquiry practices in research and scholarship. It will also enhance what we know about topics across the disciplines.

Limitations

This study has limitations in that it draws from a small participant pool. The participants were purposefully selected based on a previous awareness of their involvement in education and in Canadian poetic inquiry and scholarship which has close ties to the International Symposium on Poetic Inquiry. Also, two of the participants, Monica and Pauline, were graduate students of Dr. Carl Leggo which adds to some of the homogeneity of the group. This then limits much of the study to the work being done by a small sub-group of the larger poetic inquiry community in Canada. Yet, by the same token, poetic inquiry is about finding truths (plural) and not about identifying an absolute truth. This study highlights their experiences and truths with an aim to learn more about what poetic inquiry is and what it can do. Moreover, given the scope of the study, it also does not explore in-depth, beyond the literature review, poetic inquiry studies being done around the world by non-Canadian scholars or scholars whose work extends far beyond education-related fields. All four participants in this study are teachers and teacher educators in, or closely associated with, the Faculties of Education in Canada. While the study includes both male and female participants and those who identify as part of diverse cultural or ethnic communities, including BIPOC and/or the 2SLGBTQ+ community, the small number of participants did not include representatives from other communities, including representatives from all of Canada's provinces and territories. While each participant of this study is not currently teaching in institutions where they grew up, adding greater Canadian representation in some respects, there is a lack of representation as it relates to all facets of Canada's diverse cultural diaspora. How scholars in Nunavut approach teaching and use poetry no doubt differs from that of scholars in southern Manitoba. Gaining viewpoints from scholars across the country would add a further richness to the study and add to what is known about poetry's use in research and scholarship.

Future Research

While the scope of this research sees the study limited to a small group of Canadian, or Canadian-based educational scholars, it does however create a foundation that can be used for future research. This study, even with the findings relating to a small subset of the larger poetic inquiry community in Canada, can potentially be used to compare common characteristics of poetic inquiry scholars in Canada to other poetic inquiry scholars in the world. It can also be used, with the creation of poetic profiles and an understanding of how these participants use the functions of poetry to show voice, to further the understanding of the impacts of poetry in qualitative research studies. This is of particular note as it relates to the authentic representation of participants voices and lived experiences. There is also room to explore ways that the creation of poetry or the use of poetic representation of others voices and experiences can further elevate other research methods, such as case studies, narrative inquiry studies and phenomenological studies as they relate to data gathering, data analysis and data dissemination.

Facets of this study can also foreground a deeper examination of poetic inquiry's uses in curriculum development. This study has shown how poetry permeates all facets of the participants' lives and has provided insights into some of their teaching approaches and purposes. In my own experience, I draw parallels between poetic inquiry, with its emphasis on voice and multiple means of creating or interpreting (which connects with John's use of poetry as a support for teachers' identity development and Pauline's use of poetry as a form of making), and the tenets of Universal Design for Learning (UDL) (CAST, 2018). UDL is a framework that posits the idea that in order to reach learners with their preferred learning styles (Fleming & Mills, 1992) and multiple intelligences (Gardner, 1993), that a lesson or assignment should use a variety of techniques for engagement, representation and action, and expression (which also has echoes of Pauline's Parallaxic Praxis model, 2019). Poetic inquiry is reflected in the tenets of UDL. Through the need for the work to engage with an audience in a way that prosaic writing cannot do; poetic inquiry seeks diverse ways to represent ideas (through poetic forms and performative elements) and asks the poet or in the case of UDL, the student, to express what they have learned. With a paradigm shift occurring in many Canadian school systems, pushing away from an exclusive focus on prescriptive writing practices, poetic inquiry then functions a valuable tool for both teachers and students as they work together to strengthen students' language arts/writing skills. There appears to be further aspects to be explored in this and other areas of curriculum development that this study could support.

A final area that I believe this study has foregrounded relates to the analysis of poetic inquiry products by researchers in the poetic inquiry community, their own poetry or that of others through a close reading approach. Currently, this practice is never done. There is a generative practice, where poetry is being used in the research process and the products are shared but there lacks a wealth of deep analysis of their poetic products. This may be, as noted in the literature review, due to what Denzin and Lincoln (2011) describe as a "crisis of representation" in qualitative research (p. 3). Perhaps there is trepidation that through analysis the representation of lived experience will become hotly scientific or without feeling. Yet, the trialed methods exemplified in this study have potentially proven otherwise. Through the exemplification of a close reading practice, I was able to more e/affectively understand how and why the poems were crafted and garner a much deeper understanding and appreciation of the functions of poetry and the lived experiences shared therein. Analysis of this nature did not take away from the poetry, it added to it. Should others take up this practice and build on it, I believe that there is an abundance of knowledge to potentially uncover across the disciplines and an opportunity to develop a much-needed approach to delve more deeply into poetic inquiry products. These products are not only literary, they are research and, as such, they need a different treatment.

Poetic inquiry is far-reaching and actively in use across the disciplines. This study supports further avenues to use it, with its unique functions and purposes, in research and scholarship. This study of poetic inquiry and ways that some of its practitioners use it in their research approaches reveals that it is a research method, methodology and/or tool that is actively pushing the boundaries of arts-based research approaches, thereby bolstering the quality of contemporary qualitative research. It highlights the power that language has to impact knowledge creation and mobilization processes, thereby challenging the researcher to be conscious of their language use and its inferences as it relates to how they share their findings. Poetic inquiry also actively functions as a way to amplify the voices of others which has implications for anti-racist pedagogy, equitable and inclusive research practices and fair representation.

Concluding Thoughts on The Study

Poetic inquiry in Canadian research and scholarship is diverse at best. Yet, cohesion exists through poetic inquiry scholars' creation of poetry as ways to generate or identify knowledge and improve the lives of those who engage with it. Whether it is through creating more vivid and visceral (re)presentations of their research participants' voices or lived experiences, lessening the distance between information and understanding, using language to better know themselves as people and poets in the academy, or in using poetry to support the development of students' academics and/or identity, these poet-academics have personified key characteristics of what poetic inquiry is and what it can do that no other genre or approach can as e/affectively do.

I began this journey many years ago with little awareness of what I was doing as a novice poet-researcher. It was tacit. I was also ill-aware of the untapped power of poetic inquiry that was within my reach for conducting research due to limited exposure through standard methods texts (e.g., Creswell, 2013) in my undergraduate studies and a portion of my graduate studies. I knew at an early age that poetry did something for Zack Morris to get the attention of Kelly Kopowski. I knew that Shakespeare's lyrical language held power for me. I knew that I loved music and that writing my own poetry was an act of catharsis and initial sense-making of life events. What I was not yet aware of was the ways that I would tap into poetry, inquiry and language to create new knowledge, to delve into concepts and to articulate my own thoughts and experiences, let alone do justice to the experiences and voices of others. Through this study, and through interacting with the participants in this study, I can now say that, like them, I am "living poetically" (Leggo, 2005).

I now know, through my scholarly effort to understand more about poetic inquiry, that poetry, the foundation of poetic inquiry, functions in research as a way to use language (crafting art) to assemble knowledge (linking to epistemology), make sense of it and share it, viscerally, with others. This is unlike any other research method or tool that I have found. Other research methods ask that the researcher gather data ethically and accurately, analyze it and validate it, and coherently express the findings to others. Poetic inquiry requires another level on top of those skills and an awareness of qualitative research standards as the poet-researcher is asked to have greater dexterity with language to share their findings in e/affective ways. Poetic language and poetic devices can explicitly deliver a message or provide an opportunity to imply multiple levels of meaning in one expression. This then appeals to the pragmatic sensibilities of some and the creative sensibilities of others, depending upon how the poem is constructed and read.

I have also come to recognize how a poem provides a unique opportunity for polyphonic voices to be heard: the participant (or original author, if in the form of literature-voiced poems), the poet-researcher and the reader. This is unlike any other research method, including other arts-based methods, as the choices made in crafting the poem by the poet-researcher do not seek to marginalize the voice of their participant, but have them simultaneously ever-present in the construction of meaning. The reader chooses how to further interpret the poem, following the poet's intent that is made evident through such techniques as line breaks, enjambment and capitalization, or they can read it more prosaically (rapidly moving from line to line) to ascertain meaning. This sees the choices of the poet-researcher as potentially higher stakes than that of prose-based approaches. Verbatim quotations, in the context of the poem, have additional or fewer layers depending on where and how they appear in a poem. This therefore requires that the poet-researcher have the ability to look at the poem on a micro (word and line) and macro (whole poem and its relation to the data and research questions) level. Further, the poet cannot hide behind third-person expressions, even if they choose to use them, as their voice is present as the creator of the poem. This holds a unique degree of power and vulnerability that is unmatched in other research approaches. The poet's choices around imagery, where how they describe their experiences or the lived experiences of others through poetic language and devices, can dramatically impact understanding, alter inference and potentially make or break the study.

Through closely analyzing the poetry of the participants of this study, through pausing to analyze what they do in the construction of their poetry, through considering how poetry functions and through ruminating on why they do it, I was able to appreciate their poetry and its impacts on the study and the reader at a deeper level. Poetry has the capacity to take a simplified expression and embody it in a way that gives it substance or weight. This brings a richness to the research that may not be present through other approaches. Poetry can function in research as a way to bring lived experience(s) and/or data to life by drawing the researcher and the reader closer to the findings of the study. This provides a way to answer questions with affective impact. This study has given me a fulsome understanding of the current functions of poetic inquiry in research, where the poem is dually an aesthetic expression and a valuable form of data, and where it is or can go in qualitative research.

In addition to research, poetic inquiry also influences how teaching is and can be approached. Curriculum, as evidenced in the examples of the participants, can be adapted to include poetry as a method for knowledge creation, rumination, or dissemination. Poetic inquiry can also be more readily framed by educators as a useful and insightful approach to scholarly research. Currently, poetic inquiry is only brought to the attention of some graduate students and, as noted previously, is often omitted in major qualitative methods textbooks. Should there be a shift in how poetic inquiry is viewed, there is a potentiality for more students and researchers to use it as a mode of inquiry. Lastly, as it relates to teaching, poetic inquiry can support the formation of teacher identity by providing a critical medium to express and process emotions and give teachers a place to consider their reflexivity between their roles as educators and their students.

I believe that the researcher, teacher or reader can never fully know what others experience, but through the marrying of poetry with inquiry there is an opportunity to more viscerally understand facets of their lived experience and find ways to bridge the gap between the speaker and the receiver, the teacher and the student, the researcher, the researched and the audience. Through a greater understanding of poetic inquiry and poetry's unique functions in research, there is an opportunity to draw attention to issues and work towards solving significant problems in ways not widely in use. This not only means employing diverse poetic inquiry approaches currently in use in qualitative research, as outlined in the literature review and highlighted through a close examination of the practices of the participants, but also adopting approaches to analyzing poetic products (as exemplified in this study). Poetic inquiry's unique attributes and unparalleled functions, combining art and epistemology across a vast disciplinary network of rhizomes, as described and explored in this study and as shared in this book, see it not only as an impactful research method or methodology in its own right. It also exists as a valuable tool that can enrich teaching and strengthen qualitative research as we know it.

Study Postscript
(Adam Vincent)

I thought I saw you before.
I really did.
I read your lines,
lapping up your lyricality,
mesmerized by your metaphors,
seeing your similes,
following your found poetry,
smiling at your stories
causing me to re-think research.

But now,
I see you.
I really see you.
I see what you are doing.
Cunningly crafting comprehension,
unmasking meaning meticulously
by blending *research*and*art*
leaving me   lingering in liminal spaces
where I see   the specifics
where I feel   the facts of life
beyond the   confines of the page.

I thought I heard you.
I really did.
I said, "That can't be anyone but Carl,
Must be Monica,
Just rings of John
Has the peal of Pauline's poetry,"
yet I heard through unintentionally muffled ears.

But now,
I hear you.
I really hear you.
Your voice,
through choice,
is polyphonic.
Seeking to harmonize,
not harm the meaning of others;
not simply storytelling,
with your tonality,
but enlivening lived experience

to lessen the margins
to add meaning
and
spur change.

I see and I hear:
Your love for language, living poetically,
as an exemplar of a life well lived.
Your tactfully tenacious push for voices
and experiences to be represented, humanizing research and art.
Your ever-metamorphizing identity and storied vulnerability, making room,
showing others how to take risks and fly.
Your spotlighting of others' ideas,
illuminated brighter by your presence as dialogic interpreter, adding to what is known.

I now see for myself
>	the power of poetry,
>	functioning as
>	method and methodology,
>	research and poetry
>	art and epistemology
>	craft and tool.

I will use it more deftly.
I will show others.
I will tell others.
I will continue to look and hear.

Chapter 10
Epilogue, Post-Study Rumination on Theory and Findings

In the following chapter, I offer my thoughts on the study approximately six months after the final copy of the findings of my study, the dissertation, was approved by my university. This takes on the form of a rumination, a discussive chewing on thoughts and ideas, as it relates to the concept of a singular theory of poetic inquiry and where I see the applications of poetic inquiry on cross-disciplinary and global scales.

Does Poetic Inquiry Have a Theory?

Since the completion of this study, I have been asked by colleagues and other interested parties to define the theory of poetic inquiry. After years of research into what poetic inquiry is, does and what it can do, it seems logical to think that I have the answer. I do have an answer, but it is not the expected answer.

Poetic inquiry, with its seemingly infinite rhizomatic existence, appears across the disciplines and in diverse forms (as in Chapter 2). Whether it is in Richardson's (1993a) poetic transcription that is emulated and adapted across the social sciences (Butler-Kisber, 2002), Prendergast's (2004, 2006) approaches to finding more in found poetry being applied in educational contexts, Guiney-Yallop and Shields (2016) use of poetry for identity work, Cutts' (2020) adaptations to Faulkner's ars poetica (2007; 2019) being used to delve more deeply into lived experiences of Black women, Sameshima and Vandermause's (2008) inclusion of poetry within the parallaxic praxis research model, or Leggo's (2015) lasting request that everyone considers the value in living poetically, poetry is growing. I contend that there is no singular, bounded, theoretical underpinning related to poetic inquiry studies. As my study highlighted, and what I have unearthed in the reflective process since, is that poetic inquiry connects the poet-researcher to diverse theories, perspectives and applications; it has no discernable centre and thereby it lacks an absolute, singular theory that can be applied across the spectrum of studies. Further, proponents and scholars of poetic inquiry, most identifying as artists, do not wish to impose a singular view on what poetic inquiry should be or it loses some of its power and some of its subjective e/affectiveness for knowing and generating understanding through art. And yet, as poetic inquirers, alongside the artist's desire to not restrict, comes the researcher's intent to learn, to expand or to clarify, and to inform.

This calling to use poetry to discover, inform, and share various, subjective, approaches with other people sets it apart. It is also why the literature framed in/about poetic inquiry includes texts that offer diverse ideas or exemplify multiple ways to engage in/through poetry. These include, as mentioned in Chapters 2 and 3, the likes of Faulkner (2007; 2016a; 2016b; 2019; 2020), Owton (2017), and Leavy (2018) who give examples of how they go about crafting their research poetry. Faulkner (2020), for example, guides her reader through one of her found poem creation processes where she explains how for one poem she "used an online Diastic Poem generator [which] required a source text and a seed text" as a way to generate and "retrieve six usable poems" (pp. 147-148). She not only explains how she generated the poems but shares the final poetic product with the reader. Throughout her book, Faulkner (2020) gives numerous examples for how she approaches poetic inquiry, thereby offering ways for others to begin their own explorations.

There are many other journal articles or books found in the literature where poet-researchers offer up how they went about their research that includes the use or creation of poetry in some way, shape or form (see Chapter 2). These may have deep and rich descriptions or guides for how to engage with the poetry or may simply discuss their rationale behind the creation of their poetry. There is no explicit requirement for this element to be included in a study or dissemination of its findings, yet it is often offered up as a way of sharing the creative-analytical process and moving back the metaphorical curtain for others. There is not, as noted, a single way to use poetry for research purposes.

Back to the Original Question: Does Poetic Inquiry Have a Theory?

Yes, it does. Yet, the theory of poetic inquiry that I have unearthed and sought to clarify in this book is somewhat paradoxical. It is not a singular theory but instead a purposeful use of poetry that connects to a rhizomatic array of practices, traditions and approaches from diverse fields and disciplines. Poetry is used to connect, discover, create and/or access previously untapped knowledge.

To use a metaphor, the theory of poetic inquiry is a stanza of poetry. Depending upon who writes the poem, each stanza could have varied line length, placement on the page, use of metaphors, similes, enjambment, concrete imagery, rhyme, meter, capitalization, and the like. By the same vein, depending upon who is using poetic inquiry, why they are using it and what they are connecting with on the rhizomatic array accessed through poetic inquiry, their theoretical framework will differ. The consistency, of course, is the creation or use of poetry within the scope of the research.

It should be noted, however, that being rhizomatic does not mean that poetic inquiry is a disordered and chaotic approach, quite the contrary (as explored in Chapter 3). Poetic inquiry requires that the poet-researcher have significant experience and knowledge of poetry, poetic form and poetic devices while also having an aptitude and understanding of research and research traditions. They have to appropriately combine those two sensibilities tactfully and purposefully or they risk having their study fail or be overlooked as a valuable piece of scholarship. The rhizomes afford opportunities, but the artistry and rigour (again, returning to the notion that there must be appropriate representation of each) of all elements of the study, including the creation or use of the theory, falls on the ingenuity of the poet-researcher.

Further Explorations and Applications in Poetic Inquiry and Across the Disciplines

As I discuss in the study, and that which has been further confirmed in the months of reflection and discussion since its completion, I believe that the exemplified use of close reading and the creation of a poetics (see Chapter 3) to help to analyze what makes poetic inquiry unique will support future poetic inquiry research and qualitative research processes. This is a new way to look at poetic products from studies, beyond their generative uses, which helped me to create greater understandings of the poem's content, creation and uses within the context of the study (the research element) while adding to my appreciation of them as a form of art (the poetic element). I see this as a useful artistic-epistemological practice to use in future poetic inquiry studies, further explicating what was learned in/through poetry, and a useful practice to consider when looking at studies retroactively as I believe there remains more knowledge to unearth in the literature.

The study also re-affirmed that poetic inquiry can function as a way, or tool, to access further depths or understand further breadth in qualitative research across the disciplines, be it as a standalone approach or method or interwoven with other research approaches (see Appendix). For example, a case study could use poetic fieldnotes (see Chapter 9) or poetic transcript analysis or participant created poetry (guided or otherwise). Further, a phenomenological study may use clusters of metaphors to explain a phenomenon or group like findings, or participant created poetry may be used in a study about common identity traits of biologists who work in the Amazon rainforest, or poetry may be used to explore and explain theories in physics or math or concepts from diverse philosophies may be woven together to create new understandings through poetry. The rhizomatic array that poetic inquiry connects to and how a poet-researcher chooses to engage in the research (method/methodology) affords seemingly infinite opportunities.

This study has highlighted some of those opportunities and has used a Canadian context as a starting place to begin unearthing the rhizomes and to show others ways to unearth more (or differently) in their own research contexts, yet there remains a need to look at the use of poetic inquiry on a global scale. What similarities and differences exist? Where are the connections? Since the completion of my study, I have had conversations with colleagues from around the world, including those from India, South Africa (noting that Cape Town will be home to the 8th offering of the ISPI in May of 2022), USA, Europe and China, who are interested in either learning about poetic inquiry for the first time or who are interested in discussing how they can better unify their work as poets with their scholarly endeavours. I see this as a positive step towards exhuming and examining even more of the rhizomatic array.

Closing Thoughts

By reviewing the literature, speaking with poet-researchers (and teachers) who use poetry in their academic activities and in their personal lives, exploring their writing through close reading and creating a poetics as a way to identify similarities and differences, borrowing techniques from more traditional streams of qualitative research and combining them with poetic approaches, I feel like I have a greater understanding of poetic inquiry; its purposes, its nuances and its power both in education and beyond.

The metaphor of the rhizome to explain connectivity existed before I came to it (e.g., Irwin et al., 2006) as did the notion of poetic inquiry residing in the liminal spaces between disciplines and approaches (Sinner et al., 2006), yet I believe that I have added further dimension and clarity to those ideas. I have identified that the theory of poetic inquiry is not singular, it is instead paradoxical in that it connects the poet-researcher to various perspectives, traditions and approaches on the rhizomatic array, the caveat being that there must be an inquiry made and poetry must be used as at least one element of the research process. This is a definition that does not currently exist in the literature. My hope is that providing a more focused understanding of poetic inquiry and its diversified theorical underpinnings provides new ways to consider and to approach poetic inquiry across the disciplines. Those who choose to use poetic inquiry can draw from the now more visible rhizomatic array, with concrete examples and insights from notable scholars in the field, yet they must continue to do so purposefully and carefully, attending to both artistry and rigour.

The Array of Rhythms
(Adam Vincent)

> Poetic inquiry is not for the faint of heart
> whose rhythms must always coincide with another's
> lub-dub, lub-dub—
> instead opting for sporadic bursts of beats
> sustained rhythms of excitement
> and
> glee, immediately brought down in meter

for the moment
called for reflective pause
for a word
or
metaphor
not easily seen at a sprint.

The dusty tomes of days of yore
do call out
in necessity of understanding their meaning
then, now and implied if used
in a certain light
and
shadow that could undermine
or
refine knowing.

I must seek out more
in the array—
taking me from philosophy
to applied theory
to semantics
to hermeneutics
to stories from friends
to research journals
to conferences where on the surface I don't belong
espousing on ways that a poem gave insight
into others' lifetime fields—
looking only to share the light
looking for the shared love in knowing
how my heart can take the varied pace
of being in no place
yet a rhizomatic space of everywhere
the paradox
of being
poet-researcher-teacher
unearthing earthly delights
of knowing
risk
and
reward
exist on a <u>fine line</u>.
I reach with each beat
for the latter.

References

ABER SIG. (n.d.). In Arts-based Educational Research (ABER). http://www.abersig.com/

AERA. (2020). In American Educational Research Association. http://www.aera.net/

Allsopp, R. (2015). To step, leap, fly: On poetics and performance. *Performance Research - A Journal of Performing Arts, 20*(1), 1-3.

Anderson, C., & MacCurdy, M. (2000). *Writing and healing: toward an informed practice.* National Council of Teachers of English.

Apol, L. (2017). Writing poetry in Rwanda: A means for better listening, understanding, processing, and responding. *Journal of Poetry Therapy, 30*(2), 71-13. https://doi.org/10.1080/08893675.2017.1266188

Art/Research International. (2020). In *Art/Research International: A Transdisciplinary Journal.* https://ejournals.library.ualberta.ca/index.php/ari

ARTS. (n.d.). In Arts Researchers and Teachers Society. http://artssig.wixsite.com/artssig

Barone, T. (2001). Science, art, and the predispositions of educational researchers. *Educational Researcher, 30*(7), 24-28. https://doi.org/10.3102/0013189X030007024

Barone, T. (1995). The purposes of arts-based educational research. *International Journal of Educational Research, 23*(2), 169-180. https://doi.org/10.1016/0883-0355(95)91500-G

Black, C., & Enos, R. (1981). Using phenomenology in clinical social work: A poetic pilgrimage. *Clinical Social Work Journal, 9*(1), pp. 34-43. https://doi.org/10.1007/BF0075709

Black, M. (1944). Education as art and discipline. *Ethics, 54*(4), 290-294.

Bleicher, J. (1980). *Contemporary Hermeneutics: Hermeneutics as Method, Philosophy and Critique* (1st ed.). Routledge. https://doi.org/10.4324/9781315112558

Bloom, H. (1973). *The anxiety of influence: A theory of poetry* (2nd ed.). Oxford University Press.

Bochner, A. P. (2000). Criteria against ourselves. *Qualitative Inquiry, 6*(2), 266-272. https://doi.org/10.1177/107780040000600209

Boland, R. (1991). Information system use as a hermeneutic process. In Nissen, H., Klein, H. & Hirschheim, R. (Eds.), *Information Systems Research: Contemporary Approaches and Emergent Traditions* (pp. 439-464). North-Holland Elsevier Science Publishers.

Brady, I. (1991). *Anthropological poetics.* Rowman & Littlefield.

Brady, I. (2004). In defense of the sensual: Meaning construction in ethnography and poetics. *Qualitative Inquiry, 10*(4), 622-644. https://doi.org/10.1177/1077800404265719

Broudy, H. S. (1972; 1994). *Enlightened cherishing: An essay on aesthetic education.* University of Illinois Press.

Brown, S. L., & Melear, C. T. (2006). Investigation of secondary science teachers' beliefs and practices after authentic inquiry-based experiences: Science teacher professional continuum. *Journal of Research in Science Teaching, 43*(9), 938-962.

Butler-Kisber, L. (2002). Artful portrayals in qualitative inquiry: The road to found poetry and beyond. *Alberta Journal of Educational Research, 48*(3), 229-238.

Butler-Kisber, L. (2017). *Lynn Butler-Kisber defines poetic inquiry* [Streaming video]. SAGE Research Methods. http://methods.sagepub.com/video/lynn-butler-kisber-defines-poetic-inquiry

Butler-Kisber, L., Guiney Yallop, J. J., F, M. & Wiebe, S. (2017). *Poetic inquiries of reflection and renewal: Poetry as research.* MacIntyre Purcell Publishing Inc.

Cahnmann, M. (2003). The craft, practice, and possibility of poetry in educational research. *Educational Researcher, 32*(3), 29-36.

Carroll, P., Dew, K., & Howden-Chapman, P. (2011). The heart of the matter: Using poetry as a method of ethnographic inquiry to represent and present experiences of the informally housed in Aotearoa/New Zealand. *Qualitative Inquiry, 17*(7), 623- 630.

Carruth, H. (1948). The poet with wounds. *Poetry, 71*(4), 217-221.

CAST (2018). *Universal Design for Learning Guidelines version 2.2.* http://udl guidelines.cast.org

Charmaz, K. (2017) Constructivist grounded theory, *The Journal of Positive Psychology, 12*(3), 299-300. https://doi.org/10.1080/17439760.2016.1262612

Christianakis, M. (2011). Hybrid texts: Fifth graders, rap music, and writing. *Urban Education, 46*(5), 1131-1168. https://doi.org/10.1177/0042085911400326

Creswell, J. W. (2013). *Qualitative inquiry and research design: Choosing among five approaches* (3rd ed.). SAGE Publications.

CSSE. (n.d.). In Canadian Society for the Study of Education. https://csse-scee.ca/

Cutts, Q. M. (2019). "...Love me": A found poem exploring black Women's romantic relationships. *Qualitative Inquiry, 25*(9-10), 1123-1127. https://doi.org/10.1177/10 77800418809735

Cutts, Q. M. (2020). More than craft and criteria: The necessity of Ars Spirituality in (Black women's) poetic inquiry and research poetry. *Qualitative Inquiry, 26*(7), 908-919. https://doi.org/10.1177/1077800419884966

De Cosson, A., & Irwin, R. L. (2004). *A/r/tography: Rendering self through arts-based living inquiry.* Pacific Educational Press.

De La Lama, L. (2014). *Creating a mythopoeic graphic novel to expand self-understanding.* (Unpublished doctoral dissertation). University of Florida. http://scholarcommons.usf.edu/etd/5622

Deleuze, G., & Guattari, F. (1988). *A thousand plateaus: Capitalism and schizophrenia.* Bloomsbury Publishing.

Denzin, N. K. & Lincoln, Y. S. (2011). Introduction: The discipline and practice of qualitative research. In N.K. Denzin & Y.S. Lincoln (Eds.) *The Sage handbook of qualitative research* (pp. 1-20). Sage.

DeShazer, M. K. (1986). *Inspiring women: Reimagining the muse.* Perganon.

De Vito, J., & Johnston, L. J. (2017). *Lifting hearts off the ground: Declaring indigenous rights in poetry.* Mennonite Church Canada.

Dobson, M. L. (2012). Poetic inquiry. *The International Journal of the Arts in Society: Annual Review, 6*(5), 129-138. https://doi.org/10.18848/1833-1866/CGP/v06i05/36 082

Downey, H. (2016). Poetic inquiry, consumer vulnerability: Realities of quadriplegia. *Journal of Marketing Management. 32*(3-4), 357-364. https://doi.org/10.1080/0267257X.2015.1103301

Eiseley, L. C. (1972). *Notes of an alchemist.* Scribner.

Eisner, E. W. (1991). *The enlightened eye.* Macmillan.

Eisner, E. W. (1997). The promise and perils of alternative forms of data representation. *Educational Researcher, 26*(6), 4-10. https://doi.org/10.2307/1176961

Elbelazi, S. A., & Alharbi, L. (2020). The "exotic other": A poetic autoethnography of two Muslim teachers in higher education. *Qualitative Inquiry, 26*(6), 661-666. https://doi.org/10.1177/1077800419843943

Ellis, C. (1999). Heartful autoethnography. *Qualitative Health Research, 9*(5), 669-683. https://doi.org/10.1177/104973299129122153

Faulkner, S. (2007). Concern with craft: Using Ars Poetica as criteria for reading research poetry. *Qualitative Inquiry, 13*(2), 218-234. https://doi.org/10.1177/1077800406295636

Faulkner, S. (2016a). *Poetry as method: Reporting research through verse.* Taylor & Francis eBooks. https://doi.org/10.4324/9781315422411

Faulkner, S. (2016b). The art of criteria: Ars criteria as demonstration of vigor in poetic inquiry. *Qualitative Inquiry, 22*(8), 662-665. https://doi.org/10.1177/1077800416634739

Faulkner, S. (2018). Crank up the feminism: Poetic inquiry as feminist methodology. *Humanities (Basel), 7*(3), 85. https://doi.org/10.3390/h7030085

Faulkner, S. (2019). Poetic Inquiry: Craft, method and practice. (2nd ed. Routledge. https://doi.org/10.4324/9781351044233

Faulkner, S. (2020). Poetic Inquiry: Craft, method and practice. (2nd ed.). Routledge.

Federico, A. (2016). *Engagements with close reading.* Routledge. https://doi.org/10.4324/9781315757759

Fels, L. (2012). Collecting data through performative inquiry: A tug on the sleeve. *Youth Theatre Journal, 26*(1), pp. 50-60. https://doi.org/10.1080/08929092.2012.678209

Fels, L., & Belliveau, G. A. (2008). *Exploring curriculum: Performative inquiry, role drama, and learning.* Pacific Educational Press.

Fels, L., Leggo, C., Martin, R. E. & Korchinski, M. (2014). In Martin R. E., Korchinski M. (Eds.), *Arresting hope: Women taking action in prison health inside out.* Inanna Publications and Education Inc.

Fernández-Giménez, M. E., Jennings, L. B., & Wilmer, H. (2018). Poetic inquiry as a research and engagement method in natural resource science. *Society & Natural Resources, 32* (10), 1-12. https://doi.org/10.1080/08941920.2018.1486493

Fleming, N.D. & Mills, C. (1992). Not another inventory, rather a catalyst for reflection. *To Improve the Academy, 11,* 137-155.

Flores, T. (1982). Field poetry. *Anthropology and Humanism Quarterly, 7*(1), 16-22.

Fox, N., & Alldred, P. (2015) New materialist social inquiry: designs, methods and the research-assemblage. *International Journal of Social Research Methodology, 18* (4), 399-414. https://doi.org/10.1080/13645579.2014.921458

Furman, R. (2004). Using poetry and narrative as qualitative data: Exploring a father's cancer through poetry. *Families, Systems, & Health, 22*(2), 162-710.

Furman, R. (2014). Beyond the literary uses of poetry: A class for university freshmen. *Journal of Poetry Therapy, 27*(4), 205-211. https://doi.org/10.1080/08893675.2014.949521

Furman, R., & Cavers, S. (2005). A narrative poem as a source of qualitative data. *The Arts in Psychotherapy, 32*(4), 313-317. https://doi.org/10.1016/j.aip.2005.02.004

Furman, R., Lietz, C., & Langer, C. L. (2006). The research poem in international social work: Innovations in qualitative methodology. *The International Journal of Qualitative Methods, 5*(4), 24-34.

Galvin, K. T., Prendergast, M., & Biley, F. C. (2016). *Poetic inquiry II: Seeing, caring, understanding: Using poetry as and for inquiry.* Sense Publishers.

Gardner, H. (1993). *Frames of mind: The theory of multiple intelligences.* BasicBooks.

Gee, J. P. (1989). The narrativization of experience in the oral style. *Journal of Education, 171*(1), 75-96. https://doi.org/10.1177/002205748917100106

Glesne, C. (1997). That rare feeling: Re-presenting research through poetic transcription. *Qualitative Inquiry, 3*(2), 202-221. https://doi.org10.1177/107780049700300204

Goffman, E. (1963). *Stigma: Notes on the management of spoiled identity.* Prentice-Hall.

Görlich, A. (2016). Poetic inquiry: Understanding youth on the margins of education. *International Journal of Qualitative Studies in Education, 29*(4), 520-535. https://doi.org/10.1080/09518398.2015.1063734

Grimmett, H. (2016). The problem of "just tell us": Insights from playing with poetic inquiry and dialogical self theory. *Studying Teacher Education, 12*(1), 37-54.

Guiney Yallop, J. J., & Binder, M. J. (2017). From the edges of lateness: Finding our place in the curriculum. In E. Lyle (Ed) *At the intersection of selves and subject* (pp. 153-162). Sense Publishers. https://doi.org/10.1007/978-94-6351-113-1_16

Guiney Yallop, J. J., & Shields, C. (2015). The poetics of relationship: Thinking through personal pedagogy across time using narrative inquiry and poetic inquiry. In Ng-A-Fook N., Ibrahim A. & Reis G. (Eds.), *Provoking curriculum studies: Strong poetry and arts of the possible in education* (1st ed.) (41-54). Routledge. https://doi.org/10.4324/9781315738628

GTR language workbench. (n.d.). *GTR language workbench.* http://workbench.gtrlabs.org

Hanauer, D. I. (2010). *Poetry as research: Exploring second language poetry writing.* John Benjamins Pub. Co.

Hansen, S. & Rennecker, J. (2010), Getting on the same page: collective hermeneutics in a systems development team, *Information and Organization, 20*(1), 44-63.

Hartnett, S. J. (2003). *Incarceration nation: Investigative prison poems of hope and terror.* AltaMira Press.

Hasebe-Ludt, E., Chambers, C., & Leggo, C. (2009). *Life writing and literary Métissage as an ethos for our times.* Peter Lang.

Hasebe-Ludt, E., & Leggo, C. (2016). Provoking a curricular Métissage of polyphonic textualities. *Journal of the Canadian Association for Curriculum Studies, 14*(1), 1-5. http://jcacs.journals.yorku.ca/index.php/jcacs/issue/view/2276/showToc

Heidegger, M. (1927). *Being and Time.* Harper & Row.

Hume, M. (Director) & James, K. (Composer). (2017, April). *Knowledge through eight windows: Soundscape and poetry performed.* Presentation at the Language and Literacy Graduate Conference, The University of British Columbia, Vancouver, BC, Canada.

Iivari, N. (2018). Using member checking in interpretive research practice: A hermeneutic analysis of informants' interpretation of their organizational realities. *Information Technology & People, 31*(1), 111-133. https://doi.org/10.1108/ITP-07-2016-0168

Irwin, R. L., Beer, R., Springgay, S., Grauer, K., Xiong, G., & Bickel, B. (2006). The rhizomatic relations of a/r/tography. *Studies in Art Education, 48*(1), 70-88.

Irwin, R., Sinner, A., & Hasebe-Ludt, E. (2019). *Storying the world: The contributions of Carl Leggo on language and poetry.* Taylor and Francis. https://doi.org/10.4324/9780429025600

jagodzinski, j., & Wallin, J. (2013). *Arts-based research: A critique and a proposal.* Sense Publishers. https://doi.org/10.1007/978-94-6209-185-6

James, K. (2009). Cut-up consciousness: Poetic inquiry and the spambot's text. In M. Prendergast, C. Leggo & P. Sameshima (Eds.), *Poetic inquiry: Vibrant voices in the social sciences,* 59-74. Sense Publishers.

James, K. (2017). What lovely words might also mean. In P. Sameshima, K. Fidyk, A., James, & Leggo, C. (Eds.), *Poetic inquiry: Enchantment of place* (24-26), Vernon Press.

JCACS. (2017). In *Journal of the Canadian Association of Curriculum Studies.* http://jcacs.journals.yorku.ca/index.php/jcacs/index

Juelskjaer, M. (2013). Gendered subjectivities of spacetimematter. *Gender and Education, 25,* 754–768. https://doi.org/10.1080/09540253.2013.831812

Kincheloe, J. L. (2001). Describing the bricolage: Conceptualizing a new rigor in qualitative research. *Qualitative Inquiry, 7*(6), 679-692. https://doi.org/10.1177/107780040100700601

King, A. (1995). Giving permission to embodied knowing to inform nursing research methodology: The poetics of voice(s). *Nursing Inquiry, 2*(4), 227-234. https://doi.org/10.1111/j.14401800.1995.tb00152.x

Klecun-Dabrowska, E., & Cornford, T. (2000). Telehealth acquires meanings: information and communication technologies within health policy. *Information Systems Journal, 10*(1), 41-63.

Klein, H.K., & Myers, M.D. (1999), A set of principles for conducting and evaluating interpretive field studies in information systems, *MIS Quarterly, 23*(1), 67-93.

Kolb, D. A. (2015). *Experiential learning: Experience as the source of learning and development* (2nd ed.). Pearson Education, Inc.

Kreider, K. (2015). Material poetics and the "communication event": A theory and critical framework for artworks at a crossover between poetry and text-based art. *Performance Research - A Journal of Performing Arts, 20*(1), 80-89.

Lahman, M. K. E., Geist, M. R., Rodriguez, K. L., Graglia, P. E., Richard, V. M., & Schendel, R. K. (2010). Poking around poetically: Research, poetry, and trustworthiness. *Qualitative Inquiry, 16*(1), 39-48. https://doi.org/10.1177/1077800409350061

Lahman, M. K. E., & Richard, V. M. (2014). Appropriated poetry: Archival poetry in research. *Qualitative Inquiry, 20*(3), 344-355. https://doi.org/10.1177/1077800413489272

Lahman, M. K. E., Rodriguez, K. L., Richard, V. M., Geist, M. R., Schendel, R. K., & Graglia, P. E. (2011). (Re)forming research poetry. *Qualitative Inquiry, 17*(9), 887- 896. https://doi.org/10.1177/1077800411423219

Lambert, K. (2016). "Capturing" queer lives and the poetics of social change. *Continuum, 30*(5), 576-586. https://doi.org/10.1080/10304312.2016.1210800

Leavy, P. (2010). A/r/t: A poetic montage. *Qualitative Inquiry, 16*(4), 240-243. https://doi.org/10.1177/1077800409354067

Leavy, P. (2015). *Method meets art: Arts-based research practice* (2nd ed.). Guilford Press.

Leavy, P. (2018). *Handbook of arts-based research.* The Guilford Press.

Leggo, C. (1997; 2003). *Teaching to wonder: Responding to poetry in the secondary classroom.* Pacific Educational Press.

Leggo, C. (1998). Open(ing) texts: Deconstruction and responding to poetry. *Theory into Practice, 37*(3), 186-192. https://doi.org/10.1080/00405849809543804

Leggo, C. (1999). Research as poetic rumination: Twenty-six ways of listening to light. *The Journal of Educational Thought (JET), 33*(2), 113-133.

Leggo, C. (1999). *View from my mother's house* (1st ed.). Killick Press.

Leggo, C. (2002). A calling of circles: Ruminations on living the research in everyday practice. *Networks: An Online Journal for Teacher Research, 5*(1), 153-153. https://doi.org/10.4148/2470-6353.1208

Leggo, C. (2003). Calling the muses: A poet's ruminations on creativity in the classroom. *Education Canada, 43*(4). 12-15.

Leggo, C. (2004). Living poetry: Five ruminations. *Language & Literacy (Kingston, Ont.), 6*(2). (np). https://doi.org/10.20360/G2D307

Leggo, C. (2005). Pedagogy of the heart: Ruminations on living poetically. *Journal of Educational Thought, 39*(2), 175-195.

Leggo, C. (2007). Writing truth in classrooms: Personal revelation and pedagogy. *International Journal of Whole Schooling, 3*(1), 27-37.

Leggo, C. (2008a). Imagination's hope: Four poems. *LEARNing Landscapes, 2*(1), 31-33. https://doi.org/10.36510/learnland.v2i1.272

Leggo, C. (2008b). Autobiography: Researching Our Lives and Living Our Research. In Springgay, S., Irwin, R., Leggo C., & Gouzouasis, P. (Eds.). *Being with A/r/tography* (pp. 1-23). Brill | Sense. https://doi.org/10.1163/9789087903268_002

Leggo, C. (2008c). Astonishing silence: Knowing in poetry. In A. L. Cole & J. G. Knowles (Eds.), *Handbook of the arts in qualitative social science research* (pp. 165-174). Sage Publications.

Leggo, C. (2011a). Yearning for words, learning with words: Poetic ruminations. *LEARNing Landscapes, 5*(1), 149-155. http://doi.org/10.36510/learnland.v5i1.538

Leggo, C. (2011b). Living love: Confessions of a fearful teacher. *Journal of the Canadian Association for Curriculum Studies, 9*(1), 115-144.

Leggo, C. (2012a). Living language: What is a poem good for? *Journal of the Canadian Association for Curriculum Studies, 10*(2), 141-160.

Leggo, C. (2012b). *Sailing in a concrete boat: A teacher's journey* (1st ed.). SensePublishers.

Leggo, C. (2015). Loving language: A poet's vocation and vision. In S. Walsh, B. Bickel &. Leggo, C. (Eds.). *Arts-based and contemplative practices in research and teaching: Honouring presence* (pp. 141-168). Routledge.

Leggo, C. (2016). A poem can: Poetic encounters. *LEARNing Landscapes, 9*(2), 351-365. https://doi.org/10.36510/learnland.v9i2.780

Leggo, C (2017). The faces of love: The curriculum of loss. *Journal of the Canadian Association for Curriculum Studies, 15*(2), 64–77.

Leggo, C. (2018). Poetry in the academy: A language of possibility. *Canadian Journal of Education, 41*(1), 69-97.

Leggo, C. (2019a). The curriculum of character: Poetic ruminations on growing old(er). In J. P. Miller, K. Nigh, M. J. Binder, B. Novak & S. Crowell (Eds.), *International Handbook of Holistic Education* (240-151). Routledge. https://doi.org/10.4324/9781315112398-30

Leggo, C. (2019b). Teaching writing: Fragments of a Poet's credo. *Art/Research International: A Transdisciplinary Journal, 4*(2), 439-455. https://doi.org/10.18432/ari29466

Leggo, C., Sinner, A. E., Irwin, R. L., Pantaleo, K., Gouzouasis, P., & Grauer, K. (2011). Lingering in liminal spaces: A/r/tography as living inquiry in a language arts class. *International Journal of Qualitative Studies in Education, 24*(2), 239-256. https://doi.org/10.1080/09518391003641908

Lengelle, R. (2008). *Blossoms and balsam: Poems that reveal and heal.* Black Tulip Press.

Loads, D., Marzetti, H., & McCune, V. (2020). 'Don't hold me back': Using poetic inquiry to explore university educators' experiences of professional development through the scholarship of teaching and learning. *Arts and Humanities in Higher Education, 19*(4), 337-353. https://doi.org/10.1177/1474022219846621

MacNeil, C. (2000). The prose and cons of poetic representation in evaluation reporting. *American Journal of Evaluation, 21*(3), 359-367. https://doi.org/10.1016/S1098-2140(01)00100-X

Maarhuis, P., & Sameshima, P. (2016). Materializing the punctum: A poetic study of the Washington State University clothesline project. In Galvin, K. & Prendergast, P. (Eds.), *Poetic Inquiry II: Seeing, Caring Understanding* (pp. 279-302). Sense Publishers.

Maddalena, C. J. (2009). The resolution of internal conflict through performing poetry. *The Arts in Psychotherapy, 36*(4), 222-230. https://doi.org/10.1016/j.aip.2009.04.00

Mayo, J. B. (2020). Queer teacher to queer teacher: Reflections, questions, and hopes from current and aspiring educators. *Teaching Education, 31*(1), 32-44. https://doi.org/10.1080/10476210.2019.1709813

McCulliss, D. (2013). Poetic inquiry and multidisciplinary qualitative research. *Journal of Poetry Therapy, 26*(2), 83-114. https://doi.org/10.1080/08893675.2013.794536

Meyer, C. (2017). *Communicating for results: A Canadian student's guide.* (4th ed.). Oxford University Press.

Meyer, C. (2020). *Communicating for results: A Canadian student's guide.* (5th ed.). Oxford University Press.

Morrell, E., & Duncan-Andrade, J. (2002). Promoting academic literacy with urban youth through engaging hip-hop culture. *English Journal, 91*(6), 88-92. https://doi.org/10.2307/821822

Neilsen, L. (2008). Lyric inquiry. In J. G. Knowles & A. Cole (Eds.), *Handbook of the arts in qualitative research.* Sage. (pp. 93-102). https://doi.org/10.4135/9781452226545.n8

Ng-A-Fook N., Ibrahim A., & Reis, G. (Eds.), *Provoking curriculum studies: Strong poetry and arts of the possible in education* (1st ed.). Routledge. https://doi.org/10.4324/9781315738628

Norton, L. M. (2017). Pathways of reflection: Creating voice through life story and dialogical poetry. *Forum: Qualitative Social Research, 18*(1), Art. 9.

Norris, J. [Joe Norris]. (2014, April, 27) Carl Leggo ring around the scholar [Video]. YouTube. https://www.youtube.com/watch?v=OYfPPEDhH5Q

Öhlén, J. (2003). Evocation of meaning through poetic condensation of narratives in empirical phenomenological inquiry into human suffering. *Qualitative Health Research, 13*(4), 557-566.

Orr, G. (2002). *Poetry as survival.* University of Georgia Press.

Owton, H. (2017). *Doing poetic inquiry.* Springer International Publishing AG.

Patrick, L. D. (2016). Found poetry: Creating space for imaginative arts-based literacy research writing. *Literacy Research: Theory, Method, and Practice, 65*(1), 384- 4 0 3. https://doi.org/10.1177/2381336916661530

Pelias, R. J. (2004). Walking and writing with Laurel Richardson: A story in poems. *Studies in Symbolic Interaction, 27*(1), 41-53. https://doi.org/10.1016/S0163-2396(04)27006-5

Percer, L. H. (2002). Going beyond the demonstrable range in educational scholarship: Exploring the intersections of poetry and research. *The Qualitative Report, 7*(2), 1-13.

Piirto, J. (2002). The question of quality and qualifications: Writing inferior poems as qualitative research. *International Journal of Qualitative Studies in Education, 15*(4), 431-445. https://doi.org/10.1080/09518390210145507

Poindexter, C. (1998). Poetry as data analysis: Honoring the words of research participants. *Reflections, 4*(3), 22-25.

Poindexter, C. (2002). Research as poetry: A couple experiences HIV. *Qualitative Inquiry, 8*(6), 707-714.

Prendergast, M. (2004). "Shaped like a question mark": Found poetry from Herbert Blau's The Audience. *Research in Drama Education: The Journal of Applied Theatre and Performance, 9*(1), 73-92. https://doi.org/10.1080/1356978042000185920

Prendergast, M. (2006). *Audience in performance: A poetics and pedagogy of spectatorship.* (Unpublished doctoral dissertation). University of Victoria, Victoria, BC, Canada.

Prendergast, M. (2006). Found poetry as literature review: Research poems on audience and performance. *Qualitative Inquiry, 12*(2), 369-388. https://doi.org/10.1177/1077800405284601

Prendergast, M. (2009a). "Poem is what?" Poetic inquiry in qualitative social science research. *International Review of Qualitative Research, 1*(4), 541-568. https://doi.org/10.1525/irqr.2009.1.4.541

Prendergast, M. (2009b). The scholar dances. *Qualitative Inquiry, 15*(8), 1373-1375. https://doi.org/10.1177/1077800409332079

Prendergast, M. (2010). Reflective praxis through narrative and poetry: Performing peace mum. *Research in Drama Education, 15*(1), 79-87. https://doi.org/10.1080/13569780903481052

Prendergast, M. (2012). Education and/as art: A found poetry suite. *International Journal of Education and the Arts, 13*(2). 1-19.

Prendergast, M. M. (2014). "I contain multitudes": The challenges of self-representation in arts-based educational research. *International Journal of Education and the Arts, 15*(2). 1-16.

Prendergast, M. (2015). Poetic inquiry, 2007-2012: A surrender and catch found poem. *Qualitative Inquiry, 21*(8), 678-685. https://doi.org/10.1177/1077800414563806

Prendergast, M. (2020). anecdotal. *Qualitative Inquiry, 26*(6), 674-676. https://doi.org/10.1177/1077800419846642

Prendergast, M., & Galvin, K. T. (Eds.). (2015). *Poetic inquiry II – seeing, caring, understanding*. Springer Verlag.

Prendergast, M., & Belliveau, G. (2013). Performance and poetics. In A. Trainor & E. Graue (Eds.), *Reviewing qualitative research in the social sciences* (pp. 201-204). Routledge.

Prendergast, M., & Galvin, K. T. (2012). Editorial: Naming and expanding the borders of practice in poetic inquiry. *Creative Approaches to Research, 5*(2), 5-8.

Prendergast, M., Gouzouasis, P., Leggo, C., & Irwin, R. L. (2009). A haiku suite: The importance of music making in the lives of secondary school students. *Music Education Research, 11*(3), 303-317. https://doi.org/10.1080/14613800903144262

Prendergast, M. (2016). Tracing the journey to here: Reflections on a prison theatre devised project. *Theatre Topics, 26*(3), 343-349. https://doi.org/10.13532016-0059

Prendergast, M. (2019). anecdotal. *Qualitative Inquiry, 26*(6), 107780041984664-676. https://doi.org/10.1177/1077800419846642

Prendergast, M., Leggo, C., & Sameshima, P. (Eds.) (2009). *Poetic inquiry: Vibrant voices in the social sciences*. Sense Publishers.

Quinn-Hall, C. (2015). Poetics in a capacious landscape. In Prendergast, M., & Galvin, K. T. (Eds). *Poetic inquiry II – seeing, caring, understanding* (pp. 107-133). Springer Verlag.

Ransom, J.C. (1937). "Criticism, Inc." *Virginia Quarterly Review, 13*: 586–603.

Rapport, F., & Hartill, G. (2012). Crossing disciplines with ethnographic poetic representation. *Creative Approaches to Research, 5*(2), 11-25.

Richardson, L. (1992). The poetic representation of lives: Writing a postmodern sociology. *Studies in Symbolic Interaction, 13*(1). 19-29.

Richardson, L. (1993a). Poetics, dramatics, and transgressive validity: The case of the skipped line. *The Sociological Quarterly, 34*(4), 695-710. https://doi.org/10.1111/j.1533-8525.1993.tb00113.x

Richardson, L. (1993b). The consequences of poetic representation: Writing the other, rewriting the self. In C. Ellis & M. Flaherty. (Eds.), *Investigating subjectivity: Research on lived experience* (pp. 125-137). Sage.

Richardson, L. (1994). Nine poems: Marriage and the family. *Journal of Contemporary Ethnography, 23*(1), 3-13.

Richardson, L. (1997). Skirting a pleated text: De-disciplining an academic life. *Qualitative Inquiry, 3*(3), 295-303. https://doi.org/10.1177/107780049700300303

Richardson, L. (2000). Writing: A method of inquiry. In N. K. Denzin & Y. S. Lincoln, (Eds.), *Handbook of qualitative research* (pp. 1410-1444). Sage Publications.

Richardson, L. (2001). Alternative ethnographies, alternative criteria. In L. Neilsen, A.L. Cole & J.G. Knowles (Eds.), *The Art of Writing Inquiry* (250-252). Back-along-books.

Richardson, M. (1998). Poetics in the field and on the page. *Qualitative Inquiry, 4*(4), 451-462. https://doi.org/10.1177/107780049800400401

Roberts, S. K., Brasel, N. A., & Crawford, P. A. (2014). Poetry as praxis: An exploration of poetry discourse as qualitative inquiry. *Journal of Poetry Therapy, 27*(4), 167-181. https://doi.org/10.1080/08893675.2014.948262

Rosenblatt, L. M. (1994). *The reader, the text, the poem: The transactional theory of the literary work* (Paperback ed.). Southern Illinois University Press.

Rorty, R. (1989). *Contingency, irony, and solidarity*. Cambridge University Press.

Rothenberg, J. (1994). "Je est un autre": Ethnopoetics and the poet as other. *American Anthropologist, 96*(3), 523-524.

Saldaña, J., (2016). *Ethnotheatre: Research from page to stage*. Left Coast Press. https://doi.org/10.4324/9781315428932

Sameshima, P. (2006). *Seeing red: A pedagogy of parallax*. (Unpublished doctoral dissertation). The University of British Columbia.

Sameshima, P., Fidyk, A., James, K., & Leggo, C. (Eds.) (2017). *Poetic inquiry: Enchantment of place*. Vernon Press.

Sameshima, P., & Leggo, C. (2010). The poet's corpus in love: Passionate pedagogy. *Journal of Curriculum Theorizing, 26*(1), 65-81.

Sameshima, P., & Leggo, C. (2013). How do you spell love? Curricular conversations. *Creative Approaches to Research, 6*(1), 89.

Sameshima, P., & Sinner, A. (2009). Awakening to soma heliakon: Encountering teacher-researcher-learning in the twenty-first century. *Canadian Journal of Education, 32*(2), 271-284.

Sameshima P., Slingerland D., Wakewich P., Morrisseau K., & Zehbe I. (2017) Growing Wellbeing Through Community Participatory Arts: The Anishinaabek Cervical Cancer Screening Study (ACCSS). In Barton G. & Baguley M. (Eds.) *The Palgrave Handbook of Global Arts Education* (pp. 399-416). Palgrave Macmillan https://doi-org/10.1057/978-1-137-55585-4_25

Sameshima, P., & Vandermause, R. (2008). Parallaxic praxis: An artful interdisciplinary collaborative research methodology. In B. Kožuh, R. Kahn & A Kozlowska (Eds.), *The practical science of society* (pp. 141-152). The College of Education and Human Development & Slovenian Research Agency (AARS).

Sameshima, P., Vandermause, R., & Chamlers, S. (2009). *Climbing the ladder with Gabriel: Poetic inquiry of a methamphetamine addict in recovery*. Sense Publishers.

Saunders, V., Usher, K., Tsey, K., & Bainbridge, R. (2016). If you knew the end of a story would you still want to hear it? Using research poems to listen to aboriginal stories. *Journal of Poetry Therapy: The Interdisciplinary Journal of Practice, Theory, Research, and Education, 29*(1), 1-13. https://doi.org/10.1080/08893675.2016.1133082

Schreibman, R., & Chilton, G. (2012). Small waterfalls in art therapy supervision: A poetic appreciative inquiry. *Art Therapy, 29*(4), 188-191. https://doi.org/10.1080/07421656.2012.730924

Scruton, R. (2004). *Modern philosophy: An introduction and survey*. Pimlico.

Shakespeare, W., Taylor, G., Jowett, J., Bourus, T., & Egan, G. (2017). *The new Oxford Shakespeare: The complete works* (1st; Critical reference ed.). Oxford University Press.

Sinner, A., Leggo, C., Irwin, R. L., Gouzouasis, P., & Grauer, K. (2006). Arts-based educational research dissertations: Reviewing the practices of new scholars. *Canadian Journal of Education, 29*(4), 1223-1270.

Slattery, P. (2003). Troubling the contours of arts-based educational research. *Qualitative Inquiry, 9*(2), 192-197. https://doi.org/10.1177/1077800402250929

Smith, W. N. (2002). Ethno-poetry notes. *International Journal of Qualitative Studies in Education, 15*(4), 461-467.

Snowber, C. (2016). *Embodied inquiry: Writing, living and being through the body*. Sense Publishers.

Stake, R. E. (2006). *Multiple case study analysis*. Guilford Press.

Stapleton, S. R. (2018). Data analysis in participatory action research: Using poetic inquiry to describe urban teacher marginalization. *Action Research*, 1-23. https://doi.org/10.1177/1476750318811920

Stock, R. V., Sameshima, P., & Slingerland, D. (2016, July). Constructing pre-service teacher identities through processes of parallax. Special Issue: Artful inquiry: Transforming understanding through creative engagement. *LEARNing Landscapes, 9*(2), 489-512.

Tasker, D., Loftus, S., & Higgs, J. (2014). "From the space between us": The use of poetics as a hermeneutic phenomenological tool within qualitative physiotherapy research. *Creative Approaches to Research, 7*(2), 4-18.

Tedlock, D. (1983). *The spoken word and the work of interpretation*. University of Pennsylvania Press.

Teman, E. D. (2019). Autoethnographic poetic inquiry: Therapeutically engaging with violence toward queers. *Journal of Poetry Therapy, 32*(2), 63-77. https://doi.org/10.1080/08893675.2019.1583409

The University of British Columbia. (n.d). *Professor Carl Leggo-Faculty of Education* https://educ.ubc.ca/professor-carl-leggo

van Rooyen, H., Essack, Z., Mahali, A., Groenewald, C., & Solomons, A. (2020). "The power of the poem": Using poetic inquiry to explore trans-identities in Namibia. *Arts & Health*, 1-14. https://doi.org/10.1080/17533015.2020.1805634

Vincent, A. R. (2015). *Breaking the line*. (Unpublished master's thesis). University of British Columbia, Vancouver, BC, Canada. https://open.library.ubc.ca/cIRcle/collections/ubctheses/24/items/1.0165775

Vincent, A. (2018). Is there a definition? Ruminating on Poetic Inquiry, strawberries and the continued growth of the field. *Art/Research International: A Transdisciplinary Journal, 3*(2), 48-76. https://doi.org/10.18432/ari29356

Vincent, A. (2020a). The poetry of fieldnotes. In Burkholder, C., & Thompson, J. (Eds.). *Using fieldnotes in educational research: Approaches, practices, and ethical considerations* (pp. 138-150). Routledge. https://doi.org/10.4324/9780429275821-12

Vincent, A. (2020b). I was there, they were there: A poetic rumination of familial history, place and the concept of self. In Lyle, E. (Ed.), *Identity Landscapes* (131-151). Brill | Sense. https://doi.org/10.1163/9789004425194_013

Vygotsky, L. S. (1978). *Mind in society: The development of higher psychological processes.* Harvard University Press.

Wallace, K. O. (2015). *There is no need to talk about this: Poetic inquiry from the art therapy studio.* SensePublishers.

Walsh, S. (2006). An Irigarayan framework and resymbolization in an arts-informed research process. *Qualitative Inquiry, 12*(5), 976-993.

Whittemore, R., Chase, S. K., & Mandle, C. L. (2001). Validity in qualitative research. *Qualitative Health Research, 11*(4), 522-537. https://doi.org/10.1177/104973201129119299

Wiebe, N. G. (2008). Mennocostal musings: Poetic inquiry and performance in narrative research. *Forum: Qualitative Social Research, 9*(2), Art. 42. (np).

Wiebe, S., & Guiney Yallop, J. J.. (2010). Ways of being in teaching: Conversing paths to meaning. *Canadian Journal of Education, 33*(1), 177-198.

Wiebe, S., Yallop, J., Fels, L., Snowber, C., Richardson, P., Honein, N., . . . Leggo, C. (2016). Poetic inquiry of and on play. *Canadian Journal of Education, 39*(3), 1-26.

Wiggins, J. L., & Monobe, G. (2017). Positioning self in "figured worlds": Using poetic inquiry to theorize transnational experiences in education. *The Urban Review, 49*(1), 153-168. https://doi.org/10.1007/s11256-016-0386-5

Zimmerman, S. (2002). *Writing to heal the soul.* Three Rivers Press.

Appendix:
Interpretive Frameworks and Poetic Inquiry

Appendix Table 1: Poetic Inquiry and Philosophical/Interpretive Frameworks.

Philosophical/ Interpretive Framework	Approach to Inquiry	Current Poetic Inquiry's Uses Within the Framework	Proposed Adaptations Based on This Study
Social Constructivism	"Literary style…, inductive methods (through consensus) obtained through…interviewing, observing and analysis of texts" (Creswell, 2013, p. 36)	Transcription poetry (e.g., Richardson, 1993; Maarhuis & Sameshima, 2016) or poem-like transcripts (e.g., Glesne, 1997), field note poetry (e.g., Flores, 1982) is in use across the disciplines.	Close reading can add a layer of understanding of poetic products, while adding to the validity and credibility of the study.
Critical Feminist, Race, Queer	"Start with assumptions of power and identity struggles, document them and call for action and change" (Creswell, 2013, p. 36)	poetic inquiry is being used as a feminist approach (e.g., Faulkner, 2018) to push for social change, a way to highlight the experiences of marginalized people and their experiences (e.g., Lahman & Richard, 2014; Cutts, 2019; Teman, 2019)	Poetic inquiry can be used to trouble the status quo and highlight power disparities between the poet and the participant or the participant and society. Close reading is a way to understand the implications of language and how language is used to represent others in equitable ways.
Philosophical/ Interpretive Framework	Approach to Inquiry	Current poetic inquiry's Uses Within the Framework	Proposed Adaptations Based on This Study
Postmodernism	"Collaborative process of research…, questioning of methods, highlighting issues and concerns" (Creswell, 2013, p. 36)	Poetry is being used as a generative tool to better understand the relationships between health care workers and patients (e.g., Tasker, Loftus & Higgs (2014) who focus on physiotherapy, King (2004) who focuses on the emotional aspect of nursing and Öhlén (2003) who focuses on understanding suffering.) It is also being used as a tool for exchanging	Close reading, which can include an examination of semiotics to explore ideas akin to notions held in post-modernism, questions the use of poetry and serves to more closely consider implied issues in the content of the poem or consider issues in its creation.

Philosophical/ Interpretive Framework	Approach to Inquiry	Current Poetic Inquiry's Uses Within the Framework	Proposed Adaptations Based on This Study
		knowledge and experience between people (e.g., Wiebe & Yallop, 2010; Sameshima & Leggo, 2013)	
New Materialism	"[T]ools of interpretive research such as interviews or diary or narrative accounts…must be turned decisively to disclose the relations within assemblages (Fox & Alldred, 2015, p. 403) with less on the subjective and more on "how respondents are situated within assemblages" (Juelskjaer, 2013, p. 759).	Poetic inquiry is being used to reflect on positionality, to focus on relations (e.g., Richardson, 1994).	Close reading used to explore how a poem is created and what its creation says about the connections or interconnections of the relations.

Appendix Table 2: Poetic Inquiry and Research Approaches.

Research Approach	Approach to Data Analysis and Representation	Current Poetic Inquiry's Uses Within the Approach	Proposed Changes or Adaptations
Phenomenology	"Develop a textual description [of] 'what' happened, develop a structural description [of] 'how' the phenomenon was experienced, develop the 'essence'" (Creswell, 2013, p. 191) The "essence" is presented through narration with figures, graphs and tables where needed (p. 191)	Currently, the 'essence' of phenomena are being illustrated through field note poetry (e.g., Flores, 1982), found poetry (e.g., Richardson, 1994; Butler-Kisber, 2002; Prendergast, 2012), transcript poetry (e.g., Richardson, 1993; Maarhuis & Sameshima, 2016) and as a means for exploring lived experiences (Black & Enos, 1981).	Close reading of the poetic products of poetic inquiry studies can further understand of the phenomena through understanding why poetic choices were made and through an examination of how language is used to create meaning.
Narrative/ Narrative Inquiry	"Interpret the larger meaning of the story" (Creswell, 2013, p. 191). Presented through narration that focuses on "processes, theories and…features of the life" (p. 191)	Poetry is being used autobiographically or autoethnographically (e.g., Leggo, 2007, 2016; Yallop & Shields, 2006), as well as as a way to share other's stories (e.g., Görlich, 2016).	In analyzing autobiographic or poetry derived from narrative there is an opportunity to further understand lived experience and draw out unique features that may have gone unnoticed. Close reading can then be used to provide an additional level of understanding.
Case Study	"Use direct interpretation, develop naturalistic generalizations of what was 'learned'" (Creswell, 2013, p. 191) Presented as an "in-depth picture of the case…using narrative, tables and figures" (p. 191)	This links closely to its uses with narrative research (e.g., Yallop & Shields, 2006)	As exemplified in this study, poetry allowed for poetic play to take place that aided in the data analysis processes, while the close reading of the participants' poetics furthered an understanding of each participant's practices and furthered an understanding of poetic inquiry.

Research Approach	Approach to Data Analysis and Representation	Current Poetic Inquiry's Uses Within the Approach	Proposed Changes or Adaptations
Grounded Theory	"Engage in selective coding and interrelate the categories to develop a 'story' or prepositions" (Creswell, 2013, p. 191). Presented as "a visual model or theory" with "propositions" for how the study occurred (p. 191).	Grounded theory is not explicitly used in the poetic inquiry literature, but was used to explore the internal conflict of slam poets (Maddalena, 2009).	Grounded theory was used during this study as a way of experimentation that allowed more details of the 'story' to come to light. Through creating a new way of using literary analysis to further an understanding of the participants' poetics, more was gleaned about the power of poetic inquiry to create and mobilize knowledge.

Index

2SLGBTQ+, 4, 30, 84, 88, 140, 155

A

a/r/tography, 21, 36, 67, 75
aesthetics, 37, 148, 153
anthropology, 15, 18, 23, 24
ars poetica, 32, 53, 54, 141, 163
arts integrated, 75, 118
arts-based educational research (ABER), 20, 21, 29, 151
arts-based research, xvii, xxvi, 1, 6, 16, 27, 37, 75, 103, 111, 128, 151, 153, 157 4
autobiographical, 4, 61, 62, 67, 81, 105, 115, 116, 119, 120, 130, 138, 139, 183 autobiography, 60, 117
autoethnographic, 34, 51, 56, 72, 76, 114, 139, 170, 171, 190, 191, 194
autoethnography, 19, 94

B

Barone, T., 4, 27, 75, 102
Belliveau, G., 25, 35, 102, 105
BIPOC, 4, 84, 88, 155
Brady, I., 11, 23, 24
Butler-Kisber, L., 18, 21, 22, 31, 88, 94, 95, 102, 163

C

Cahnmann, M., 11, 22
close reading, xv, 2, 7, 47, 49, 50, 51, 52, 55, 56, 127, 141, 150, 154, 156, 165, 166, 181, 182, 183

craft, xx, 4, 6, 11, 22, 27, 31, 32, 33, 40, 55, 57, 58, 63, 69, 76, 90, 94, 95, 96, 97, 102, 104, 106, 112, 113, 120, 127, 128, 129,130, 142, 154, 160, 164
Creswell, J. W., 2, 37, 39, 41, 43, 46, 53, 128, 157, 181, 182, 183, 184
curriculum, xix, 2, 3, 5, 20, 29, 37, 49, 70, 75, 82, 118, 152, 156, 159
Cutts, Q. M., 4, 32, 54, 84, 139, 163, 181

D

data analysis, 6, 14, 40, 43, 44, 46, 47, 48, 49, 109, 116, 145, 150, 156, 183, 184
data collection, 6, 39, 40
dialogic, 43, 52, 78, 81, 83, 86, 103, 104, 110, 144, 161
dissemination, 1, 5, 22, 37, 40, 55, 56, 150, 152, 156, 159, 164

E

Eisner, E. W., 14, 18, 55, 76, 102
ekphrasis, 77, 78, 81, 106, 118, 131
enjambment, 4, 74, 80, 139, 158, 164
epistemological, 36, 39, 78, 110, 111, 141, 154, 165
epistemology, xx, 37, 48, 54, 159, 161
ethnographic, xv, 4, 22, 23, 152
ethnography, 22, 33

F

Faulkner, S., 1, 15, 27, 28, 30, 31, 32, 33, 53, 54, 55, 95, 100, 110, 141, 163, 164, 181
Fels, L., 4, 25, 84, 105
field note poetry, 18, 143, 151, 181, 183
field notes, xviii, 10, 21, 37, 40, 152
Flores, T., 17, 18, 22, 31, 37, 144, 181, 183
found poetry, 18, 19, 21, 22, 46, 70, 83, 97, 97, 99, 100, 101, 102, 105, 129, 137, 141, 151, 160, 163, 183
Furman, R., 4, 15, 16, 19

G

Galvin, K., 12, 30, 38, 144 0
GTR Language Workbench, 45, 46
Guiney Yallop, J. J., xvii, 4, 38, 41, 42, 49, 58, 86, 90, 92, 94, 116, 125, 135

H

health care, 4, 15, 18, 24, 181
hermeneutic, 2, 3, 20, 46, 51, 52, 56, 121, 148, 167
higher education, xxvii, 75, 116, 138
hybrid texts, 26

I

identity, xx, 16, 30, 36, 62, 64, 73, 81, 85, 86, 87, 88, 90, 91, 93, 94, 115, 116, 118, 132, 149, 156, 157, 159, 161, 163, 165

International Symposium on Poetic Inquiry (ISPI), xvi, 29, 38, 61, 75, 87, 88, 95, 117, 155, 166
Irwin, R., 6, 12, 24, 36, 63, 64, 75, 166

J

jagodzinski, j. & Wallin, J., xxvi, 2, 4, 37, 128
James, K., xv, xxvi, 1, 3, 9, 12, 24, 30, 31, 37, 38, 95, 153

K

knowledge creation, 5, 141, 157, 159

L

Leavy, P., 1, 10, 11, 13, 22, 23, 164
Leggo, C., xv, xvi, xvii, xxiv, 4, 5, 9, 12, 14, 16, 18, 19, 21, 24, 25, 26, 28, 29, 31, 32, 35, 38, 41, 49, 58, 61, 62, 63, 64, 66, 69, 70, 71, 72, 73, 75, 79, 81, 87, 95, 102, 114, 115, 118, 121, 122, 129, 149, 155, 163, 182
limits, 28, 40, 63, 70, 76, 87, 98, 99, 113, 114, 154, 155
line breaks, 4, 7, 46, 68, 74, 78, 79, 94, 97, 101, 104, 137, 140, 142, 147, 158
literacy, xvii, xxiv, 26
living poetically, xix, 19, 62, 66, 70, 72, 112, 114, 118, 128, 129, 130, 158, 161, 163

M

metaphor, 4, 6, 7, 17, 18, 24, 26, 32, 74, 80, 84, 86, 94, 95, 96, 98, 99, 138, 147, 164, 166
métissage, 25, 26, 29, 142

N

New Critical approach, 51, 52

O

Orr, G., 4, 16, 70

P

performative inquiry, 21, 25, 105
phenomenological approaches, 152, 183
philosophy, 92, 128, 167, 181
Piirto, J., 27, 28, 32
poetic data analysis, 19, 22
poetic devices, 4, 7, 37, 50, 51, 52, 53, 66, 67, 68, 69, 80, 81, 84, 90, 91, 101, 116, 119, 120, 127, 130, 141, 147, 148, 151, 158, 165
poetic form(s), 13, 17, 23, 37, 50, 51, 66, 67, 69, 73, 78, 90, 100, 102, 121, 144, 148, 149, 153, 157, 165
poetic inquirer, xvii, xix, xxvi, 21, 25, 55, 61, 62, 85, 112, 148, 163
poetic inquiry paradox, 7, 112, 148
poetic inquiry, functions of, 28, 38, 66, 76, 84, 98, 116, 149, 152, 154, 157, 158
poetic inquiry, history of, 12, 18, 33, 49
poetic inquiry, theory of, 5, 163, 164, 166

poetic representation, 18, 21, 22, 31, 155
poetic transcription, 14, 18, 19, 21, 22, 98
poetic voice, xxiii, 20, 35, 73, 94, 99, 103, 144
poetics, xv, xviii, xix, xxvi, 13, 14, 49, 66, 72, 77, 81, 83, 90, 93, 99, 104, 109, 119, 127, 130, 154, 165, 166, 184, 184
poet-researcher, 1, 4, 27, 36, 38, 40, 55, 99, 129, 143, 148, 151, 157, 158, 163, 164, 166, 167
poetic rumination, 19, 31, 62, 128
polyphonic, 97, 98, 120, 129, 133, 150, 158, 160
Prendergast, M., xvi, xxvi, 1, 3, 9, 10, 11, 12, 15, 17, 18, 19, 21, 22, 24, 25, 25, 30, 33, 37, 38, 40, 41, 43, 58, 61, 96, 98, 99, 102, 103, 104, 105, 116, 126, 135, 138, 144, 153, 163

R

research method(s), xvii, 2, 3, 11, 24, 35, 36, 37, 39, 40, 49, 56, 148, 153, 155, 158,
research poetry, 13, 14, 21, 22, 28, 31, 54, 151, 164
rhizomatic array, 6, 164, 165, 166
rhizome, 5, 6, 18, 20, 27, 28, 29, 32, 33, 36, 54, 119, 159, 165, 166
Richardson, L., 12, 13, 14, 18, 19, 21, 22, 27, 31, 36, 37, 102, 163, 183

S

Sameshima, P., xvii, 4, 30, 38, 41, 42, 50, 58, 63, 68, 75, 77, 79, 81,

82, 83, 116, 123, 124, 135, 136, 163, 181, 182, 183
Sinner, A., 5, 9, 20, 21, 64, 77, 82, 166
social justice, 10, 22, 30, 77, 88, 94, 141
social work, 17, 32
Stake, R., 39, 43, 46, 47
storytelling, 14, 31, 70, 86, 94, 116, 160
synesthesia, 80, 84, 120, 123, 124, 129, 141, 150

T

terminology, 21, 24, 153
transcript poetry, 78, 79, 83, 141, 151, 183
trustworthiness, 6, 53, 54, 141

U

Universal design for learning (UDL), 156

V

Vincent, A., xv, 1, 26, 31, 37, 38, 49, 95, 142, 147
vox, 10, 22, 26, 99, 102, 153

www.ingramcontent.com/pod-product-compliance
Lightning Source LLC
Chambersburg PA
CBHW070608300426
44113CB00010B/1448